"Patrick Johnson's work on missional preaching is very appropriate and timely for pastors serving congregations in these very tense and challenging times. Whether you are an urban, suburban or rural pastor, Johnson's work will aid you in developing sermons that speak prophetically to what God has called your congregation to be at this time in its history. Johnson's missional hermeneutic provides the preacher/pastor an interpretive lens to exegete culture, the congregation and the biblical text. The book is a great read for all preachers and pastors but especially for those who are looking to prepare their churches to engage their communities, address social justice issues or simply redefine the church's mission for today. It underscores for its readers the importance of the church being a witness of Christ to the world."

Tasha Vinson Brown, assistant dean, Northern Seminary

"With *The Mission of Preaching* Patrick Johnson focuses the continuing investigation of the missional church on the theology and practice of preaching. He ably engages the primary resources for this undertaking, especially Lesslie Newbigin and Karl Barth, and lays out the trajectories for the missional renewal of preaching in our post-Christendom context. Combining scholarship and pastoral passion, he is profoundly broadening and deepening the exploration of the missional church with this pioneering work."

Darrell L. Guder, Henry Winters Luce Professor of Missional and Ecumenical Theology, Princeton Theological Seminary

"I've been waiting for a solid book on missional preaching, and it has finally arrived. Patrick Johnson brings into conversation some of the best writers in homiletics and missional ecclesiology, then invites us to practice confessional preaching that is centered on the person and work of Jesus, formed by a missional hermeneutic, and is contextual and communal. This book will help you equip the church for the sake of the world."

JR Woodward, national director, V3 Church Planting Movement, and author of *Creating a Missional Culture*

THE

MISSION

OF

PREACHING

Equipping the Community for Faithful Witness

PATRICK W. T. JOHNSON

Foreword by DAVID J. LOSE

IVP Academic

An imprint of InterVarsity Press
Downers Grove, Illinois

InterVarsity Press
P.O. Box 1400, Downers Grove, IL 60515-1426
ivpress.com
email@ivpress.com

InterVarsity Press® is the book-publishing division of InterVarsity Christian Fellowship/USA®, a movement of students and faculty active on campus at hundreds of universities, colleges and schools of nursing in the United States of America, and a member movement of the International Fellowship of Evangelical Students. For information about local and regional activities, visit intervarsity.org.

Scripture quotations, unless otherwise noted, are from the New Revised Standard Version of the Bible, copyright 1989 by the Division of Christian Education of the National Council of the Churches of Christ in the USA. Used by permission. All rights reserved.

While any stories in this book are true, some names and identifying information may have been changed to protect the privacy of individuals.

Cover design: Cindy Kiple
Interior design: Beth McGill
Images: © Jamie Farrant/iStockphoto

ISBN 978-0-8308-4070-0 (print)
ISBN 978-0-8308-9712-4 (digital)

Printed in the United States of America ∞

Library of Congress Cataloging-in-Publication Data

Johnson, Patrick W. T., 1979-
The mission of preaching : equipping the community for faithful
witness / Patrick W. T. Johnson.
    pages cm
  Includes index.
  ISBN 978-0-8308-4070-0 (pbk. : alk. paper)
  1. Preaching. 2. Witness bearing (Christianity) 3. Evangelistic
work. I. Title.
BV4221.J64 2015
251—dc23

                                                    2015001566

P   23   22   21   20   19   18   17   16   15   14   13   12   11   10   9   8   7   6   5   4   3   2   1

Y   35   34   33   32   31   30   29   28   27   26   25   24   23   22   21   20   19   18   17   16   15

To Isla, Luke and Claire

Contents

Foreword

To understand the import of the book you hold in your hands, it's vital to give attention to a fact of congregational life that is as blatantly obvious as it is frequently overlooked: *The dominant culture in the United States no longer has any vested interest in supporting church participation.* From Benjamin Franklin to Dwight David Eisenhower, it was commonplace for politicians not simply to invoke God's blessing over their work or at the end of their speeches (which, ironically, has become more common recently), but to urge citizens to attend church. It was Eisenhower, for instance, who is reported to have said, "I don't care what church they go to, as long as they go to church." The source of their earnestness about church attendance was their well-founded belief that church participation helped to nurture a loyal and active citizenry. For this reason, it was only natural—and in the government's self-interest—to promote church attendance.

But while the mixture of faith and politics has become both more explicit and more partisan in recent decades with the development of movements like the "moral majority," the general cultural expectation that one needs to attend church to be a good citizen has waned significantly. Church attendance is now a matter of personal discretion, much like being a member of a fitness club or fraternal organization. In short, it is one of a number of activities by which one may spend one's time, but it is not particularly necessary and therefore not particularly urged by public leaders.

With that dimension of immediate culture in mind, now consider two observations that Diana Butler Bass, in *Christianity After Religion*, draws from one of the longest running religious polls in recent history, which asks respondents a single question: Do you consider yourself (a) religious but not spiritual, (b) spiritual but not religious, (c) both, or (d) neither?

First, Bass points out that across the twenty-five years that the poll has been given, the largest change in these answers has been between the first and second possible responses. That is, whereas a generation ago most respondents answered that they were "religious but not spiritual," today most respondents answer the opposite, that they are "spiritual but not religious." Second, she reminds us that most of the practices that now inform and govern congregational life were solidified a generation ago. In other words, the dominant patterns of congregational life were formed by, and constructed to serve a population that is only shrinking while having little to commend them to that segment of the population that is growing.

Now circle back and join Bass's analysis with our earlier observation about the decline of cultural support for church participation and it's difficult to avoid a simple, nearly irrefutable and rather devastating observation: if we wanted to construct a church that does not in any way, shape or form speak to the identified needs of the current generation and runs contrary to the spiritual impulses of the contemporary culture, we have most certainly done so. We are set up to care for the religious lives (keep in mind the previous generation's disdain of "spirituality") of ready-made Christians that the culture produced and sent to church. We are manifestly not prepared to equip Christians to strengthen their spiritual lives, navigate a complex world via the compass of a robust Christian faith or even help would-be spiritual people understand why Christianity might matter to them.

This is why Patrick Johnson's *The Mission of Preaching* matters. For, in the pages to follow, Johnson challenges us to shift our understanding of preaching from a clearly defined practice employed by a single practitioner and the delight, wonder and appreciation of a receptive but largely passive audience to an emerging, but still under construction, practice that seeks to equip both more traditional and seeking Christians alike not only to understand their faith but to share it. Ultimately, the result of such preaching is that the appointed and authorized testimony of one (the "preacher") equips, supports and authorizes the testimony of many (the "congregation").

I describe this development as the move from performative preaching to formative preaching. To most easily appreciate that move and the significant contribution Johnson makes, we need only consider the criteria for "good preaching" each model assumes. In traditional, performative preaching, the criteria for faithful proclamation is that the preacher him- or herself is capable of interpreting the text, sharing where he or she sees God's activity in the world and inviting others into the discipleship community. In the kind of formative, missional homiletic that Johnson argues for, however, the criteria of competent and faithful proclamation is no longer the *preacher's* ability to do these things, but rather the growth over time of the *congregation's* competence and confidence in performing these primary elements of the Christian faith.

In order to accomplish this goal, Johnson makes three significant moves before articulating most fully a missional homiletic that seeks to equip twenty first–century Christians with the ability to claim and share their faith as a meaningful, relevant and compelling narrative with which to understand their lives. First, he assesses several sympathetic homiletical proposals that help him articulate the significance of understanding preaching as a particular kind of testimony that ultimately reaches its goal as it enables the testimony of others. Second, he develops the work of Karl Barth to ground his homiletic in a theological understanding of the church that views the community of faith as not just benefitting from, but actually participating in the present, ongoing and coming reign of God in the world. Third, he distills the best of current missional theology in order to develop a more robust vision of how preaching functions within a larger set of practices and characteristics distinct to communities animated by their participation in the *missio Dei*.

From this solid grounding in current homiletical theory, classic neo-orthodox theology and current missional convictions, Johnson moves to articulate a theology of the practice of missional preaching that is simultaneously three-dimensional, accessible and relevant. I won't say more, because I don't want to deprive you of the thrill of discovery as you, with Patrick Johnson as your mentor, guide and conversational partner, reimagine the potential and possibility of your preaching to nurture the testimony of a whole community of disciples and, in this way, spark a renewal of the church in our day.

David J. Lose
President, the Lutheran Theological Seminary at Philadelphia

Acknowledgments

Writing *The Mission of Preaching* has been like discovering an answer to a burning question, and I am grateful to Princeton Theological Seminary for providing the resources that make answering a question like "What is missional preaching?" possible and fun. I am especially grateful to several of the faculty for their wisdom and mentorship, including James Kay, Darrell Guder and Nancy Lammers Gross. Along the way, I have been blessed with colleagues for whose friendship and stimulating conversation I am thankful. Kamalesh Stephen, Dave Ward and Adam Hearlson have been good friends and great conversation partners during the writing of this book, and Angela Hancock, Shauna Hannan, Charles "Chip" Hardwick and Peter Henry are wise colleagues with the gift of genuine enthusiasm.

In bringing this work to publication, I am very grateful to my editor, David Congdon, whose close reading has strengthened the book and saved me from hundreds of mistakes, and to the editors and staff of IVP Academic for their support and wisdom. By them I have been truly blessed! The church where I have served as pastor during these last several years, Frenchtown Presbyterian Church in Frenchtown, New Jersey, has inspired and sharpened the ideas of this book. They have generously shared their pastor with the library, the seminary community and the ministry of writing.

In the often solitary work of writing, I have found no substitute for family. My family has been unfailingly supportive and encouraging, often spurring me on and encouraging me with their unmerited pride. Most especially I am grateful to my wife and partner, Caitlin. Her shared commitment to the gospel, her belief in the importance of this project and her willingness to "send me off to write" have been a blessing beyond measure. From the time I began this work to its completion, we have been blessed with twin children, Isla and Luke, and a daughter, Claire. As I finish this project, I am especially hopeful for them. I hope that they will grow up in a church that bears faithful witness, that they will hear great preaching and come to love it, and most of all, that they will love Jesus Christ, who first loved them.

Abbreviations

CD   Karl Barth. *Church Dogmatics.* Edited by G. W. Bromiley and T.
           F. Torrance. Translated by G. W. Bromiley, G. T. Thomson, et al.
           4 vols. Edinburgh: T & T Clark, 1936–1977.

KD   Karl Barth. *Die kirchliche Dogmatik.* 4 vols. Zollikon-Zürich:
           Evangelischer Verlag A.G., 1932–1970.

Introduction

I first encountered the work of J. E. Lesslie Newbigin, a.k.a. Bishop New-bigin, during a seminary course on his life and theology. Originally a missionary to India from the Church of Scotland, Newbigin developed a wide-ranging ministry as an ecumenist, theologian and pastor to pastors. He served as associate general secretary of the World Council of Churches and was one of the first bishops of the Church of South India. In the opening of his biography, *Lesslie Newbigin: A Theological Life*, Geoffrey Wainwright compares Newbigin to the early fathers of the church, writing,

> As rarely in modern times, the Church had in Lesslie Newbigin a bishop-theologian whose career was primarily shaped by his evangelistic and pastoral responsibilities and who yet made contributions to Christian thought that match in interest and importance those of the more academic among his fellow bishops and teachers. . . . On any reckoning that takes seriously the ecclesial location and reference of theology, Newbigin must be accounted an ineluctable presence of his era.[1]

As I encountered Newbigin's life and writing, I found him to be a compelling figure and a prophetic voice for my own context.

When Newbigin returned to Great Britain, he turned his theological and missionary focus on the "West," those nations and cultures that for many centuries had been Christian and were understood together as "Christendom" but that Newbigin saw in a missionary context. In a small pamphlet titled *The Other Side of 1984*, which was originally delivered as

---

[1]Geoffrey Wainwright, *Lesslie Newbigin: A Theological Life* (New York: Oxford University Press, 2000), v.

the Warfield Lectures at Princeton Theological Seminary and later expanded into the book *Foolishness to the Greeks: The Gospel and Western Culture*, Newbigin considered what would be involved in a "genuinely missionary encounter" between the gospel and Western culture.[2] He argued that Western culture could no longer be considered Christian and, more importantly, that it should not be considered "secular" either. Rather, he proposed, the implicit and explicit beliefs and plausibility structures found in Western culture function as a pagan religion. As such, the church in the West is presented with a missionary challenge.

When I encountered Newbigin's work, his challenge to the church in the West resonated deeply with my own experience as a Christian and a pastor. In the churches where I had participated and served, on both the Atlantic and Pacific coasts of the United States, I sensed that active Christian discipleship was more and more a countercultural lifestyle. Moreover, the core beliefs of Christian faith seemed at odds with the implicit and explicit beliefs common in the wider culture. I sensed this most keenly on Easter, as I and others struggled to bear witness to and grasp the meaning of the resurrection in a swirl of Easter eggs, pastel colors and odes to spring. Newbigin's work helped me both interpret my experience and think more deeply about it.

Specifically, Newbigin's inquiry prompted me to ask homiletical questions in the same vein. If we are now in a missionary context, then how does preaching in this missionary context differ from that in a Christendom context? What homiletical models and assumptions arose from a Christian cultural context and are no longer useful in a missionary context? What kind of preaching equips the church for its missionary existence? What kind of preacher? How does homiletics form such preachers and help them guide the church in their preaching? These are the questions that fueled the fire of this book and led to this proposal for "missional preaching."

The best way to understand this book is to see it as a conversation. If we move momentarily out of the theological disciplines and into the field of rhetoric, this conversation is best understood as ironic discourse, to use the language of Kenneth Burke. Burke posits that language creates

---

[2]Lesslie Newbigin, *Foolishness to the Greeks: The Gospel and Western Culture* (London: SPCK, 1986), 1.

meaning, and he analyzes four master tropes, or literary devices, to demonstrate how it does so. The metaphor is Burke's foundational trope, and it teaches us that knowledge is perspectival. Sounding almost like Dr. Seuss, Burke writes, "Metaphor is a device for seeing something in terms of something else. It brings out the thisness of a that, or the thatness of a this."[3] In other words, metaphors create new perspectives from which to view an object. These perspectives do not dissolve objective reality by introducing multiple relative viewpoints but enable us to establish reality by viewing it from various angles. Only by viewing an object from many perspectives can we approach the truth, which for Burke is "the sublimity of an object in the world."[4]

The next trope is metonymy, which is a figure of speech in which one concept is substituted for another with which it is closely associated. Each of the remaining tropes operates by the invention of metaphor, and all four overlap. If the metaphor teaches us that knowledge is perspectival, "the tutelage of metonymy is that language demands such perspectivism."[5] In order to know truth, which is utterly sublime, we must appeal to symbolic language to describe the truth, though any description is partial and incomplete. According to Burke, this partial, symbolic and reductive construction is a metonym; a metonym attempts to "convey some incorporeal or intangible state in terms of the corporeal or tangible."[6]

Now if a metonym is a reductionistic representation of the truth, then the next trope, synecdoche, is its complement. To define synecdoche, Burke uses conventional phrases such as "part for the whole, whole for the part, container for the contained, sign for the thing signified ... cause for effect, effect for cause" and so forth.[7] In each of these expressions, Burke notes a "relationship of convertibility," which implies "a connectedness between two sides of an equation, a connectedness that, like a road, extends in either direction."[8] In this way, metonymy is a special

---

[3]Kenneth Burke, "Four Master Tropes," *Kenyon Review* 3 (1941): 421.
[4]David Tell, "Burke's Encounter With Ransom: Rhetoric and Epistemology in 'Four Master Tropes,'" *Rhetoric Society Quarterly* 34 (2004): 39.
[5]Ibid., 37.
[6]Burke, "Four Master Tropes," 424.
[7]Ibid., 426.
[8]Ibid., 428.

application of synecdoche that extends in only one direction: reduction. Synecdoche, on the other hand, is primarily concerned with moving in the other direction, abstracting from the metonym and correcting its reductionistic excess. David Tell, interpreting Burke, writes, "If metonymy is the reduction from the immaterial experience of shame to the material experience of colored cheeks, synecdoche is the 'conversion upwards' by which the poet understands that colored cheeks represent shame."[9] Whereas metonym reduces intangible truth to the tangible, synecdoche allows us to move from the tangible toward the truth. In this sense it is the vehicle for human knowledge.

However, this carries with it a troublesome question: can one extrapolate from a reduction toward the truth? To put it differently, using Burke's phrase, can one describe the complex in terms of the simple? To respond to this question, one must first understand Burke's use of the concept of recalcitrance. Although Burke does not mention recalcitrance in "Four Master Tropes," Jeffrey Murray has argued convincingly that it must be recognized as logically prior to and a necessary condition for irony in a Burkean epistemology. According to Burke in *Permanence and Change*, recalcitrance is the resistance offered by reality against our symbolic constructions of reality. It is the resistance of reality to any totalizing perspective. Murray argues that recalcitrance is Burke's way of achieving a balance "between phenomenology's insistence that the universe can be discovered as it is 'in-itself' and the opposite inclination that *any* meaning can be laid upon the universe."[10] Recalcitrance, then, is the disruption of perspective, the very first crashing-in of the "other" that resists totalizing claims to knowledge or understanding. Moreover, it is the condition for irony, the dialogical trope that will bring multiple perspectives into a dialectical tension.

Turning to irony, Burke writes, "Irony arises when one tries, by the interaction of terms upon one another, to produce a development which uses all the terms."[11] In irony, each synecdochal term is a relative perspective that is brought into a dialectical relationship with other relative perspec-

---

[9]Tell, "Burke's Encounter," 43.
[10]Jeffrey W. Murray, "A Dialogue of Motives," *Philosophy and Rhetoric* 35 (2002): 28.
[11]Burke, "Four Master Tropes," 432.

tives. From the standpoint of an observer who considers the participation of all the terms, irony offers a "perspective of perspectives," which is then able to produce a "resultant certainty." This certainty is necessarily ironic because it requires that "all the sub-certainties be considered as neither true nor false, but contributory."[12] Each relative perspective is qualified and disrupted by competing perspectives, such that no one perspective can claim superiority. Rather, each perspective is partial and needs the other perspectives to describe a "truth" that is fundamentally recalcitrant.

While he stresses that each perspective is contributory, Burke cautions against a simplification that would treat all perspectives in a dialogue as the same. He writes, "Although all the characters in a dramatic or dialectic are necessary qualifiers of the definition, there is usually some one character that enjoys the role of *primus inter pares*."[13] For example, Burke notes that in Plato's dialogues Socrates is both an interlocutor and also the "*end or logic*" of the dialogical development. He continues this point, arguing that the most representative anecdote, or metonym, will be one that has a dual function in the dialectic: "one we might call 'adjectival' and the other 'substantial.'" In its adjectival role, the anecdote will be one perspective cast alongside many other perspectives. Yet in its substantial role, the anecdote will "embody the conclusions of the development as a whole."

The substantial character gathers the insights of the ironic dialogue into a tentatively certain understanding of the truth. Moreover, this tentative certainty prompts the audience "not only to induce knowledge from a reduction, but also to seek further reductions from which they might induce knowledge."[14] It prompts the audience—in this case, the reader—to seek other perspectives, more conversation partners, and to arrive at new and different "tentative certainties."

Now, returning to the book in hand, the substantial and adjectival character of this conversation is "missional homiletic," or more precisely my proposal of a missional homiletic. Throughout this conversation, "missional homiletic" is both one concept among many and the concept that gathers the insights of these various perspectives in a tentatively

---

[12]Ibid., 433.
[13]Ibid., 436.
[14]Tell, "Burke's Encounter," 47.

certain way of understanding preaching. In its essence, here is what I am proposing as a missional homiletic: Preaching confesses Jesus Christ through a missional interpretation of scripture in order to equip the congregation for its confession to the world. This is my tentative answer to the question that emerged for me in my encounter with Newbigin's *Foolishness to the Greeks*: What would be involved *homiletically* in a genuinely missionary encounter between the gospel and Western culture?

But that takes us to the end of the conversation before it has started! The point of an ironic dialogue is to see the "thing"—the question of what is involved homiletically in a missionary encounter—from a variety of perspectives. The specific perspectives here, or conversation partners, are three "testimonial" homileticians, the ecclesiology of Karl Barth, and missional theological literature from the United States. In chapter one we will examine the proposals of three homileticians who all understand the preacher as a form of witness and preaching as a form of testimony or bearing witness. Thomas G. Long, in his seminal book *The Witness of Preaching*, argues that the image of preacher as witness is superior to other images common in homiletics (e.g., herald, pastor and storyteller), comprehending their strengths and avoiding their weaknesses. As he develops his proposal, Long relies particularly on the hermeneutics of testimony put forward by Paul Ricoeur. Similarly, Anna Carter Florence understands preaching as testimony and relies on Ricoeur, yet she comes from a feminist theological perspective and her work moves far beyond Long's proposal. Finally, David Lose proposes preaching as confession, which is a specific form of testimony, and he argues that it is theologically and philosophically the most appropriate model for preaching in the postmodern context.

As a group, these three make a strong case for preaching as a form of testimony. Moreover, they each raise crucial and different homiletical questions and in their interacting perspectives form an excellent mutual critical dialogue. The risk in bringing these three proposals together under one heading is the assumption that they all say the same thing, which they do not. Though they all operate within a testimonial framework, there are substantive differences among their proposals. These differences will not be glossed over but will in fact provide the impetus for crucial homiletical and theological decisions in the development of this missional homiletic.

Chapter two will be an in-depth examination of Barth's "The Holy Spirit and the Sending of the Christian Community," which is section 72 of *The Church Dogmatics: Doctrine of Reconciliation* and part of Barth's ecclesiology. It is crucially important, especially for a homiletic that takes seriously the missionary existence of the church, that preaching be situated in a robust ecclesiology. There are ecclesiological implications in the homiletical proposals examined in chapter one, but they are not developed. Barth's ecclesiology provides an understanding of the "sent church" in which to situate a missional homiletic. Indeed, Barth is an excellent conversation partner for this project because of his importance within the broader missional theological conversation. David Bosch, the late South African missional theologian, has argued that Karl Barth develops the sending nature of the triune God and the missionary nature of the church more fully than any other theologian.[15] Moreover, Barth understands the commission given to the church and individual Christians as bearing witness to Jesus Christ. In this sense, Barth understands the whole task of the church to be that which testimonial homiletics assigns to preaching: witness. Thus, Barth's ecclesiology not only provides a framework in which to understand preaching, but provides a strong link to testimonial homiletics.

Moving from Barth's ecclesiology into the lived experience of the church in North America, chapter three will explore missional literature to bring out implications for the practice of preaching. Unfortunately, the word "missional" has been vastly overused and has come to mean too many things, so a bit of background on what I mean by "missional" will be helpful. I use the term in a specific sense to refer to the literature that arises out of the conversations of the Gospel and Our Culture Network (GOCN). The GOCN is a network of churches and organizations "who are working together on the frontier of the missionary encounter of the gospel with North American assumptions, perspectives,

---

[15]David J. Bosch, *Witness to the World: The Christian Mission in Theological Perspective* (Eugene, OR: Wipf & Stock Publishers, 2006), 373.

preferences, and practices."[16] It began in the late 1980s as the North American continuation of the gospel and culture discussion started in Great Britain by Newbigin in the early 1980s. Following up on his insights in *Foolishness to the Greeks*, Newbigin encouraged North American missiologists, in particular George Hunsberger, to begin the work that became the GOCN. The activities of the network—which focus on theological reflection, cultural research and church renewal—are based on the conviction that "genuine renewal in the life and witness of the church comes only with a fresh encounter of the gospel within our culture."[17]

In 1995 the GOCN announced a research project funded by a grant from the Pew Charitable Trusts, the goal of which was to "identify the crucial components for a missiological ecclesiology for the North American mission field." The research team included people from a variety of ecclesiastical traditions and vocational backgrounds. Their three-year project progressed in four stages: (1) they shared with each other their approaches and questions about a missiological ecclesiology and developed a consensus statement regarding basic assumptions and questions to be discussed with outside experts; (2) they met with individuals whose writing they felt could contribute substantively to a missiological ecclesiology, and in the course of discussion looked for signs of an emerging consensus; (3) they continued their reading and research to develop a consensus about the probable shape of a missiological ecclesiology; and (4) they developed this outline into a book written by the whole team and polished by one editor.[18]

The results of their research were published in 1998 with the title *Missional Church: A Vision for the Sending of the Church in North America*, edited by Darrell L. Guder. The writers set a large goal for themselves: to go beyond "tips and tricks" solutions to the problem of the church's displacement in North America and instead to deal with the fundamental issues. They write that the problem "has to do with who we are and what

---

[16]"Why Join?" The Gospel and Our Culture Network, accessed March 7, 2013, www.gocn.org /network/why.

[17]"About the GOCN," The Gospel and Our Culture Network, accessed March 7, 2013, www.gocn.org /network/about.

[18]Darrell L. Guder, "A Missional Vision of Church for North America: A Research Project of the Network," *The Gospel and Our Culture Network Newsletter* 7, no. 4 (December 1995): 1-3.

we are for. The real issues in the current crisis of the Christian church are spiritual and theological."[19] This seminal work first gives a thick description of the North American cultural context, then sketches the outlines of a missionary ecclesiology and its implications in the North American context, and finally explores the implications of this vision for ministerial leadership and church polity.

In its immediate reception, it became clear that *Missional Church* had both put its finger on a problem of widespread concern and raised more questions than it answered. In an *International Bulletin of Missionary Research* review, Lutheran missiologist Robert Scudieri wrote, "I found myself reading *Missional Church* and saying 'Yes, yes! That's us. That is our mission field. That is how we need to work in North America.'"[20] Less enthusiastic but still appreciative is the *International Review of Mission* review by Dennis Smith, a mission coworker for the Presbyterian Church (U.S.A.) in Guatemala. Smith is not dismissive of the study, and indeed writes that he likes its "feisty and prophetic quality." But he sums up his nagging doubt—which he says is no fault of the authors'—by saying, "The book is proposing such fundamental change that it leaves me perplexed as to what those changes would look like if implemented."[21]

Smith is not alone in his doubt, and indeed the question of practicability was recognized by the *Missional Church* team from the start. They knew they were not offering "solutions." But since the publication of their study, they have been actively spreading the good news of their vision for the sending church in North America and trying to flesh out the implications of these changes through numerous books, articles and lectures. Moreover, they have been encouraging others to join the effort. Indeed, this book can be considered an attempt to provide a homiletical answer to the question "What would this change look like?"

So when I say that chapter three will explore missional literature to uncover possible implications for a missional homiletic, I mean specifi-

---

[19]Darrell L. Guder et al., *Missional Church: A Vision for the Sending of the Church in North America* (Grand Rapids: Eerdmans, 1998), 3.

[20]Robert Scudieri, review of *Missional Church: A Vision for the Sending of the Church in North America*, by Darrell L. Guder, *International Bulletin of Missionary Research* 22 (1998): 178.

[21]A. Dennis Smith, review of *Missional Church: A Vision for the Sending of the Church in North America*, by Darrell L. Guder, *International Review of Mission* 87 (1998): 574.

cally the work that has arisen in relation to the Gospel and Our Culture
Network. The chapter will be structured in relation to one particular
piece of missional literature, *Treasure in Clay Jars: Patterns in Missional
Faithfulness*. This work is the fruit of research into the characteristics of
missional congregations in North America. The research was conducted
by a team involved in the Gospel and Our Culture Network that specifically set out to follow up on the ideas proposed in *Missional Church*. The
researchers first identified congregations that could be considered "missional" according to the ecclesiological traits identified in *Missional
Church*, then visited and interviewed them. From those interviews and
visits they developed nine characteristics that they discerned to varying
degrees in these congregations, and they called these characteristics "patterns of missional faithfulness."

These patterns will form the basic outline for exploring a range of
missional literature and developing missional implications for preaching
in chapter three. The use of *Treasure in Clay Jars* makes an important
contribution to this conversation of practical theology because it brings
the "theory" of missional theology into critical dialogue with the lived
experience and practices of missional churches. By allowing the patterns
developed in *Treasure* to shape the exploration of missional literature—
rather than, for example, the imperatives developed in *Missional
Church*—I am explicitly privileging a praxis-oriented theological method.
That is to say, a theological method that places theological norms in
mutual critical dialogue with lived experience and practice.

Speaking of lived experience and practice, while I have been re-
searching and writing this book I have also been "experiencing" and
"practicing." My primary work has been as what my denomination calls
a "solo pastor," the only pastor on staff in a village church that counts
about 170 souls in weekly worship. In this town by the Delaware River I
do all the things that solo pastors in churches like this ordinarily do:
preach, teach, baptize, marry, bury, counsel, visit, cut grass, shovel snow
and unlock doors. And along the way I try to lead the church to be the
church, to understand itself as a parable of the kingdom of God, to live
as the body of Christ in our community and in the world. My secondary
work is as a seminary professor, teaching students in the areas of speech

communication, worship leadership, and preaching. In this work I have the opportunity to think and learn alongside others as we try to understand the shape of Christian ministry today. What should characterize preaching and worship leadership in the church? What is faithful preaching and communication—both faithful to the gospel and to the context in which we are called to bear witness? How can our preaching, communication and leadership address the pressing questions of our time with the good news of the gospel?

This proposal for missional preaching arises from both those areas of work, as a pastor and as a teacher, and is presented in response to the needs and possibilities I have perceived there.

One recent Thanksgiving I was in my study preparing a sermon for the annual Thanksgiving worship service that a group of local churches holds each year. The phone rang, and a person in our town who leads a weekly meditation group was on the line. He told me that his group, which incidentally is not religious, was a planning a community-wide Thanksgiving potluck, and he wondered if I would come and say a blessing before the meal. The potluck was on the same night as the worship service, so I told him I could stop by to say the blessing but would have to leave before dinner.

I arrived early at the local restaurant, which had closed for the night to host the potluck, and chatted with folks as they came. People walked in of every stripe: well-heeled and down-at-the-heels, healthy and sick, young families and widows, luxury sedans parked next to rusted-out vans. They trudged through pouring rain and were glad to do it. They all brought a dish and sat it on the long table and found their place for the meal. After saying the blessing I left and went to the worship service— reluctantly. The worship was also a feast, but it did not leave the same impression as the potluck.

I drove home that night asking myself, where was the kingdom of God breaking in that evening? Ultimately, signs of the kingdom were present both in the worship service and at the potluck, but the events were completely disconnected. The churches were conducting the same Thanksgiving service they had done for decades, while the local community leaders were trying to create table fellowship across socioeconomic and cultural lines. How I wished those two events were part of one witness to Christ! How can preaching form a church that will think beyond its traditions in order to participate in or host a community-wide Thanksgiving potluck with the kind of joy I saw in that restaurant? How can preaching inspire and shape a church to share the goodness of God in Jesus Christ with neighbors near and far, in words *and deeds*? How can preaching equip and send the people of God to be the people of God in the world and for the world? Because the only way the world will possibly believe this good news is if they see a community of people who live it and invite them to live it too. This is the hope of missional preaching.

1

The Preacher as Witness

In recent years many homiletical proposals have cast the preacher as a witness, using witness as a metaphor to understand the identity of the preacher and the work of preaching. In that sense, describing a missional preacher as a witness is claiming common ground with a variety of proposals that understand the preacher as a type of witness. Rather than begin from scratch, I will build off of other witness-oriented homiletical proposals and extend the concept in the direction of missional preaching. Framing the witness of preaching in a missional context means understanding the preacher not only as a witness, but as a witness who equips the congregation for its own witness.

In this chapter we will examine three homiletical proposals that each present the preacher as a witness and together will serve as conversation partners in the development of a missional homiletic: *The Witness of Preaching* by Thomas G. Long, *Preaching as Testimony* by Anna Carter Florence and *Confessing Jesus Christ: Preaching in a Postmodern World* by David J. Lose. These proposals share a strong family resemblance when seen from the perspective of witness because each proposal understands the preacher as a type of witness and preaching as a form of witness, and each relies on common philosophical and hermeneutical underpinnings. Indeed, given the many theological and theoretical differences among them, it is remarkable that these three authors are unanimous in arguing that witness is the most appropriate way to understand and practice the ministry of preaching today.[1]

---

[1]There are more than simply theoretical connections among these three authors and proposals

Despite this strong unifying theme, there are many differences among these proposals and we should not elide these differences under one totalizing perspective. Each proposal has a different animating concern, a different theological frame of reference and different conversation partners, and they each examine a distinctly different dimension of the broad concept of witness. Indeed, these differences are what help make the conversation among these proposals so rich and offer the resources to develop a more nuanced missional homiletic. In what follows, we will first attend to the basic theoretical and theological outlines of each proposal. By doing this we will gain a rich sense of why the metaphor of witness is the most appropriate way to understand preaching in our context, both in comparison to other metaphors and in response to contemporary philosophical and cultural challenges. For some homiletical readers this will be familiar material, but for other readers, especially those coming from the missional theological conversation, this groundwork is essential to understanding the current homiletical landscape, which has moved far beyond "three points and a poem." In order to move our conversation forward, I will then draw out the way each proposal understands the relationship between the preacher and the congregation, and the preacher's witness and the congregation's witness, as these relationships are essential to understanding a missional homiletic.

THE WITNESS OF PREACHING

The Witness of Preaching by Thomas G. Long is intended as an introductory textbook on Christian preaching, and as such most of the book is practical instruction on interpreting a biblical text for preaching, developing that interpretation into a sermon and delivering the sermon. What makes his proposal unique—and after twenty-five years it endures as a widely used textbook—is that Long tries to "allow the theological image of *bearing witness to the gospel* to govern and organize every aspect of the process of creating a sermon from beginning to end—from the

---

and this book. Each proposal was developed at Princeton Theological Seminary. Long was a professor of homiletics in 1989 when he wrote *Witness*, Florence was a doctoral student a decade later when she wrote the dissertation that developed into her book, and Lose was a doctoral student a few years after Florence. In addition, Long is one of the teachers whom Florence credits in her dissertation.

interpretation of the biblical text to the oral delivery of the sermon."[2]

In the first chapter, Long develops this theological image in contrast with other images of preaching by using four basic tropes that describe who the preacher is in the event of preaching. While contrasting each image with the metaphor of witness, Long argues that the preacher as witness "gathers up the virtues of the others and holds their strongest traits in creative tension."[3] So the first image Long explores is the "herald," which he roots biblically by referencing the Greek term *kēryssō* and by which he means the action done by a herald, which is usually translated to the English "preaching."[4] He also connects this image to the early-twentieth-century theological movement that came to be called "neo-orthodoxy," which was closely associated with the work of Karl Barth and helped bring the herald motif to prominence in contemporary homiletical literature.[5]

The essence of the herald metaphor is the very strong connection between the words of the preacher and the voice of God speaking to the congregation. The sermon is an occasion for God to speak, and one

---

[2]Thomas G. Long, *The Witness of Preaching*, 2nd ed. (Louisville: Westminster John Knox, 2005), ix. This quote belongs to the preface to the second edition, and thus is not in the first edition. In the footnotes below, I will note if any quotation in the second edition differs from the first edition: Thomas G. Long, *The Witness of Preaching*, 1st ed. (Louisville: Westminster John Knox, 1989).

[3]Ibid., 45.

[4]I would argue that this image of the preacher as herald is not nearly as biblically rooted as Long allows. There is a slight non sequitur here in that Long uses a Greek verb to give biblical warrant for the use of an English noun. As a verb, *kēryssō* refers not to the herald as a person but to the preaching the herald does. Forms of this verb are used throughout the New Testament to describe various forms of preaching (with the notable exception of the Johannine literature and Hebrews). On the other hand, the nominative form *kēryx*, which we would translate as "herald," appears only three times and only in later writings. The term is never applied to Jesus, is applied to Paul twice (1 Tim 2:7; 2 Tim 1:11) and is used in reference to Noah once (2 Pet 2:5). Thus, while the New Testament writers describe preaching as "heralding," they do not ordinarily describe the preacher as a herald. Why? In his article on *kēryx* and associated words in the *Theological Dictionary of the New Testament*, Gerhard Friedrich posits two possible reasons: (1) In the New Testament the focus is on preaching and not the preacher because God or Christ is the true preacher, and there is thus little place for the human herald as such, and (2) in Greek history, *kēryx* had the specific meaning of an "inviolable sacred personage," which contrasts sharply with Christian preachers who are persecuted and given up to death for Jesus' sake (2 Cor 4:11). See Gerhard Kittel and Gerhard Friedrich, eds. *Theological Dictionary of the New Testament* (Grand Rapids: Eerdmans, 1965), 3:s.v. "kerus."

[5]Though Long connects the use of "herald" to Barth, the connection appears to be somewhat tenuous. In *Preaching and Theology*, James F. Kay notes that Barth himself orients preaching around the term *epangelia* (verb, *epangellomai*), while Rudolf Bultmann orients preaching around the term *kērygma*. See James F. Kay, *Preaching and Theology* (St. Louis: Chalice Press, 2007), 35. Moreover, Long notes that the weaknesses he identifies in the herald image do not come so much from Barth as from his "over-zealous disciples." See Long, *Witness of Preaching*, 28.

listens in order to hear not the preacher but the living voice of God. Long explains three basic implications of this image for preaching. First, "What truly becomes important about preaching . . . is the message, the news the herald proclaims."[6] The message is the gospel, which is the good news of Jesus Christ entrusted to the preacher through the scriptures. Thus the herald "has one clear task with two parts: to attend to the message of the Bible, and to proclaim it plainly."[7] As preachers do this, they rely on God's promise to be present and to speak through the scripture and the sermon.

Second, just as this image emphasizes the divine presence in preaching, it consequently de-emphasizes the human presence in preaching. The focus is not on the preacher's personality, style or skill in developing and delivering the message. Rather, it is on the one whom the preacher represents and on the faithfulness of the sermon to the message of the gospel. Third, and finally, "The herald preacher is both an outsider and an insider and bears, therefore, a paradoxical relationship to the congregation, the church."[8] That is to say, on the one hand, the preacher brings a divine message that comes from outside the congregation. On the other hand, the preacher speaks as one who is part of the church, and the church provides for and nourishes this preaching ministry through which they expect to hear word from God.

Long argues that the strengths of the herald image are that it (1) recognizes the importance of what preachers have to say, (2) reinforces the biblical and theological character of preaching, (3) provides a strong basis for prophetic preaching and (4) insists on the transcendent dimension of preaching. However, there are also significant weaknesses in the herald image. The most important weakness is the motif's marginalization of the humanity of the preacher and the human work of preaching, which entails several problems: (1) it is contrary to what we know of the importance of rhetorical and literary forms of scripture and the importance of those forms for shaping the interpretation of the text, (2) it seriously undercuts

---

[6]Long, *Witness of Preaching*, 20.
[7]Ibid., 21.
[8]Ibid., 22. In the first edition this sentence reads, "The herald preacher has a paradoxical relationship to the congregation, the church" (*Witness*, 1st ed., 27).

efforts to theologically critique the practical aspects of crafting sermons and (3) it is not consonant with a theology of the incarnation of the Word. Finally, in addition to marginalizing the preacher, the image also ignores the context of preaching and the impact of context on the sermon.

The second image Long explores for the preacher is the "pastor." Long writes, "If the herald image focused on the biblical word, on being faithful to God's message, then the pastor image moves all the way to the other end of the spectrum and focuses on the listener, on the impact of the sermon on the hearer."[9] The essence of the pastoral motif is that the preacher seeks to help the listeners and to provoke some change in them through the sermon. Long highlights Harry Emerson Fosdick as the pastoral preacher par excellence, who had the unusual ability to make a personal connection with each hearer even in a large congregation and who encouraged other ministers to follow his therapeutic aim of preaching.[10]

Long lists three basic implications of the pastor image for the practice of preaching, each of which contrasts with the preacher as herald: (1) the most important dimension of preaching for the pastor is what happens inside the hearer, that the hearers are different or better people at the end of the sermon than they were at the beginning, (2) the image of the pastor shines a spotlight on the person of the preacher, "the preacher's personality, character, experience, and relationship to the hearers," and (3) this motif creates a hermeneutical lens through which the preacher interprets the biblical text; the preacher is looking for an interpretation that involves personal issues and offers the possibility of healing.[11]

The strength of this image, Long argues, is that it gives serious attention to the healing power of the gospel and how the gospel affects hearers' lives. In addition, the preacher as pastor provides a much stronger basis on which to consider practical aspects of sermon development and delivery. Despite these strengths, however, Long sees many

---

[9]Ibid., 28. This sentence is not in the first edition.

[10]While Fosdick preached in the early part of the last century, I would argue that contemporary examples of pastoral preaching par excellence come from the movement of "felt need" sermons in the latter half of the twentieth century. Rick Warren is perhaps the most famous contemporary example of the preacher as "pastor."

[11]Long, *Witness of Preaching*, 31. The first edition reads, "The preacher's relationship to the hearers— in terms of style, personality, character, previous experiences, and so on . . . " (*Witness*, 1st ed., 32).

weaknesses with significant implications. First, the preacher as pastor (or equally as counselor) implies a one-to-one, individualized relationship between preacher and hearers. Long writes, "To think of the preacher as pastor almost inevitably views the hearers as a collection of discrete in-dividuals who have personal problems and needs, rather than as a con-gregation, as a church, as a community with a mission."[12] Second, pas-toral sermons almost always focus on the needs and deficits of the hearer and the problems that need to be fixed while forgetting that they also have gifts and assets that can be celebrated and potential that can be challenged. Third, and this is a particularly important point for Long, the pastor image tends toward a utilitarian understanding of the gospel in which the sermon begins with a problem and the gospel yields a solution. Long wants to stress that the eschatological nature of the gospel pre-cludes immediate solutions to all problems. There are some areas of life, such as tragic suffering or inexplicable evil, in which the victory of God is not yet realized and the gospel offers us no immediate answer. Finally, the fourth weakness Long notes is that this motif "runs the risk of re-ducing theology to anthropology by presenting the gospel merely as a resource for human emotional growth."[13]

Long's third image for describing the preacher is "storyteller/poet." This motif focuses on the narrative dimension of the sermon and the poetic expression of language. Moreover, its proponents argue that it can combine the strongest traits of the preacher as herald and as pastor. The storytelling poet/preacher can give serious attention and care to the bib-lical text and to the hearer's communicational needs. Long identifies several possible ways in which homileticians identify the preacher as a storyteller/poet. Some simply intend a more critical and effective use of illustrations, while others want the whole sermon to be narratively struc-tured. Some want to the sermon to be narratively "open-ended" so that listeners help make meaning, others focus on the imaginative experi-ences that can be communicated through poetic language, and still

---

[12]Ibid., 32. The first edition reads, "To think of the preacher as pastor almost inevitably views the hearers of sermons as a collection of discrete individuals who have personal problems and needs rather than as a group, a community, a church with a mission" (*Witness*, 1st ed., 33).

[13]Ibid., 35. The first edition reads, " . . . runs the risk of reducing theology to anthropology by presenting the gospel merely as a resource for human growth" (*Witness*, 1st ed., 35).

others see narrative as a biblical and theological category rather than a form of artistic expression.

Through this variety of possibilities, Long draws implications that set this image in relation to the others considered: (1) like the herald, the storyteller/poet is interested in the content of the gospel "but refuses to divorce that content from the rhetorical forms in which it is found," (2) like the pastor, the storyteller/poet is concerned with the hearer, except in this case the focus is on the listening process, (3) also like the pastor, the storyteller/poet shines a spotlight on the person of the preacher, this time as a narrative artist, and (4) like the pastor, the storyteller/poet is most interested in what happens experientially to the hearer as a result of the sermon.[14]

The storyteller/poet image has several strengths and goes a considerable way toward capturing the strengths of the other motifs while avoiding their weaknesses. It is able to attend to both the message of the gospel and the experience of the hearer; it utilizes rhetoric in a way that is sensitive to the rhetorical form of the gospel; it helps to knit the individual and the community together by creating a common world in the experience of the story; the church is understood as an active teller of the story and not simply a passive hearer; and, finally, it uses a style that is interesting and memorable, making the storyteller/poet a welcome voice.

As with the other images, however, Long sees weaknesses. First he notes that this style tends to "underplay the non-narrative dimensions of Scripture and to narrow to a single method the communicational range of preaching."[15] Even though the broad sweep of the gospel is narrative, the biblical witness includes non-narrative texts that Long argues require a different rhetorical form. Second, he is again very suspicious of placing too much emphasis on the experiential dimension of the preaching event, specifically of measuring the success of a sermon by its effect on the listeners. As he puts it succinctly, "God does not always move us when we desire to be moved, and everything that moves us deeply is not God."[16]

Thus all three images—herald, pastor and storyteller—have strengths and weaknesses. Moving into his own proposal, Long argues that the

---

[14]Ibid., 42.
[15]Ibid., 44.
[16]Ibid.

image of the preacher as a witness and preaching as an act of bearing witness to the gospel is more suited to "disclose the true character of Christian preaching" than any of the others.[17] Moreover, he believes it is able to draw together their strengths and hold them in creative tension.

Long begins by grounding his own proposal in biblical imagery. He notes as an example Acts 20:24, "where Paul is reported to have said, 'But I do not count my life of any value to myself, if only I may finish the course and the ministry that I have received from the Lord Jesus, to testify to the good news of God's grace.'"[18] He also notes the Old Testament usage of witness, out of which the New Testament usage develops, specifically citing Isaiah 43:8-13. In two places in this passage the Lord through the prophet says to the people, "You are my witnesses."[19]

This Isaiah passage is important not only for Long; it is also crucial for Paul Ricoeur, the Christian hermeneutical philosopher on whom he relies. Long writes that in his comments on this passage, Ricoeur deduces four features of witness:

1. The witness is not a volunteer, not just anyone who comes forward to give testimony, but only the one who is *sent* to testify.

2. The testimony of the witness is not about the global meaning of human experience but about God's claim upon life. It is Yahweh who is witnessed to in the testimony.

3. The purpose of the testimony is proclamation to all peoples. It is on behalf of the people, for their belief and understanding, that the testimony is made.

4. The testimony is not merely one of words but rather demands a total engagement of speech and action. The whole life of the witness is bound up in the testimony.[20]

---

[17]Ibid., 45.

[18]Ibid.

[19]Given that I am arguing that missional preaching shifts the focus of witness from the individual to the community, it is interesting to note that in Isaiah the prophet treats the witness as the corporate community. It is "you, O Jacob," "you, O Israel" who are the witnesses (Is 43:1).

[20]Ibid., 46. Long is relying here on Ricoeur's essay "The Hermeneutics of Testimony," in *Essays on Biblical Interpretation*, ed. Lewis S. Mudge (Philadelphia: Fortress, 1980), 131. Ricoeur's larger point, in making the connection between testimony and interpretation, is that a witness must interpret an event in order to give testimony and that giving testimony is an essential element of interpretation.

In addition to adopting these characteristics of witness from Ricoeur, Long also follows Ricoeur by locating the image of witness in the context of a legal trial.[21] As in a trial, preachers are witnesses who give public testimony about what they have seen and heard and what they believe about it. They come from the people, as one of them, to a particular place in order to testify to the truth. The truth is ultimately what the court is interested in, and in this sense the person of the witness is not the focus of the proceeding. On the other hand, though, the court has access to the truth only through witnesses and their testimony, thus making their personal character and experience vitally important. In this sense the life of the witness is bound to the testimony, and as such witnesses put their life and reputation at risk.

From this Long draws several important implications for the preacher as witness, each of which explains his claim that this image gathers up the strengths of the others and holds them in tension. First, the preacher as witness presents the authority of the preacher in a new light. The preacher's authority does not come from education, experience, depth of faith, rank or power. Rather, it comes from the preacher's encounter with God while wrestling with the biblical text. Long writes, "When [this encounter] happens, the preacher becomes a witness to what has been seen and heard through the Scripture, and the preacher's authority grows out of this seeing and hearing."[22] Moreover, in Long's view, the crucial formal event that gives authority to the witness is ordination, wherein the church sets the witness apart as the one whom they send to the text in order to have an encounter to which the preacher will then bear witness.[23]

The second implication Long notes is that the image of witness offers

---

[21]Long suggests that homileticians have historically been reluctant to embrace this image because the courtroom connotation implies that the preacher is condemning the congregation rather than offering a word of grace and mercy. One may recall the preaching style and theory of Charles Finney, who conceived of the preacher as a prosecutor and the hearer as a sinner being cross-examined. While Long follows Ricoeur by taking up the image of juridical testimony, David Lose, as we will see later in this chapter, argues on biblical grounds that juridical testimony should not be the governing motif for preaching.

[22]Long, *Witness of Preaching*, 47.

[23]As we will see later in this chapter, Anna Carter Florence argues against ordination as a formal authorization for preaching on the basis of its embeddedness in oppressive patriarchal structures. This is a key point of disagreement between Long and Florence, who was his student. Moreover, the question of whether ordination is a requirement for preaching leads directly into missional theological debates over clericalism and ordered offices.

a distinct way of approaching the Bible. The preacher does not go to scripture in order to gather timeless principles about God, but rather goes in order to encounter God through scripture. Long understands the Bible as a "faithful witness to the interactions of God with the whole creation."[24] Moreover, as one studies this witness one comes to know God and is potentially able to encounter the living presence and voice of God. Crucially, it is this encounter—apparently not the text, nor a summary of the gospel—that is the basis for and the content of the preacher's testimony. As Long puts it, "Witnesses testify to events, and the event to which the preacher testifies is the encounter between God and ourselves."[25]

Third, the image of witness provides a place for rhetoric and rhetorical form, which will be shaped by the preacher's encounter with God through the text. Rhetoric here is not simply ornamentation to the sermon, like a moving illustration, but is the whole way the preacher shapes the words and patterns of the sermon to correspond to the truth the preacher has heard and seen. As such, the rhetorical styles of the sermon will be as varied as the preacher's experience.[26] The fourth implication is that the witness is not a neutral observer. Witnesses are not neutral, first, in the sense that their testimony is bound and deeply connected to their lives, and they stake their reputation and life on the truth of their testimony. In the second place, witnesses are not neutral because they are located in a particular community and context that shapes their understanding of scripture and encounter with God.

---

[24]Long, *Witness of Preaching*, 48.

[25]Ibid. By framing it this way, grounding preaching on a preacher's experience, one wonders what the objective criteria are—if there are any—for faithful Christian preaching. This question follows us in our examination of the other two homiletical proposals and later in the development of a missional homiletic.

[26]At various points in his writings, it seems that Long has different understandings of the use of rhetoric in the development of the sermon. Sometimes he argues as he does here, that the rhetorical form of the sermon flows from the preacher's experience of God through the text (*Witness*, 49). At other times, the rhetorical form appears to be shaped more by the literary form of the text (see *Preaching and the Literary Forms of the Bible* [Philadelphia: Fortress, 1989], 33-34) and at other times by the response the preacher desires from the congregation (*Witness*, 137-48). I asked Long to clarify this point and he responded that, while the sermonic form will in some way reflect both the literary form of the text and the preacher's experience, ultimately it is guided by how the preacher can best carry out the focus and functional intentions of the sermon (Thomas G. Long, personal communication, June 24, 2011). In this sense it appears that, for Long, homiletical rhetoric is aimed more toward influencing the congregation than communicating the preacher's experience.

Finally, "The witness image underscores the ecclesiastical and liturgical setting of preaching."[27] Here Long envisions Christian worship as a reenactment of a cosmic trial, wherein God is set against all that opposes his will and way and in which Christ is the only true and faithful witness. "All human testimony," Long writes, "is authentic only to the extent that it remains faithful to the witness of Christ."[28]

As he moves from this initial chapter into the remainder of the textbook, Long extends this image of the preacher as witness into various aspects of developing and delivering a sermon. We now have, though, a broad sense of Long's proposal for preaching as witness, and so we can turn to his understanding of the role of the congregation relative to the preacher. Though he mentions the congregation, community or church often in his description of the event of preaching and the preacher as a witness, he never specifically outlines his understanding of the congregation relative to the preacher. Implicitly, I see four clear lines of thought that emerge.

First, Long stresses repeatedly that the preacher comes from the congregation as one of the congregation. He begins the book with an engaging story of a guest preacher trying to find his way to the chancel and turns the story into a theological question of how the preacher gets to the pulpit. However the logistical reality works out, Long's theological answer is that the preacher comes from the pew, which is to say from the congregation. Moreover, this is the case in two specific senses. First, the preacher has been with the congregation immediately before the event of preaching (in fellowship, education and so on) and has been involved in their lives throughout the week. Second, the preacher is, like the whole congregation, one of the baptized, and though the preacher has received a special calling to preach, the preacher shares in the baptismal calling of the whole church. In his proposal for the preacher as a witness, one can see this understanding of the preacher as one of the congregation unfold as Long discusses the social and theological situatedness of the preacher and the impact it has on the interpretation of the text and on the sermon.

Second, the preacher is sent by the congregation to the text in order to encounter the presence of God and bear witness to that encounter.

---

[27]Long, *Witness of Preaching*, 50.
[28]Ibid.

Preachers do not go to the text simply on a whim. Indeed, as Long understands it, preachers' formal authority rests precisely in that they do not go on their own but are sent by the community. He writes, "To call the preacher an authority does not mean the preacher is wiser than others. What it does mean is that the preacher is the one whom the congregation sends on their behalf, week after week, to the Scripture."[29] This act of sending is formalized in ordination, and it receives practical expression as the church sends its ministers to seminary to receive training in how to listen to scripture.

In addition, this act of sending by the congregation means that preachers do not go to the text by themselves. The encounter between the preacher and the text is not simply one person's encounter but is also the encounter of the whole community with the text through the preacher. Long writes, "The preacher goes on behalf of the faithful community, and, in a sense, on behalf of the world."[30] Preachers approach the text not simply with their own questions, concerns and needs, but with those of the community that has sent them there and that awaits a word from them.

Third, the event of preaching takes place in the context of the community that is gathered for worship. Of course, preaching happens in other settings, but corporate worship is the paradigmatic setting. Moreover, Long argues, "preaching and the community of faith . . . are reciprocal realities." The witness of preaching gathers the community of faith, and the community of faith "continues to bear witness to Christ in and for the world through every aspect of its life, including preaching."[31] This reciprocal relationship, which Long does not unfold, points precisely in the direction of missional preaching, wherein the witness of the preacher equips the congregation for its witness.

Finally, Long understands the preaching ministry as a form of the ministry of proclamation that is given to the whole community. He writes, "The whole church proclaims the gospel, and the preaching of sermons is but one part of this larger ministry. So when a preacher stands in the pulpit, reads the Scripture, and preaches the sermon, this action is but another

---

[29]Ibid., 48.
[30]Ibid., 49.
[31]Ibid., 51.

form of the one common ministry to which the whole church is called."[32]

Furthermore, even the ministry of preaching does not belong to the preacher or the community. The ministry of preaching belongs to Christ and is given to the community, and it is then entrusted to and exercised through the preacher. At no point is the ministry of preaching not a ministry of the whole community. It is exercised in the context of and in connection to the other elements of worship in which the people of God proclaim the gospel.

As we turn from Long's *Witness* to another homiletic proposal, I want to briefly highlight what I see as the strongest contributions of Long's work to a missional homiletic. First, Long surveys the field of homiletics and places the image of witness in relation to other images as one that embraces their various strengths and holds them together. In this sense he makes a strong case for the preacher as witness in the context of the wider field of homiletics and offers a sturdy bridge into the missional theological conversation. Second, he concisely and clearly lays out his understanding of the preacher as a witness, building his motif on Ricoeur's hermeneutics of testimony. This becomes a common thread that links the homiletical proposals we will consider and provides a hermeneutical basis on which to understand the preacher as witness. Third, and especially important for this project, Long situates preaching firmly in the context of the Christian community, identifying the "reciprocal reality" that is the primary interest of a missional homiletic.

Preaching as Testimony

In *Preaching as Testimony* Anna Carter Florence also understands the preacher as a witness and the act of preaching as bearing witness, or giving testimony, and she uses Ricoeur's Christian hermeneutics of testimony to develop her work. In this sense her work shares a familial relationship to Long's. That said, Florence's vision of preaching as testimony is very different from Long's understanding of preaching as bearing witness to the gospel.

To understand her proposal it is important first to understand the perspective from which Florence writes and the deep concern that ani-

---

[32]Ibid., 4.

mates her work. She writes from a feminist perspective, a point that is clearer in the dissertation on which her book is based than in the book itself. At the outset of the dissertation, published in 2000, she notes that a recently developed branch of homiletical theory is feminist homiletics, which seeks "to critique and reconstruct the practice of preaching from the perspective of feminist theory."[33] Florence understands her distinct contribution to this effort as uncovering historical accounts of women who were noted for their preaching and extrapolating contemporary implications. Thus, the first section of *Preaching as Testimony* tells the stories of Anne Marbury Hutchinson (1591–1643), Sarah Osborn (1714–1796) and Jarena Lee (1783–?), each of whom was a noted preacher and persecuted for preaching.

Florence discovered in mining these historical narratives that each of these women described their preaching as "testimony." They did this in part because at the time "preaching" was understood as a certain liturgical activity reserved exclusively for men, and in this androcentric context these women could defend themselves by claiming they were testifying and not preaching. Whatever the women called it, both supporters and opponents called it preaching, and there was an intense public reaction to it. These discoveries led Florence to wonder, "Does testimony blur the boundaries of what a sermon is and who may preach it?"[34] Thus she began to explore preaching as testimony.

While Florence's perspective is feminist, the deep concern that animates her work is the authority by which the preacher preaches. This concern connects with her feminist perspective because she argues that traditional understandings of authority in preaching were used to oppress women and prevent them from preaching. For instance, formal authority to preach was traditionally conferred by ordination and often predicated on formal education, both of which were customarily denied to women. However, in the historical examples she uncovered, Florence discovered that the women who preached had enormous actual authority that was conferred by their witness. She writes, "The authority of their

---

[33] Anna Carter Florence, "Preaching as Testimony: Towards a Women's Preaching Tradition and New Homiletical Models" (PhD diss., Princeton Theological Seminary, 2000), 1.

[34] Anna Carter Florence, *Preaching as Testimony* (Louisville: Westminster John Knox, 2007), xx.

witness convicted them and others, and their engagement with it—how fully they gave themselves over to their testimony—proved to be more powerful than any other skill or asset."[35]

Florence also connects her concern for the source of authority in preaching to the postmodern milieu. She claims that in the contemporary situation, traditional understandings of knowledge and power, who has it and where it comes from, are no longer valid. Florence writes, "When church and society face challenges to orthodoxy, tradition, and leadership, preachers are continually forced to ask themselves by what authority they stand in the pulpit as interpreters of Scripture, and whether that authority 'allows' them to speak openly."[36] As she reflects on her interactions with preachers and students learning to preach, particularly those who are questioning traditional sources of authority, Florence writes that she finds:

> More and more . . . preachers are relying not on outside authorities as the proof of their words . . . but on the authority of testimony. . . . More and more, preachers are finding that what makes their sermons authoritative for their people is not the number of footnotes but the depth of the preacher's engagement with the Scriptures and life itself.[37]

In other words, preachers are finding that testimony is a key source—perhaps the only source—of authority in the contemporary situation, and thus Florence sets out to develop a homiletical proposal that understands preaching as testimony.

By testimony, Florence means "both a narration of events and a confession of belief: we tell what we have seen and heard, and we confess what we believe about it."[38] Her thesis is that "preaching in the testimony tradition provides us with a historical, biblical, theological, and homiletical memory of women's preaching: in short, a women's preaching tradition."[39] As she unfolds her thesis, she uses historical accounts of

---

[35] Ibid., 67.
[36] Ibid., xvi.
[37] Ibid., xvii.
[38] Ibid., xiii. In Ricoeur's understanding, confession is that part of testimony in which the witness makes a claim about the significance of the events she has seen and heard. As we will see, David Lose develops his theory of preaching as confession in relation to this aspect of testimony.
[39] Ibid., xvii.

women's testimony to provide backing for her claim, and theories of biblical testimony and feminist theology provide warrants for her argument. When seen together, Florence argues that the interplay of these resources reveals something that has been invisible on the homiletical landscape: an authentically feminist homiletic that can help both men and women who seek to preach in a postmodern environment.

To explain the distinctive characteristics of biblical testimony, Florence relies on the hermeneutics of Paul Ricoeur and the biblical scholarship of Walter Brueggemann. As noted earlier, Florence's reading of Ricoeur is largely similar to Long's reading, though she draws slightly different implications. For Florence, the essence of Ricoeur's theory is that "testimony gives something to be interpreted and, at the same time, calls for an interpretation."[40] The act of giving testimony is an act of interpreting an experience one has had. Moreover, since testimony is both narration and confession, it resists certitude and therefore others must make a judgment—an interpretation of their own—about the truthfulness of the testimony. Furthermore, Florence argues, the engagement of the witness who gives the testimony is crucial because those who hear the testimony have no access to the originating experience; they must make their judgments based only on the character of the witness and the testimony given. Florence notes that, as with Jesus Christ, the "trial may turn against us," the judgment may be negative and suffering the result. Yet that is the cost of true testimony, of witness that is fully engaged.[41]

Based on Ricoeur's theory of Christian interpretation, Florence draws two specific implications for homiletics. First, the authority of the preacher's testimony now rests not on ordination or rhetorical skill but on the preacher's engagement as a witness. Florence finds this consonant with the experience of Hutchinson, Osborn and Lee, whose authority came from "how fully they gave themselves over to their testimony."[42] Because the authority of preaching comes from the engagement of the witness, this means that preaching "is open and available to anyone willing to pattern

---

[40]Ibid., 63.
[41]Ibid., 64.
[42]Ibid., 67.

herself after the testimony of Christ."[43] Note that this is different from Long's proposal, in which the formal authority of the preacher comes from the congregation sending the preacher to the text, a sending made explicit in ordination. Indeed, it is Florence's specific intention to remove ordination as a necessary source of authority for preaching.

Second, the content of preaching is experience, but not experience so broadly conceived that it could include anything that ever happened to the preacher. Instead, "Ricoeur suggests that we simplify things, as follows: *experience, as it relates to testimony, is an encounter with God.*"[44] Thus, Florence argues that human experience has a central place in preaching but only the experience in which God meets us and about which we then confess what we believe. This sounds very similar to Long's approach, and indeed he also claims that the content of preaching is not facts about God gleaned from the text but the encounter the preacher has with God through the text. The important difference between them on this point is the relative weight they are willing to place on the preacher's experience. Florence places the whole burden of homiletical authority on the preacher's experience, while Long locates the preacher's authority in the sending of the congregation as well as the experience with God through the text.

In addition to Ricoeur, Florence uses Walter Brueggemann's *Theology of the Old Testament* to argue that Israel's speech patterns for God in the Old Testament are a model for biblical interpretation and that those speech patterns most closely fit the category of testimony. Of the four types of testimony Brueggemann discerns in the Old Testament (core, counter, solicited and embodied), Florence focuses only on core and counter testimony. The core testimony of the Old Testament, according to Brueggemann, is "God is incomparable."[45] This is the essential thing that Israel says throughout the various events of its history, even when the circumstances of its existence oppose the truth of the confession. Moreover, such contrary circumstances are not hidden in Israel's history but are brought out in its countertestimony, which is the way in which

---

[43]Ibid.
[44]Ibid., 69.
[45]Ibid., 71.

Israel challenges its own core testimony. For instance, declaring God's hiddenness, ambiguity or instability, and negativity are ways that Israel bears witness to its experience and counters the core testimony.

From Brueggemann's theory Florence draws several implications for preaching as testimony. First, as she writes, "Brueggemann takes Ricoeur a step further: testimony is not only the distinctive Christian way of speaking and knowing but also the distinctive biblical way of speaking and knowing."[46] In other words, there is biblical warrant for preaching as testimony, and there is a wide range of testimonial types and models found in the Bible. Second, there is now more specificity to what authoritative engagement of the witness means: it means hearing and embodying the biblical text, and then speaking what we see and believe. Such speech is "true speech" because it intends "to interrupt the order and bring about justice."[47] Finally, those who offer this "true speech" do so as God's partner. Preachers are not neutral, objective or detached in their speech; rather, they speak as ones who have encountered God, who live with God and who speak in partnership with God.

Thus Florence uses the work of Ricoeur and Brueggemann to understand testimony from a hermeneutical and biblical perspective. For the theological criteria by which to interpret scripture and assess the content of testimony, Florence turns first to Mary McClintock Fulkerson's feminist theology of biblical interpretation and then to Rebecca Chopp's feminist theology of proclamation. In Changing the Subject: Women's Discourses and Feminist Theory, published in 1994, Fulkerson argues that the trouble with feminist theology is that it universalizes "women's experience" and does not pay significant attention to the particular experience of women. So she proposes that feminist theology understand itself as testimony and focus on the interpretive meaning-making done by particular women in particular communities. To illustrate this, she studies the ways poor Pentecostal women and middle-class Presbyterian women interpret the same scripture and arrive at different meanings.

Fulkerson's conclusion is the assertion that texts themselves are inherently unstable: they lend themselves to a variety of readings and meanings.

---

[46]Ibid., 74.
[47]Ibid., 77.

As Florence writes, "The thing that stabilizes the biblical text . . . is a community's reading of it: what they are interpreting it *for*. Meaning emerges from practice. Meaning depends on performance."[48] So when a person reads a text, her reading is a "graf(ph)t," a term Fulkerson coined to express the sense that an interpretation is both a new creation and dependent on the host (the text) for its life. In the case of the poor Pentecostal women, they graf(ph)ted an understanding of God's empowering presence onto texts that would traditionally prohibit women from preaching in order to neutralize the patriarchal oppression inherent in the text. The key homiletical implication Florence draws from this theory is that experience is not only part of the interpretation of a text, and therefore of preaching, but is necessary: experience is a sine qua non of preaching. As Florence writes, "If you haven't experienced the text, you can't preach. You haven't seen anything and you haven't earned the right to say a blessed word."[49]

Thus preaching as testimony requires an experience of the text, yet there must be criteria by which to assess the experience lest it become pure subjectivity. For that criteria, Florence turns to Rebecca Chopp's feminist theology of proclamation. First, Florence draws on Chopp's understanding of the word of God "as perfectly open sign." Essentially, this means that the word is not bound within the cultural system of the "present age," a system that oppresses and marginalizes women. Rather, the word is always disrupting that system by its very openness. Florence writes, "It is a Word that opens up many voices, any of which can push and challenge and transform the present order. This Word is always open

---

[48]Ibid., 84.

[49]Ibid., 91. I assume here that Florence is calling for the preacher to have a personal experience with the text, but this conclusion does not seem to necessarily follow from Fulkerson's argument. If we agree that (1) texts are inherently unstable and that a community's interpretation provides stability, and that (2) some texts call for new interpretations graf(ph)ted from the experience of the reader, it does not necessarily follow that the preacher must have an "experience" of the text in order to preach a sermon based on it. It is possible, for instance, for the preacher to preach based on the community's experience of the text, though it may not be her own. Or it is possible to preach based on the graf(ph)ted interpretation of someone else in the community, not the preacher. In fact, I would argue that this characterizes most preaching. To put it in classical language, preachers preach the "deposit of faith," the faith that is experienced and passed on in and by the church. Only on occasion do preachers preach what they have personally experienced.

to new meaning; it is perfectly open sign; it is God."[50] Preaching, which is the word that proclaims the word, must therefore be like the word itself: it must be an open sign.

Florence makes two notes in relation to how preachers may use scripture in order to preach as an "open sign." First, scripture is prototypical rather than archetypical. This means it is a model or paradigm for future proclamation, but it is not a decisive or final proclamation. Scripture is ancient proclamation through which the perfectly open word moved, and the sermon is analogously contemporary proclamation. Second, scripture is interpreted by women through a hermeneutics of marginality, which construes scripture in the context of an "open dialogue about freedom." Florence writes, "A feminist reading of Scripture searches for freedom in the text and in life."[51] Thus when preachers go to the text in order to experience the presence of God, they must assess their experience according to the way of the perfectly open sign and the prototype of scripture: it must come from the margins to challenge the present system, always moving toward liberation and freedom.[52]

Having now seen the broad contours of Florence's proposal, I want to highlight how she understands the congregation relative to the preacher. While Florence does not make these relationships explicit, I see three basic implications emerge in her proposal. First, the congregation includes those who are possibly resistant to preaching as testimony, who cling to systems of oppression and resist the liberating word. Indeed, Florence's whole proposal is set against the backdrop of the "system"—including preachers and congregations—that resists "true preaching." In congregations, Florence suggests that this primarily refers to listeners who want "orthodox" interpretations, who listen for sermons with clear answers in black-and-white terms, and who trust in systems of authority such as education and ordination. Likewise, preachers caught in the

---

[50]Ibid., 95.

[51]Ibid., 96.

[52]In contrast to Florence, Long does not give similar theological criteria by which to assess the preacher's encounter with God through the text. He argues that whatever claim the preacher makes must develop directly out of the exegesis of the text (*Preacher as Witness*, 108-12). Furthermore, he encourages preachers to reflect on their own theological heritage and core theological affirmations before going to the text. These reflections could provide criteria for assessment (59-63).

"system" believe that if they give these congregations what they want, then the gospel will be heard and their ministry will be a success. Throughout her proposal, Florence encourages preachers to resist and challenge the system, to take the risk of preaching as testimony and lead their congregations in a new direction. To put this implication in other language drawn from missional theological conversations, Florence is characterizing the congregation and the preacher as being in need of continuing conversion.

Second, an unspoken implication of Florence's homiletic is that members of the congregation are themselves preachers, called to testify to their experience with God. The readership audience Florence has specifically in view are preachers who preach on Sunday morning, but the thrust of her theory opens the door to preaching at anytime, by anyone. As Florence notes, the preaching ministry traditionally has been restricted on the basis of education and ordination, the two authority structures that Florence overturns because they have been used to oppress women. By contrast, drawing on the history of women's preaching, Florence asserts that testimony has an intrinsic authority that arises from one's experience with God. Florence clearly recognizes that construing homiletical authority in this way opens the pulpit to women. A more far-reaching implication, though, is that this understanding of preaching makes anyone at anytime a potential preacher.[53] Here, Florence is touching on what missional theologians describe as the common vocation to witness that is given to all the baptized: every Christian is called and gifted to bear witness to the gospel.

Finally, the third understanding of the relationship between the preacher and the congregation is that the preacher lives among the congregation as a "theologian in residence," one who knows them and loves

---

[53]At this point Florence's work brings us into a debate that reverberates through the Protestant Reformation and that also bears on a missional homiletic. Florence's contention that anyone is authorized to preach resembles an Anabaptist understanding of preaching, despite Florence's own Reformed roots. One may think here of Quaker meetings in which the ministry of the word is undertaken by anyone of the congregation who feels moved to stand and speak. On the other hand, the Reformed stream of the Reformation has typically restricted the ministry of the word to those who meet certain qualifications in order to guard against false teaching or "fanaticism." See Kay, *Preaching and Theology,* 16–19. This debate bears on a missional homiletic because these two perspectives are also in tension in missional literature: on the one hand, the desire to empower the whole congregation to perform the tasks of ministry and, on the other hand, the theological and practical need for ordered offices. We will return to this point in more detail in chapter four.

them. As theologian in residence, the preacher is one who speaks of God while living among a particular people, in their context and sharing their life. Moreover, the relationship between the preacher and the congregation is characterized fundamentally by love. Florence writes that she has found it helpful in her homiletical teaching to remind a preacher that "everything she says is with and for these people, not apart from them or against them. Preachers and listeners share the same interpretive space. They practice and receive the same love."[54] Thus the mutual life and love of the preacher and congregation is the context in which the sermon arises and in which it is delivered.

Before we turn to our final homiletical proposal, I want to conclude this discussion of *Preaching as Testimony* by highlighting what I see as its strongest contribution to a missional homiletic. By repositioning homiletical authority on the structure of testimony rather than education and ordination, Florence has opened a homiletical path for breaking out of a clerical paradigm and authorizing people who are not ordained, indeed all the baptized, to preach. What Florence says of preachers and preaching could easily be said of all Christians and all proclamation. Indeed, I believe Florence has made a homiletical argument for what I would call the witness of the congregation. She argues that testimony is the essential form of Christian speech and that it is available to all Christians without educational or ordinational distinction. This affirmation resonates deeply with a theology and homiletics that takes seriously the vocation of the Christian community in light of the mission of God.

CONFESSING JESUS CHRIST

We turn now to the final homiletical proposal, in which David Lose offers a homiletical theory that specifically engages postmodern epistemological critiques and responds to them by construing preaching as a form of witness. In the sense that both Lose and Florence propose preaching as a form of witness and both respond to the "authority challenge" of postmodernism, they offer homiletic proposals that share a family resemblance. Like Florence, Lose is concerned with the authority

---

[54]Florence, *Preaching as Testimony*, 154.

structure underlying contemporary preaching and offers a form of testimony as an adequate authority structure on which to understand preaching. Beyond these general similarities, however, their work differs widely and is often in disagreement. Within the context of developing a missional homiletic, their divergent work on the same theme offers a mutually critical dialogue.

In *Confessing Jesus Christ: Preaching in a Postmodern World*, David Lose begins by articulating his understanding of the challenge posed to preaching by the postmodern situation. Lose understands postmodernism "chiefly as a reaction to modernist assumptions about: (1) the basis for knowledge and (2) language's ability to represent reality."[55] These modernist assumptions are otherwise known as "Enlightenment" assumptions, those beliefs and ways of knowing that arose from the various enlightenments that swept across Europe from the mid-seventeenth century. The Enlightenment era, Lose argues, was essentially an effort to construct a universally valid rationality that would not rely on theological or philosophical speculation to ground its assertions. On the one hand this pursuit took the form of Descartes's process of discerning first truths through rational and logical deduction, and on the other hand it took the form of Locke's process of empirical observation and verification. Both men, together with the rational and empirical traditions of inquiry they espoused respectively, were seeking the same goal: "indubitable 'first truths' or 'universal foundations' . . . on which to ground all knowledge."[56] Modernity for Lose is thus characterized as the "resolute and optimistic desire to discover, study, describe, and ultimately harness the universal laws of the created order."[57] Likewise, postmodernity is typified by the dissipation of this optimistic resolve.

Postmodernity then is an assault on modernist assumptions about: (1) the basis of knowledge and (2) language's ability to represent reality. In

---

[55]David J. Lose, *Confessing Jesus Christ: Preaching in a Postmodern World* (Grand Rapids: Eerdmans, 2003), 7. This book is a further development of Lose's dissertation at Princeton Theological Seminary, "Confessing Jesus Christ: Preaching in a Postmodern World" (PhD diss., Princeton Seminary, 2000). Whereas there are significant differences between Florence's dissertation and book, differences which made exploration of her dissertation fruitful for understanding her work, Lose's book and dissertation are nearly identical and thus reference will made only to the book.

[56]Ibid., 10.

[57]Ibid.

the modern milieu, certain philosophical foundations were considered to be the basis of knowledge, which Lose describes as "unquestioned assertions of what is undeniably and self-evidently true, assertions that serve to undergird our sense that the world is, ultimately, a coherent, unified, and meaningful place."[58] Postmodern critics gladly point out that what one person takes to be a universally valid foundation is another person's unfounded and unquestioned assumption. Moreover, they argue, this unquestioned assumption masquerading as an unquestionable foundation is used to exclude (and discriminate against) whatever does fit into the established order and thus to perpetrate oppression and injustice. Postmodernists, therefore, relentlessly press against "foundations" and "agreed assumptions" to create a world characterized by competing voices and claims where no idea is privileged or excluded. Rather than a universally valid ontology or epistemology, postmodernists seek "pragmatic, ever-local determinations of the good, the true, and the beautiful."[59]

In addition to launching an assault on a modernist basis of knowledge, postmodernist critics also challenge language's ability to represent reality. In a modernist view, language describes and helps us engage with the world in which we live. To put it another way, language is a tool we use to interact with the world around us. From a postmodernist perspective, however, language does not simply represent reality, it creates reality; it does not describe the world around us, it produces the world around us. As Lose writes, "Our various characterizations of the 'world' are not neutral descriptions of 'reality' but rather imaginative sociosymbolic constructs that produce, rather than reflect, the world(s) we inhabit."[60]

This insight implies a profound "loss of innocence" for humanity and has at least four important implications: (1) if reality is a sociosymbolic construction, then history loses its teleological dimension, (2) humanity is culpable for the reality it constructs, (3) while language creates worlds, each world is self-contained and unable to refer beyond itself, and (4) if reality is constructed, then "truth" must ultimately be judged as relative to its "reality." These implications in turn have profound and severe implica-

---

[58]Ibid., 13.
[59]Ibid., 17.
[60]Ibid., 18.

tions for homiletics and indeed for anyone who wishes to speak meaningfully about reality and truth. If reality is linguistically constructed and truth is thus relative, is it possible to speak meaningfully to those outside one's cultural-linguistic community? On this point, Lose argues that perhaps "the most damaged item in the postmodern fray is not so much a unified sense of the truth . . . but the very possibility of even speaking about . . . a truthful description of our physical and moral world."[61]

Lose has intentionally presented the postmodern challenge in such stark terms because he intends to chart an epistemological middle way, a way that avoids the alternative traps of foundationalism and relativism. In his view, those who have attempted to resolve the conflict directly have been drawn back into problems that arise from the assumptions that frame the argument itself. Thus, he proposes that "the only way to 'resolve' these philosophical deadlocks is to sidestep them altogether and reframe the questions at hand by paying attention, not first to the metaphysical issues involved but instead to our actual practices."[62] To do this he will direct his attention to three crucial issues: (1) an epistemology characterized by critical fideism, (2) the ability of language to refer beyond itself and (3) our limited ability to speak of the real and the true.

Lose's exploration of critical fideism begins with an observation that boils his argument down to its essence: "Regardless of our ability to prove *whether we know* or demonstrate *how we know*, on a day-to-day basis we in fact *believe that we do know*."[63] He is concerned less with philosophical inquiry into the foundations of knowledge and much more with the practical use of knowledge. Thus he wishes to set aside the question of ultimate epistemological foundations, which he believes to be a dead end, and deal instead with the penultimate epistemological foundations that undergird everyday life. In everyday life, communities share penultimate epistemological foundations that help them make sense of the world and describe their encounter with and experience of what they call reality.

Moreover, as Richard Rorty has argued, these penultimate foundations

---

[61]Ibid., 27.
[62]Ibid., 33.
[63]Ibid., 35.

are not rooted in universally valid criteria but in communally held sets of beliefs. Furthermore, using the work of Ihab Hassan, Lose argues that communities develop these deep beliefs because human beings have an innate desire to make sense of their world and to structure their conversation and action according to their convictions. Hassan himself draws on the work of William James and argues that not only is belief necessary to knowledge but it should celebrated because "it is from belief that all of our other creations derive."[64] In Lose's view, this way of building an epistemology on belief is not a simple "foundationalism" because these communities do not claim warrant for their foundations with universally valid external criteria, nor is it "relativism" because those who structure their lives on these penultimate foundations do in fact live as if these are "true."

In short, Lose is arguing for a kind of knowledge that is culturally conditioned, communal and rooted in belief. The question lingers, though, whether this is simply an elaborate version of "mere fideism." That is to say, is this epistemology based on an "uncritical, almost blind commitment to a basic set of beliefs?"[65] Lose's response to this question is that, first, all knowledge is fideistic to some degree. Nevertheless, he is proposing a critical fideism, not a blind fideism. His fideism is critical on two accounts: (1) there is enough diversity within the community itself that the community's penultimate foundations are regularly questioned and critiqued, and (2) the community makes a case for its belief in the public arena and submits its beliefs to the questions and critique of other communities.

Still, for a set of beliefs to be critically assessed in a public dialogue, language must be able to refer beyond itself. That is to say, mutually critical crosscultural conversation requires that the language of one community be understandable to another community, and this is the second issue to which Lose turns.[66] Those who argue that language creates reality, and therefore that each distinct language creates its own distinct reality, argue that this kind of crosscultural conversation is virtually impossible. To give a theological example of this sort of position, Lose examines

---

[64]Ibid., 37.
[65]Ibid., 39.
[66]One must be clear that Lose, like Lindbeck and others, intends "language" to refer to the complex semiotic web of a distinct culture.

George Lindbeck's *The Nature of Doctrine*, in which he articulates a non-foundational cultural-linguistic model of religion. According to Lindbeck's theory, a religion like Christianity can be understood only from within, according to its own rules and grammar, and is incommensurable with other religions.

While this understanding of religion has brought some benefits, Lose argues that Lindbeck and his followers have gone too far in asserting that Christianity is a closed linguistic system. First, incommensurability is not the same as incomparability. For instance, while a Buddhist understanding of nirvana and a Christian understanding of heaven are ultimately two discrete concepts, they nevertheless can be compared. Moreover, not only is comparability possible, it is in fact necessary for understanding. In the same way that certain concepts are defined in their interdependent relationship to other concepts within a system, so certain systems are defined in their interdependent relationships to other systems. For instance, we can understand a distinct Christian view of heaven more clearly when we understand the ways in which is it like and not like a Buddhist understanding of nirvana. Indeed, the relative difference is necessary for understanding a Christian view of heaven as a distinct concept.

This example represents a "borderlands" concept where there is enough overlap between two "languages" to build meaningful and critical interaction. This, Lose argues, is the place to start in crosscultural communication: at the overlapping borders of a cultural linguistic system and not at the distinct core of a system. By comparing two languages in this way, one does not say they are ultimately commensurable, nor that one can arrive at an understanding of another culture that leaves no remainder. Lose agrees that cultures can be fully understood only from within. However, this kind of crosscultural comparison can produce an "adequate translation" that is the basis of a meaningful mutually critical conversation.

The final question Lose addresses in relation to postmodern challenges is whether we can speak about a reality that transcends our cultural-linguistic traditions. Once again he sidesteps the terms of debate set up in a modernist-postmodernist dichotomy and says at the outset that regardless of our theoretical doubts we do in fact talk about reality all the time, either in talking about love and loss or about tonight's dinner plans. Lose believes that the best model for how we talk about reality is presented by Donna Haraway and echoed by Calvin Schrag and Paul Ricoeur. According to Haraway, we describe the "real" from a position of "situated knowledge," which acknowledges its own position and passionate involvement in the act of knowing and does not appeal to a foundationally guaranteed objectivity. To speak of the "real," Haraway argues, we must undertake our own responsibility for speaking from our position and undertake the accountability of listening to the critique of others. Lose sees Haraway's position echoed in Calvin Schrag's interplay between distanciation and participation and Paul Ricoeur's understanding and explanation.[67] That is to say, our descriptions of reality are always in process, always being developed in a complex interplay of conversation. Every time we describe reality from the perspective of our situated knowledge, we are then compelled to listen to the critique of others, and that in turn influences our situated knowledge and brings us to a new description of reality.

This understanding of the way we speak about reality leads directly into Lose's proposal for homiletics. He believes that, far from crippling faith, the postmodern critique of modernism has created greater freedom for religious belief and speech because faith is now understood as a necessary basis of knowledge. In this sense postmodernism has rendered Christianity a service by clarifying that Christian claims ultimately rest on faith. In addition, understanding speech about reality as a dialogical conversation leads directly into the Christian practice of confession, a practice that Lose argues can provide constructive direction for speaking in the postmodern situation.

Lose explores the practice of confession from three perspectives: biblical, theological and linguistic. From a biblical perspective, he explores the various New Testament usages and meanings of the Greek word *homologeō* (confession) and the words associated with it. The word has a variety of meanings and undergoes development as one traces it from the Gospels through the Epistles. In particular, Lose notes that as the

---

[67]In a dissertation on the subject, Michael Brothers explores this interplay of "nearness and distance" in relation to homiletical theory through the lens of speech performance theory and practice. See Michael Brothers, "The Role of Distance in Preaching: A Critical Dialogue with Fred Craddock and Postliberal Homiletics" (PhD diss., Princeton Theological Seminary, 2003).

early Christian community develops, "confession" gradually takes on the sense of a specific liturgical act and a doctrinal content. Nevertheless, there is also great continuity in meaning in the New Testament, and Lose summarizes the usefulness of the concept for preaching in two aspects. First, "Confession designates a summary of the church's essential assertions concerning God's decisive activity in Jesus of Nazareth, the one crucified and raised from the dead."[68] In other words, confession summarizes the essential content of the kerygma, as when Paul writes in 2 Corinthians 9:13 that the Corinthians are glorifying God through their obedience to the confession, or when the writer to the Hebrews urges them to hold fast this confession (Heb 4:14).

Second, confession "denotes articulating that faith as a living response both to this proclaimed word and to the current situation and crisis of the world."[69] It is particularly this last aspect of confession, as a response to the current situation, that sets confession concept apart from its near relative, witness. For instance, Lose notes that *homologein* and *martyrein* are used nearly synonymously in the New Testament, except that *homologein* has the distinct sense of being a response to a situation of duress. While he says he does not want to make too much of this distinction because the biblical terms are so nearly synonymous, he clearly considers the notion of confession as a response to an external challenge a key aspect of the term's homiletical usefulness.

In his theological analysis, Lose finds broad affirmation for this twofold understanding of confession, and his conversation partners extend and deepen his biblical findings. In examining the writings of Miroslav Volf, Brian Gerrish and Douglas John Hall, Lose further argues that confession is central to the life of faith, that it provides a pattern for making sense of the world, and that it is an intentional articulation of Christian faith in response both to the biblical promise and "specific

---

[68]Lose, *Confessing Jesus Christ*, 102. Given that Lose argues that confession articulates a concise summary of the faith, there is surprisingly little in his proposal that unpacks the content of the confession. It is clear that in his view the core Christian confession is something like "Jesus Christ was crucified and is risen," but what this means is more or less assumed along the way. In *Confessing Jesus Christ*, Lose tackles the question of *how* one can preach in the postmodern milieu, but he has left the question of *what* one can preach quite ambiguous.
[69]Ibid.

needs and crisis of the age."[70] In his linguistic analysis Lose draws on the work of J. L. Austin and John Searle along with Mikhail Bakhtin to describe confession as a specific kind of speech act. Using Searle's interpretation of Austin, Lose argues that confession is an assertive form of an illocutionary speech act, which is to say that confession "commit[s] the speaker to something's being the case" and implicitly calls for a response of belief from the hearer.[71] Furthermore, drawing on Bakhtin, Lose describes confession as a prompting, catalytic word in the larger conversation of faith, rather than an isolated, individual word.

So how does all of this shape a homiletical proposal of preaching as confessing Jesus Christ? Drawing again on his understanding of the way in which we can speak meaningfully about "truth" and "reality" in the postmodern context, Lose casts confession as a dialectical act of participation and distanciation or, to use Haraway's terms, responsibility and accountability. Faithful preaching, Lose argues, articulates the Christian tradition in response to the current situation (participation) but leaves the hearer free to respond without coercion (distanciation).

As conversation partners to help develop this proposal, Lose examines and critiques two proposals that he believes represent an extremist form of the two poles of preaching. On the one hand, he argues that Charles Campbell's *Preaching Jesus: New Directions for Homiletics in Hans Frei's Postliberal Theology* has a strong vision of participation in the Christian tradition, but the vision is so strong that the preacher and hearer are "absorbed" into the world of the text. In other words, there is no "distance" for critical appropriation by the hearer. On the other hand, in *Sharing the Word: Preaching in the Roundtable Church*, Lucy Rose so strongly emphasizes the critical distance of the hearer that she gives no attention to the participation of the hearer in the Christian tradition. By contrast, Lose intends his proposal to hold the dialectic of participation and distanciation in appropriate tension, and three aspects of his work that give shape to that claim.

He first draws on biblical scholars Meir Sternberg, Robert M. Fowler and R. Alan Culpepper to argue that biblical narratives themselves offer

---

[70] Ibid.
[71] Ibid., 104.

both narrated information and critical distance by which to appropriate that information. He then references homileticians Jana Childers and Robin R. Meyers to make the same point, as they both argue that preaching must offer not only narrative content but also critical distance for the hearer to appropriate the message. Furthermore, he claims that confession is particularly suited for this delicate task because confession "implies *simultaneously* (1) a grounding in a communal understanding of the gospel and (2) an articulation of that identity that does not demand from the hearer its own validation and therefore preserves the critical distance in which the hearer might appropriate the confession."[72] In other words, this is not a situation in which the hearer first gets the narrative and then gets the critical space. Rather, in preaching as confession Lose argues that both narrative participation and distance come in roughly equal measure.

Finally, Lose notes the theological character of the critical distance he believes is necessary between the sermon and the hearer. It is not a distance in which the hearer is simply free to choose, because there is always a sense in which a hearer feels pressed upon or compelled by the reading or preaching of scripture. Rather, Lose understands this space as the arena in which "a lively encounter between Word and hearer can take place through the power of the Holy Spirit."[73]

As he concludes his homiletical proposal, Lose turns his attention to the two distinct conversations that characterize the ministry of preaching: a conversation with the text, followed by a conversation with the congregation. Regarding the conversation with the text, Lose notes first that Walter Brueggemann has often argued that scripture should be understood as testimony, a theory on which Anna Carter Florence built part of her proposal. However, Lose disagrees with Brueggemann's theory of scripture as testimony for several reasons: (1) in Brueggemann's theory, the "truth" of scripture becomes solely dependent on the reader, (2) the Bible is understood to refer only to itself and within itself, and not to an external reality, and (3) while Brueggemann emphasizes juridical testimony as the biblical motif, other types of testimony such as religious confession are far more prevalent in the Bible.

---

[72]Ibid., 138.
[73]Ibid., 141.

In contrast to Brueggemann's understanding of the Bible as witness, Lose argues that the Bible should be understood paradigmatically as confession.[74] Once again he turns to linguistic analysis to elucidate what he means by the Bible as confession, specifically to the work of John Searle. Searle describes a genre he calls "serious discourse," which is assertive and purports to correspond to reality. The four rules Searle outlines for serious discourse are:

> (1) The speaker commits himself or herself to the truth of the statement; (2) the speaker must be in a position to give some reason for the truth of the statement; (3) the statement must not be obviously true to both speaker and hearer; and (4) the speaker believes that the statement is true.[75]

Lose believes that on the whole, at least on an illocutionary level, the biblical authors meet these stipulations and the Bible functions as this kind of serious discourse. It is especially important, Lose notes, that the biblical authors believe that their statements are true. While he recognizes that there are a variety of literary genres in the Bible, including the narrative genre so important to Brueggemann, Lose contends that the overarching intent of the biblical authors is to make an assertive confession of what they believe to be true. Moreover, insofar as the biblical texts seriously intend to speak for God, they open at least the possibility that they may indeed function as God's word to us.

Thus, when preachers go to the biblical text in preparation for preaching, they should understand that they are going primarily to hear a confession of faith. Indeed, preachers should ask themselves explicitly what confession of faith is being made by the text and what confessions of their own enable or limit their ability to make sense of the text's confession. As preachers hear the text's confession, it will call forth from them a response, which is in fact the sermon.[76]

---

[74]Lose notes that Ricoeur discusses religious testimony and in that context religious confession. Ricoeur argues that religious confession is the meaning or significance assigned to religious testimony.

[75]Lose, *Confessing Jesus Christ*, 161.

[76]In reference to Florence's emphasis on the preacher's experience of God through the text, I noted that there is a difficulty inherent in making the sermon dependent on the preacher's own experience of God. The difficulty is that preachers often preach "the deposit of faith" given to the church and not always or necessarily their own experience of it. Moreover, preachers often deliver sermons

In the last chapter of his proposal, Lose turns to the second conversation that characterizes the ministry of preaching, the preacher's conversation with the community. Specifically, he asks, how should the preacher shape his or her conversation with the community? What is a rhetoric appropriate to preaching as confession? In short, Lose argues that form should follow content, that a rhetoric of confession should match the content of the confession. As the content of the confession is Jesus Christ crucified and risen, so Lose's rhetoric of confession follows a similarly cruciform pattern.

To construct this rhetoric, Lose draws first on the work of André Resner in *Preacher and Cross: Person and Message in Theology and Rhetoric* to argue that the apostle Paul in his pastoral ministry inverted the classical notion of ethos and interpreted it in light of the cross. In classical rhetoric, the ethos appropriate to the rhetor involved such characteristics as nobility, strength, wisdom and courage. Paul, however, stressed his own sinfulness, foolishness and weakness in order that his hearers might rely on the trustworthiness of God and not himself. This inverse ethos, Lose argues, is a rhetoric appropriate to the content of the Christian confession and the work of the Holy Spirit in the ministry of preaching.[77]

Lose finds a secular analog to this reinterpretation of classical rhetoric in the feminist rhetoric of Sonja K. Foss and Cindy L. Griffin. They propose an invitational rhetoric that is not explicitly or coercively persuasive but invites the audience to see from the rhetor's perspective. The two main components of their rhetoric are: (1) "offering perspectives" and (2) "creating external conditions of safety, value, and freedom."[78] Lose understands these two components as akin to the two primary emphases of his understanding of confession: (1) offer a communal narrative identity and (2) create the critical distance necessary for the hearer to appropriate the preacher's confession.

---

that arise from others' experience, or the experience of the community as a whole, and not from their own. In articulating the sermon as the preacher's personal response to the confession of the text, it appears that Lose has similarly placed great weight on the individual preacher's experience.

[77] Lose and Resner may be overstating Paul's inversion of classical rhetorical ethos. In her review of Lose's *Confessing Jesus Christ*, Susan Bond references James Thompson's *Preaching Like Paul: Homiletical Wisdom for Today* (Louisville: Westminster John Knox, 2000) as he points to Paul's use of Greco-Roman strategies in his rhetorical inventions and decisions. L. Susan Bond, review of *Confessing Jesus Christ: Preaching in a Postmodern World*, by David J. Lose, *Homiletic* 28 (2003): 27–29.

[78] Lose, *Confessing Jesus Christ*, 200.

From these resources, Lose proposes what he calls a "kenotic" rhetoric for preaching as confession, by which he means a rhetoric of self-emptying after the pattern of Christ as Paul describes it in Philippians. Christ emptied himself, became vulnerable, "he humbled himself and became obedient to the point of death—even death on a cross" (Phil 2:6-8). The preacher who wishes to confess the crucified Christ, Lose argues, should confess according to the pattern of Christ. Rather than offer a "strong" word of certainty intended to persuade coercively, the preacher should offer the "weak" word of confession, in response to the grace of God and the need of the world. The preacher offers a confession characterized by vulnerable humility that is nevertheless assertive and calls for a response of belief or unbelief from the hearer.

As Lose himself concludes, he has proposed a way of preaching as confession, in which the content and delivery are shaped by the core Christian confession that Jesus Christ was crucified and is risen. As with Florence's proposal, the theoretical and theological foundation of Lose's proposal forms what might be called a general theory of proclamation. That is to say, his analysis of the postmodern problem, his proposal of an epistemological middle way and his use of the Christian practice of confession as a model for faithful communication today can be applied to all forms of Christian confession by all the baptized.

However, particularly in the latter half of the book, Lose turns his focus specifically to the ministry of preaching as distinct from other forms of confession and points toward the relationship between preaching and other forms. Preachers are distinct, first, because they "occupy a unique role in relation to confessing faith in the weekly worship service as they are both recipients of confession and confessors."[79] This is true in in two ways. First, it is true given the dialogical nature of worship, as preachers confess their faith and also hear the confession of the hearers. Second, it is true in that the preacher is specifically sent by the congregation to hear the confession of the biblical text and then articulate a confession to the congregation. Still, as Lose notes, this could also be said of the confession of all the baptized: confession is in response to what they have heard, and

---

[79]Ibid., 142.

their confession then prompts further confession.

The real distinction of the preaching ministry is the role preaching plays in relation to the larger conversation of the faithful. He writes, "It is also important to recognize that the preacher has been set apart by the community to engage both canon and community so as to prompt, focus, and nurture the conversation of faith by publicly 'confessing Christ.'"[80] Preaching is a catalyst, he writes, "a prompting, focusing, shaping, and nurturing" word in the larger conversation of the congregation.[81] Preaching plays a vital role, yet it plays only one role in the witness of the community. Preaching does not bear the whole burden of gospel communication; rather it shares the burden with other elements of the liturgy and other works of the congregation. The important task of preaching, Lose argues, is what he identifies as the twofold work of confession: "[Preaching as confession] both grounds the hearers in a narrative, communal identity while simultaneously preserving the space in which they are able not simply to listen to, but also be encountered by and appropriate, the gospel proclaimed."[82]

As I conclude this discussion of David Lose's work, I want to note the distinctive ways I think his project contributes to this missional homiletic. First and most importantly, he offers a sustained analysis of the epistemological challenges presented to homiletics by the postmodern situation and a creative response that provides a theoretical foundation for the possibility of preaching. Missional theology also self-consciously understands itself as a response to challenges presented by the postmodern situation, as missional theologians attend to the post-Christendom and postcolonial aspects of postmodernism as well as to the postfoundational challenges Lose addresses. Second, Lose's notion of confession brings a new dimension to the broad category of witness, specifically understanding confession as a response to a situation of duress and challenge, which is consonant with missional concerns. Finally, Lose addresses directly the relationship between the preaching ministry and the broader witness of the congregation. He acknowledges

---

[80]Ibid.
[81]Ibid., 146.
[82]Ibid., 145.

the limited nature of preaching and the multiform nature of the church's witness, and he identifies what he understands as the distinct contribution of preaching to the community's larger witness. Lose does not, however, discuss the nature of the congregation's witness, describing it only as "the larger conversation of the faithful" and alternatively as the appropriation of the preacher's confession by the hearer.

TOWARD A MISSIONAL ECCLESIOLOGY

Thomas Long, Anna Carter Florence and David Lose each offer a theory of preaching that casts the preacher as a type of witness and preaching as a form of witness, and these proposals offer suggestive connections to missional theology and a missional homiletic. The interaction of their homiletical proposals, especially in places where they disagree, raises crucial questions for homiletics, for the development of a theory of missional preaching, and for preachers and teachers of preaching. These questions will become important in chapter four when I outline the contours of a missional homiletic, but I list them here in order to prompt your own thinking and reflection about these homiletical issues.

1. *What or who is the object of the preacher's witness?* Each of these authors offers a different answer, and there is both confusion within the proposals and disagreement among them. Long says in one place that the gospel is the object of witness and later that the preacher's encounter or experience with God through the text is the object of witness. Florence is clearer in saying that the preacher's encounter with God is the object of witness. Alternatively, for Lose the object of witness is the essential Christian confession of the crucifixion and resurrection of Jesus Christ, though he adds little substance to that statement. In short, the question for us is, to whom or to what does the preacher bear witness in a missional homiletic?

2. *By what criteria should one assess the faithfulness of the preacher's witness?* These proposals have offered several options: Long seems to leave criteria to the theological tradition of the preacher; Florence argues in tandem with Chopp that the sermon must be a word of liberation coming from the margins; and Lose argues that the sermon must be consonant with the essential Christian confession of Jesus Christ, though

he says little about its material content. What are criteria of faithfulness in a missional homiletic?

3. What kind of witness is scripture? Each of these proposals understands scripture as a kind of witness, but each understands it as a slightly different kind of witness. Long is the least explicit in describing what he means by saying the Bible is "the faithful witness to the interactions of God with the whole creation," though his primary conversation partners are Paul Ricoeur and Walter Brueggemann.[83] Florence relies more explicitly on Ricoeur and Brueggemann for her understanding of testimony as juridical and scripture as core and counter testimony, and she calls scripture a perfectly open sign, again using the work of Chopp. Lose on the other hand argues that confession is the paradigmatic form of scripture, not juridical testimony as Florence argues. This question for us is, in a missional homiletic, what type of witness is scripture?

4. What of ordination? Long argues in support of ordination as a formal authorization by the church given to the preacher to go to the text on its behalf. Florence, on the other hand, argues strongly against ordination as providing authorization for preaching. Lose does not specifically address the issue but clearly sees the preacher as a unique witness who has a relationship to the text and the community that other witnesses do not. What should be the status of ordination relative to preaching in a missional homiletic?

5. In what ways does the congregation bear witness? All three homiletical proposals understand preaching as a specialized form of the ministry of proclamation given to the whole church. However, none of the proposals gives a concrete sense of how that ministry expresses itself in the corporate life and individual lives of a congregation. In a missional homiletic, what specifically characterizes the witness of the congregation?

6. How does the witness of the preacher relate to the witness of the congregation? Long and Florence, while they understand the preacher's witness as distinct, do not elaborate on the ways in which it is related to the congregation's witness. Only Lose answers this question specifically, and he understands the preacher's witness as a catalytic, prompting, nur-

---

[83]Long, *The Witness of Preaching*, 48.

turing word in the larger conversation of the faithful. I have already
given away my answer to this question in the premise of the book! The
witness of the preaching equips the congregation for its manifold witness
to the world.

2

The Witness of
the Christian Community

As we saw in the last chapter, witness is an increasingly common way to understand the preacher and the ministry of preaching in the field of homiletics. Though each author we looked at understands witness from a different theological orientation, they share common hermeneutical and philosophical interests, and they each are convinced that witness/testimony/confession is the best metaphor for understanding who the preacher is and what the preacher does. The congregation, though, is in the background. In the proposals we explored, little or no reflection is given to the theological nature of the audience the preacher addresses, otherwise known as ecclesiology. In order to describe preaching as a form of witness that equips the congregation for witness, we need to bring other theological resources, and specifically ecclesiological resources, to this conversation. First, we need a more robust understanding of the congregation and its witness; that is to say, we need an ecclesiology that has witness as its point of orientation. Second, we need a more precise understanding of preaching within the context of this ecclesiology, what it is and how it functions relative to the witness of the congregation.

In this chapter, we will attend to Karl Barth's ecclesiology as it relates to the witness of the congregation and the nature and function of preaching relative to that witness. For clarity and depth we will carefully unfold one section of his ecclesiological writing in which he most fully describes the witness of the local congregation: "The Holy Spirit and the Sending of the Christian Community." This is a section within Barth's chapter "Jesus Christ, the True Witness," which is found in part two of *The Doctrine of Reconciliation*, the fourth volume of the *Church Dogmatics*.

As the preaching proposals of the last chapter might have been familiar territory for homiletical readers, so Barth's ecclesiology might be familiar terrain for the missional theological reader. For those who are new to the missional conversation, however, this in-depth exploration of Barth's understanding of the vocation of the Christian community is an excellent way to become familiar with the core theological concerns of missional theology. Before turning to Barth, though, I want to explain first why Barth is a natural conversation partner for developing a theory of preaching as a missional practice and why this section of his ecclesiology is the decisive one for developing a missional homiletic. It will also be helpful to understand how Barth structures his ecclesiology as part of the larger "Doctrine of Reconciliation," since this section is connected to Barth's larger work.

BARTH'S ECCLESIOLOGY AND ITS PLACE IN MISSIONAL THEOLOGY

The animating contention of missional theologians is that Christian vocation and mission typically have been underdeveloped in systematic and dogmatic theology. The problem as they see it is that traditional theology characterizes the church as justified and sanctified, gathered and upbuilt, while its vocational and missionary activity is understood as an optional and additive enterprise. In the Payton Lectures to Fuller Seminary in 2007, Darrell Guder writes of the beginnings of the missional movement:

> We were following through on Wilbert Shenk's assessment that Western Christendom is Christianity without mission, although we moderated that statement by concentrating on the curious silence about mission in western ecclesiologies— a theological lacuna that characterizes virtually all systematic theologies in the West until Barth made mission the pervasive theme of his *Church Dogmatics*.[1]

David Bosch, in *Transforming Mission*, fills in the historical details of Guder's contention. He writes that until the sixteenth century the term "mission" was used exclusively with reference to the doctrine of the Trinity. The Jesuits then used it with reference to spreading the Christian

---

[1]Darrell L. Guder, "Walking Worthy: Missional Leadership After Christendom," *Princeton Seminary Bulletin* 28 (2007): 252.

faith to those who were not members of the Catholic Church (including Protestants). From that point until the twentieth century, mission was primarily understood as an activity of the church, often done by a special few in faraway places.[2]

In the twentieth century, understandings of mission began changing to become more theologically integrated with ecclesiology, with the decisive shift coming in the Vatican II document *Lumen Gentium* (Light to the Gentiles). Bosch writes, "Vatican II reflects a convergence in Catholic and Protestant views on the missionary nature of the church, even if one has to add immediately that the Catholic documents show far greater consistency and lucidity than those produced by the Protestant conferences."[3] Among several common characteristics of this emerging ecclesiology, Bosch identifies first that "*the church is seen as essentially missionary:* . . . Its mission (its 'being sent') is not secondary to its being; the church exists in being sent and in building up itself for the sake of its mission."[4] Thus mission is not something that is added on to the life of church but that constitutes the life of the church. Likewise mission is not something that is optional for the church; rather, where there is the church, there is necessarily mission. This what it means for the church's very being to consist in its "sentness" or its "missional character."

In missional theology, the church's nature as mission is derived from God's nature: as God is a sending God, so the church is a sent church. Or, to use Bosch's well-worn phrase, "Since God is a missionary God, God's people are a missionary people."[5] This theology of God is commonly referred to as *missio Dei*, and Bosch gives a brief account of the development of this idea in ecclesiological thought through the middle and late

---

[2]David J. Bosch, *Transforming Mission: Paradigm Shifts in Theology of Mission,* American Society of Missiology 16 (Maryknoll, NY: Orbis Books, 2011), 1-2. Darrell Guder describes this phenomenon in relation to nineteenth-century theological education at Princeton Seminary in his inaugural lecture as the Henry Winters Luce Professor of the Theology of Mission and Ecumenics at Princeton Theological Seminary. He argues that, though mission was a strong commitment of the seminary in the nineteenth century, it was understood as one of the many activities belonging to the study of practical theology. "The relation of mission to theology was that of a subsidiary ministry practice, training missionaries next to the formation of local pastors." Darrell L. Guder, "From Mission and Theology to Missional Theology," *Princeton Seminary Bulletin* 24 (2003): 39.

[3]Bosch, *Transforming Mission*, 372.

[4]Ibid., 381 (italics original).

[5]Ibid.

twentieth century. It is hard to say precisely what is now meant by *missio Dei* because theologians have differing perspectives. At its core, though, this approach to ecclesiology derives the church and its mission from the nature of the triune God and puts them into the context of the doctrine of the Trinity. In short, it goes like this: the Father sent the Son, the Father and the Son send the Spirit, and the Father, Son and Holy Spirit send the church into the world.[6] Rather than understand mission as a function of the church, the church is now understood as a result of God's original sending.[7] Whereas in the past mission was understood reductively as part of a doctrine of the church, missional theology understands the church as part of an encompassing doctrine of God and God's mission.[8]

According to Bosch, the theologian who most fully developed this understanding of the triune sending God and the missionary church is Karl Barth. Bosch writes, "Johannes Aagaard calls him 'the most decisive Protestant missiologist in this generation.' In light of Barth's magnificent and consistent missionary ecclesiology there may indeed be some justification for such a claim."[9] Indeed it is Barth's "missionary ecclesiology" and his extraordinary treatment of the sending of the Christian community that makes him an ideal resource for the development of a theory of preaching as a missional practice.

Barth's theological magnum opus, the *Church Dogmatics*, is divided into four multipart volumes: *The Doctrine of the Word of God*, *The Doctrine of God*, *The Doctrine of Creation* and *The Doctrine of Reconciliation*. Our focus will be on the fourth volume, *The Doctrine of Reconciliation*, in which Barth develops his ecclesiology. *The Doctrine of Reconciliation* is presented

---

[6]This formula, of course, includes the *filioque* clause and thus represents a Western theological orientation. Given that the missional discussion understands itself as an ecumenical enterprise, one wonders whether the Eastern church could accept a theology developed along these lines.

[7]It is helpful in this literature to recall that the Latin *missio* means "sending," and "mission" is the English cognate of *missio*. See Oxford English Dictionary, s.v. "mission."

[8]John Flett has chronicled the history of the *missio Dei* concept in the ecumenical conversations of the twentieth century and unpacked the "being-in-act" nature of God and the church in Karl Barth's theology. In his historical research, Flett found no evidence that Barth initiated the "*missio Dei*" language, contrary to claims by Bosch and others. See John G. Flett, "God is a Missionary God: Missio Dei, Karl Barth, and the Doctrine of the Trinity" (PhD diss., Princeton Theological Seminary, 2007). His theological work with Barth in the dissertation has been published in a book: John G. Flett, *The Witness of God: The Trinity*, Missio Dei, *Karl Barth, and the Nature of Christian Community* (Grand Rapids: Eerdmans, 2010).

[9]Bosch, *Transforming Mission*, 373.

in four parts, three of which have five main parallel points. The table below illustrates the conceptual framework:

Table 1.1 Karl Barth's *Doctrine of Reconciliation* Metastructure

The Doctrine of Reconciliation	Part 1	Part 2	Part 3
Jesus Christ is . . .	very God (§59)	very man (§64)	God/man (§69)
The sin of man is . . .	pride (§60)	sloth (§65)	falsehood (§70)
The event of reconciliation is . . .	justification (§61)	sanctification (§66)	calling (§71)
The Holy Spirit and the_____ of the Christian community	gathering (§62)	upbuilding (§67)	sending (§72)
The being of Christians in Jesus Christ in . . .	faith (§63)	love (§68)	hope (§73)

Barth describes this structure at the beginning of *The Doctrine of Reconciliation*, and his written description is represented graphically here. It is helpful to see the structure illustrated this way because not only do the sections relate vertically down the columns, they also relate horizontally across the rows. For instance, Barth develops his ecclesiology in the fourth section of each part, illustrated across the row: the Holy Spirit and the gathering of the Christian community, the Holy Spirit and the upbuilding of the Christian community, and the Holy Spirit and the sending of the Christian community. Yet in each case the particular ecclesiological doctrine flows from an aspect of his soteriology, illustrated vertically: justification leads to gathering, sanctification leads to upbuilding, and vocation leads to sending. Indeed, the decisive aspect of this structure for our purpose is the way Barth connects soteriology and ecclesiology. In each case, ecclesiology is developed as an aspect of soteriology and is understood as the subjective active participation of humanity in the event of reconciliation. This will become more clear if we review how the gathering and upbuilding of the Christian community are connected to the soteriological events that precede them.

In his transition from the doctrine of justification to the Holy Spirit and the gathering of the Christian community, Barth explains this part of the doctrine of reconciliation by using a "simple picture": the sin of humanity is depicted as a horizontal line and the atoning work of God in Jesus Christ as a vertical line. The point of intersection of the horizontal and vertical represents the doctrine of justification. Barth then describes his doctrine of the church and faith again on the horizontal, but this time *as intersected by the vertical*. In other words, the church is described in terms of humanity as justified; the outworking of this is the Holy Spirit and the gathering of the Christian community.

Barth describes the "particular problem" involved in this doctrine as the "subjective realization of the atonement." The atonement has both an objective side, in which it is a divine act and offer, and a subjective side, which is humanity's "active participation" in the divine act of justification. Barth understands each part of his ecclesiology as the way in which humanity participates subjectively in the objective act of reconciliation. So active participation in the reconciling event of justification means being gathered by the Holy Spirit into the Christian community. Likewise, active participation in the event of sanctification means being upbuilt by the Holy Spirit in the Christian community. So Barth writes in his transition from sanctification to upbuilding, "The Holy Spirit . . . effects the upbuilding of the Christian community, and in and with it the eventuation of Christian love; the existence of Christendom, and in and with it the existence of individual Christians."[10]

In this last statement, it is important to note—especially for our purposes—that the community is placed prior to the individual: first Christendom, then individual Christians. Barth wonders in the next paragraph whether the two ought not to be reversed: first individual Christians, then Christendom. But he then argues that they should not be reversed because the individual Christian always exists "on the basis and in the meaning and purpose of the community." He even goes so far as to affirm Calvin's statement, made alongside Tertullian and Augustine, that in this sense the church is the "mother of all believers" (though he is quick to limit the force of the metaphor).[11]

It is not that Barth is describing the church as an end and individual Christians as means to that end. Barth is quite clear that he understands both the individual and the community as means and ends; they are mutually interrelated. Rather, he is arguing that the Christian com-

---

[10]Karl Barth, *CD* IV/3.2, 615. In the German, the word that is translated here "Christendom" is the word *Christenheit*. It is interesting that he uses this term in a positive, or at least neutral, sense because the general force of his theological argument is contrary to a "Christendom" concept, as we will see later in his discussion of "nominal Christians."
[11]Ibid.

munity is conceptually prior to the Christian individual, for this reason:

> Because we cannot see and understand the individual Christian except at the
> place where he is the one he is, and because this place is the community, we
> have first to consider the community, although remembering at every point
> that in it we have to do with the many individual Christians assembled in it.[12]

To summarize, in the flow of Barth's ecclesiological development, each
act of reconciliation leads to an understanding of the Spirit-initiated community. The doctrine of justification leads to the doctrine of the gathering
of the community, the doctrine of sanctification leads to the doctrine of the
upbuilding of the community and the doctrine of vocation leads to the
doctrine of the sending of the community. The community is composed of
individuals, and the individuals are understood in light of their place in the
community. Of course, these are doctrinal distinctions and connections. In
the actual life of the community, all of these "participations" occur at the
same time, and together they constitute an understanding of the church.

We turn now to the section that speaks most directly to the church's
mission in the world, "The Holy Spirit and the Sending of the Christian
Community." At this point, one might ask whether it is sufficient to focus
on one piece of Barth's ecclesiology since there are actually three main
components. In my judgment, Barth's theological style lends itself to this
approach because (1) he writes in a "spiral" way, returning again to themes
he has previously developed, and (2) each of his ecclesiological sections
evokes and presupposes the others. By focusing in depth on this last piece
of his ecclesiology, the contours of the whole also come to light.

"THE HOLY SPIRIT AND THE SENDING OF THE CHRISTIAN COMMUNITY"

As he does in the other sections of his ecclesiology, Barth begins by connecting the reader to the event of reconciliation he has just finished de-

---

[12]Ibid., 616. In his transition from the doctrine of justification to the Holy Spirit and the gathering of the Christian community, Barth makes this same point by way of the Apostles' Creed. In
turning to the work of the Holy Spirit, Barth is turning from the second article to the third article of the creed. The justified person, the Christian individual, is found in the creed as part of
the community: "I believe . . . in the holy catholic *church*." Barth argues that the existence of such
individuals is not self-evident but is only known through faith. That is to say, it is only known
through belief in the community that comprises these individuals. See ibid., 645-46.

scribing—in this case, vocation. "As we have tried to explain and affirm
in the preceding section, the vocation of man is his vocation to be a
Christian."[13] Moreover, a person's vocation to be a Christian does not
come before or after one's calling into the church, but a calling into the
church is simultaneous with the calling to be a Christian. Thus, as before,
this discussion leads immediately to a consideration of the church.

Barth bases this movement on Christ's intention for the one who is
called. Christ, he argues, did not envision individual followers, nor desire
to "set [each one] in a kind of uni-dimensional relationship to Himself."
Rather, Christ's desire is to unite Christians both with himself and with the
others whom he calls. Thus, one's calling to be a Christian is at once a
calling to be united into the community. Barth writes that "in his ministry
of witness . . . [the Christian] is from the very outset, by his very ordination
to it, united not only with some or many, but . . . with all those who are
charged with this ministry."[14] Thus, a consideration of the vocation of the
Christian leads necessarily into a discussion of the community of Christians: the church.[15] Specifically, to the church from the standpoint of its
mission or sending.

The people of God in the flow of human events. Barth develops his
discussion of the sending of the church in four parts, and the first part
considers the "sheer fact of its existence as the people of God in world-
occurrence."[16] The Christian community, he argues, exists in and with
the whole cosmos. The history of the people of God occurs within and
alongside the history of the cosmos; the people of God affect the cosmos,
and the cosmos affects the people of God. In considering the sheer fact

---

[13] Ibid., 681.

[14] Ibid., 682.

[15] When he introduces this section of his ecclesiology, Barth writes, "*Das Phänomen und Problem, die Wirklichkeit der Kirche interessiert uns in diesem dritten Teil der Versöhnungslehre.*" It appears that Barth is referring here to the universal church (*Kirche*). But throughout the section, including in the title, he much more often refers to "*der Gemeinde Jesu Christi,*" or simply "*der Gemeinde.*" Here it appears that Barth is referring not to the universal church, but to the parish or flock, which is translated in English as the "community." It is important to note therefore, especially for practical theology, that Barth is developing his ecclesiology with the local congregation in the foreground. So, later, when he describes the function and task of "*die Gemeinde,*" he means to describe the function and task of the church that is gathered in one particular place and time.

[16] Barth, *CD* IV/3.2, 684. "World-occurrence" translates the German "*Weltgeschehen,*" but it is a somewhat awkward English compound. By this Barth means the everyday happenings of the world, and a more contemporary English translation would be "the flow of human events."

of this coexistence, Barth's first task is to explain the nature of the historical environment in which the community exists. True to his theological method, Barth does not seek to explain this environment philosophically or from a perspective of social science, that is, from a standpoint outside Christian theology. Rather, he aims to describe the world theologically in relation to the people of God.

So his first description of the world-occurrence in which the people of God find themselves is a theological one: the sphere of God's providence. The Lord of the community is not simply a lord but the Lord of lords; the God whom the community serves and who reveals himself in Jesus Christ is also the God who rules the world in absolute authority. Indeed, there is much in world affairs that is opposite to God's will and way. Yet the community should not think because of this that world affairs are under the authority of another god, in the sphere of no god at all, or under the direction of a different will of the one God revealed in Jesus Christ. Rather, Barth argues that the providence of God and God's authority in every sphere of world-occurrence must be the first step in Christian thinking about the world, "the positive sign before the bracket of whatever else may have to be considered."[17]

If world affairs is the sphere of God's providence, though, it is also the sphere of *confusio hominum*, the confusion of humanity. By this Barth means: (1) this is not a state in which people find themselves but is the activity and work in which they are engaged, (2) it is people, *homines*, who create and are engaged in this confusion and not God or the devil, and (3) it is genuine confusion, which means that while world affairs surely involve "folly" and "wickedness," it is not "a night in which everything is black."[18] The *confusio hominum* is the entanglement and intertwining of God's good creation, including humanity and the cosmos, and the negation of God's good creation, "the reality and operation of the absurd, grounded in no possibility given by God."[19] Moreover, it is truly entanglement and not admixture in the sense that God's good creation

---

[17]Ibid., 688. In a lengthy exposition of scripture, Barth compares his understanding of the church vis-à-vis world-occurrence and God's providence with the Old Testament depiction of Israel in the midst of the nations.

[18]Ibid., 695.

[19]Ibid., 696.

is not lost or diminished in this confusion, though it surely suffers and is often turned toward negative ends.

Now if this were all that could be said about world-occurrence, then the Christian community would have to simply exist in the tension between God's providence and humanity's confusion. However, Barth contends there is a third view, a view that is obligatory for the Christian, one that is superior to and comprehends the other two: "the reality and truth of the grace of God addressed to the world in Jesus Christ."[20] This, Barth argues, is a new reality, not coming from within world-occurrence but being revealed by God from without; it is shown to the community as that new reality to which they must attest in the twofold aspect of world affairs. Barth writes:

> The open secret of what has happened in Jesus Christ is that in Him the transcendent God who yet loves, elects, and liberates the world, and lowly man who is yet loved, elected and liberated by Him, are indeed distinct and yet are not separated or two, but one.[21]

This does not mean the twofold aspect of world-occurrence is dissolved or has been merged into Christ; that would be Christomonism. Rather, it means the apparent autonomy and finality of the tension between God and humanity has been reconciled in Jesus Christ, who has removed human confusion, restored order and concluded peace between God and humanity.

Now, while Jesus Christ is the new reality of world history as such, Barth makes an important restriction to the revelation and knowledge of this new reality. It can be known only in faith; it is known to the community only in faith, and it cannot be known "to the world which does not participate in the knowledge of Jesus Christ."[22] The new reality is hidden in world affairs, and the world appears only in its twofold antithesis and conflict. The reconciliation of God and humanity appears only as yet in Christ and only by faith. Yet by faith the community is given knowledge of this new reality in Christ, and "it is precisely this distinction which empowers

---

[20]Ibid., 706. In making this assertion, Barth is careful to avoid implying that Jesus Christ is a Hegelian synthesis of his foregoing thesis and antithesis. The problem with this would be that Barth would then have to posit some positive connection or common denominator between God's providence and human confusion, which he does not intend to do. Compare 703-6.

[21]Ibid., 712.

[22]Ibid., 714.

and obligates the church to confront the world with its witness."[23]

The community that is given this knowledge participates in world affairs on the basis of this new reality, and it sees things differently and conducts itself differently than those who do not have this knowledge. Though the community's knowledge is the knowledge of faith, it acts in world affairs with resolute confidence in Jesus Christ. In the light of God's decision in Jesus Christ, the community makes purposeful decisions that erect signs pointing to this new reality. And no matter how the world may appear to others, the community lives in and with a firm hope in Jesus Christ and for the world and humanity.

The second question Barth asks on the subject of the people of God in world-occurrence is how the Christian community is to understand itself within world affairs. The first answer is that the community is visible in the world, like any other organization or institution, and it is *ad extra* within world-occurrence. By this Barth means the church does not hover above world affairs nor exist within world affairs as an embedded foreign object but lives on the same level with the world, in the flesh as Christ was in the flesh, a people like many other peoples. This understanding of the church-with-the-world is essential to the community's witness because in this way the community lives in solidarity with the world and in "honest and sober correspondence to [Christ's] coming in the flesh."[24]

Yet, on the other hand—and this is the second answer to the question—this people is not simply any people but the community of Jesus Christ and the people of God in world-occurrence. This is what Barth describes as the inner life of the community and, in that sense, the invisible aspect of the community, though it is visible to some by faith. The movement of the community's life is thus inward to outward as it seeks to be become *ad extra* what it truly is *ad intra*: the earthly-historical form of Jesus Christ.[25] Barth writes, "Its true invisible being, and therefore its real dis-

---

[23]My translation, found in Karl Barth, *KD* IV/3.2, 820. The original text: *Und eben diese Auszeichnung befähigt und verpflichtet sie zum Zeugnis ihr gegenüber.* The published English translation is: "And it is this distinction which capacitates it for witness to the world, and commits it to this witness."

[24]Barth, *CD* IV/3.2, 725.

[25]Note here that Barth understands the two natures of the church analogously to the twofold nature of Christ. The visibility and invisibility of the community correspond to "true man" and "true God" in Christ. See ibid., 728.

tinction from and superiority to the world, is that it is elected and called to be a people alongside and with Jesus Christ . . . and that it is given to it to be appointed his witness."[26]

In concrete terms, Barth argues that this twofold nature of the church means, first, that the community exists in total dependence and total freedom in relation to its environment. For instance, in the sphere of speech the community is utterly dependent on human language and thus is open to the risk of misunderstanding and self-deception. Yet in its witness the community attests to the free and omnipotent word of God, which is not limited by the conditions of human speech and can "very well make use even of these human conditioned words"; thus the "whole sphere of human speech and wealth of its possibilities is open to them."[27] As a second example, the community is totally dependent and totally free with respect to its sociological structure. The community necessarily takes its structure from surrounding culture and social forms, yet as the people of God it is free to invest these forms with new meaning and determination.

Secondly, the twofold nature of the church means it exists in total weakness and in total strength relative to world affairs. By this Barth means that the people of God do not have a constant place in the world, as does the government or work, and thus exist in total weakness.[28] Yet in this very weakness is strength, shown by the fact that the community has nevertheless continued, grown, reformed and renewed; this is nothing other than the power of God. This weakness and strength is seen in the success of the community's work in the world. On the one hand, the work of the community consists in witness to something other than itself; even in this its

---

[26]Ibid., 729.

[27]Ibid., 737-38. It is interesting to note the connection of this point to a well-worn debate in the field of homiletics. Based on the small volume *Homiletics*, some have argued that Barth eschewed the use of rhetoric in preaching. In this same passage from which I quote, Barth gives a lengthy apology for the use of rhetoric (that is, the intentional use of language) in the community's speech based on its freedom, given by the sovereignty of God, to speak the word. In her book *Karl Barth's Emergency Homiletic: 1932-1933* (Grand Rapids: Eerdmans, 2013), Angela Dienhart Hancock greatly nuances our understanding of Barth's *Homiletics* and calls into question many common views of Barth's understanding of preaching.

[28]Here Barth draws again on his distinction between religion and the "people of God." Religion, he argues, may well have a constant place in the world, but he is not willing to subsume the "people of God" under the category of religion. Barth might categorize "Christianity" as a species religion, but the gospel itself would not be subsumed under a category of religion.

work is small compared to the work of the world, and even its successes are limited in scope. Yet its strength is concealed, for the church is concerned with what lies at the very center of human existence, though to others it may appear to lie on the edge. Barth writes, "Its strength consists in the fact that it and it alone is occupied with that which alone within world-occurrence is full of promise and originally and finally has the future for it."[29]

The final question to which Barth turns within this discussion of the people of God in world-occurrence is, how does the Christian community live in world-occurrence? By this Barth is turning to the fundamental question of how the community, which he has been describing, *can* actually exist. The first and general answer he gives is that it exists "in virtue of its secret." In other words, the community does not live by virtue of its own power, freedom or capacity; it has a secret power, freedom and capacity by which it lives. Moreover, this secret can be described by two names, Jesus Christ and the Holy Spirit, which Barth connects in two related statements.

"The first is that the Christian community exists as called into existence and maintained in existence by Jesus Christ as the people of His witnesses bound, engaged, and committed to Him."[30] This means that the being of the community is grounded in God and in Jesus Christ as its Lord. Moreover, the community exists as Christ exists, not simply because he exists. By this Barth means that the being of the community is "a predicate, dimension and form of existence of His."[31] Thus the community lives only

---

[29]Barth, *CD* IV/3.2, 750.

[30]Ibid., 752.

[31]Ibid., 755. Note that the community is *a* predicate, but is not the only predicate. In other words, the community exists as Christ exists, but Christ does not exist as the community exists. In light of God's sovereign freedom, the community must always remember that Christ is free to act in ways other than through the community. This point is important as a distinction between Barth's ecclesiology and the ecclesiology of Stanley Hauerwas, who draws on Barth. In *With the Grain of the Universe*, Hauerwas criticizes Barth for not acknowledging that the church is "constitutive of gospel proclamation" and the "binding medium in which faith takes place." See Stanley Hauerwas, *With the Grain of the Universe: The Church's Witness and Natural Theology* (Grand Rapids: Brazos Press, 2001), 145. In this critique, Hauerwas is right that Barth does not afford the church such a high status. But for Barth this circumscription of the church in the economy of salvation is essential if the church is to follow Christ and not substitute itself for Christ. See in this regard Nicholas M. Healy, "Karl Barth's Ecclesiology Reconsidered," *Scottish Journal of Theology* 57 (2004): 287-99. This distinction between Barth and Hauerwas is germane to homiletics in the work of Charles Campbell, *Preaching Jesus: New Directions for Homiletics in Hans Frei's Postliberal Theology*. Campbell worked under Hauerwas in developing his proposal, and Campbell's work affords the church the same high status as Hauerwas does in the economy of salvation.

as it lives in Christ. As the community acknowledges and confesses Christ as Lord, as it bears witness to Christ in speech and action, thought and choices, whether its witness is born well or poorly, then Christ is present and alive in the community and the community lives in him. This union with Christ is the basis and secret of the community's existence.

Barth understands this first statement about the secret of the community as an elaboration of the second statement, with which Barth actually begins this section on the sending of the Christian community: "The Holy Ghost calls, gathers, enlightens, and sanctifies all Christians on earth, keeping them in the true and only faith in Jesus Christ."[32] In other words, the Holy Spirit is the power that effects the union of Christ and the community, a relationship Barth understands as dynamic and historical rather than static and immobile.[33] He explains, "The Holy Spirit is the power, and His action the work, of the co-ordination of the being of Jesus Christ and that of His community as distinct from and yet enclosed within it."[34] That the people of God are in fact the people of God in the world, that the community of Jesus Christ hears Christ's call and is able to bear witness to Christ in world affairs, is possible only by the continuing work of the Holy Spirit to gather, upbuild and send the community.

In summary, in the first division of this section, Barth has explained the nature of the existence of the people of God in world affairs and the basis for that existence. The people of God live in a historical environment that is the sphere of God's providence and also the sphere of human confusion, yet in Jesus Christ the conflict between these two has been resolved and this new reality is revealed to the community by faith. The community understands itself in the world as a visible people and worldly people, yet with an inward and invisible life. Because of this dual nature, the community lives in total dependence on its environment and in total freedom relative to it, in total weakness with respect to its ability to carry out its work and yet in total strength to do it. Finally, the basis

---

[32]Barth, *CD* IV/3.2, 758.

[33]John Flett has elucidated this point at great length, connecting the being of God to the being of the church and arguing that Barth's conception of God and of the church is not as a static being but as a "being-in-act." See Flett, *The Witness of God: The Trinity, Missio Dei, Karl Barth, and the Nature of Christian Community* (Grand Rapids: Eerdmans, 2010).

[34]Barth, *CD* IV/3.2, 760.

of the very existence and possibility of this community is that it exists in Jesus Christ, a union that is effected continually by the Holy Spirit.

The community for the world. So Barth has given a theological description of the people of God as they find themselves immersed in the flow of human events. In the second subsection of his treatment of the sending of the Christian community, he comes to the primary issue at hand for us: the vocation of the community. Barth writes, "The community of Jesus Christ exists for the world." More precisely, the community of Jesus Christ exists first for God. Yet because God exists for the world, the community has no option but to also exist for the world. As Barth asks, "How else could it exist for God?"[35]

The very fact that Christ is Lord of the community, and the community is shaped by his existence, means that the community exists for the world. It is called out of the world and gathered as the people of God, upbuilt by the Holy Spirit and sanctified, in order that it might then live for the world. Here Barth is addressing the crucial issue raised by missional theologians, and it is worth quoting at length:

> Called out of the world, the community is genuinely called into it. . . . The work of the Holy Spirit in the gathering and upbuilding of the community cannot merely lead to the blind alley of a new qualification, enhancement, deepening and enrichment of this being of the community as such. Wonderful and glorious as this is, it is not an end in itself even in what it includes for its individual members. The enlightening power of the Holy Spirit draws and impels and presses beyond its being as such, beyond all the reception and experience of its members, beyond all that is promised to them personally. And only as it follows this drawing and impelling is it the real community of Jesus Christ.[36]

In a moment, Barth will examine the way in which the community follows this impulsion and lives out its commission in the world. First, though, Barth aims to show the essential elements that lie at the foundation of its activity in the world.

---

[35]Ibid., 762.

[36]Ibid., 764. We should note here, as Barth does, that the sending of the church into the world is not a repetition of Christ or a continuation of Christ; the church is not a *Christus prolongatus*. Christ's sending does not cease as the church is sent, nor does Christ's sending disappear into the church's sending. Christ is sent into the world, and the church is sent to follow him on his way. See ibid., 768.

Barth writes "that the true community of Jesus Christ . . . is the fellowship in which it is given to men to know the world as it is."[37] The world does not know the truth about itself, and it is given to the church to know God and humanity and the covenant between them, and to know the decisive action that God has taken in Jesus Christ. Because of this grace given to the people of God, the community is able to know human beings, to see their potential and their limitations, and to know that Jesus Christ died and rose for them and that the grace of God is addressed to them. As the community engages with the world and acts in it on the basis of this knowledge, then those in the world will at least see that they are addressed not as strangers by strangers, "but rather as those who are well acquainted."[38]

Second, the true community of Jesus Christ is "the society in which it is given to men to know and practice their solidarity with the world."[39] This does not mean conformity to the world, for in a sense the community has to keep its distance from the world and even oppose it. But, Barth asks, of what purpose would be its opposition if it did not display a profound commitment to the whole of humanity and each individual person? The solidarity of the community with the world is on the basis of what the community knows to be true of the world and each person it encounters: "The indestructible destiny of this man, his aberrations and confusions, and the universally applicable Word of his justification and sanctification accomplished in Jesus Christ."[40] This bond of solidarity between the community and world is so strong that Barth argues no concern about reputation or purity should prevent the community from taking it up, from being in the world and with humanity in its joys and struggles, sharing and bearing its burdens and hopes.

Third, the true community of Jesus Christ is the society in which "it is given to men to be under obligation to the world."[41] As the community has this knowledge and solidarity with the world, so it is made jointly responsible for the world and its future. This means that the community

---

[37]Ibid., 769.
[38]Ibid., 772.
[39]Ibid., 773.
[40]Ibid., 774.
[41]Ibid., 777.

is sent into the world to cooperate with Christ in his work. This sending thus precludes the community from withdrawing from the world or resting in itself, for the community exists only as it actively reaches beyond itself to the world. Barth further clarifies that, first, it is *given* to people in this community to exist in the way he has described. It is not self-evident, it does not belong to their human nature, and is not of their own intention. Second, it is given to a *fellowship* to exist in this way, not to isolated individuals and not for their personal enrichment or enjoyment. The freedom to know the world and be in solidarity with it is given to individuals personally, and they are personally responsible for it, but they are given this freedom to exercise as members of the community and to represent the community in their own place and way. Finally, it is given to *persons* to exist in this way, not the community as a whole. In other words, one is not free to know the world and exist in solidarity with it and be under obligation to it simply because one is a member of the community. This would violate both God's freedom and the freedom of the human person. No, as Barth writes, "The union of men with God, as the purpose of their history with Him, has always to be specifically and personally realized by each of them."[42] Thus, it is given to *persons* in the community to exist in this way, with some of the members taking greater part in its mission than others, and by the Spirit's power the distinction between the two fluidly changes over time.

Finally, in this section on the community for the world, Barth examines the basis of his presupposition that the community is the society that exists for the world. In everything else that will be said about the sending of the Christian community, Barth wonders how we can be sure about what has been said regarding the giftedness of the community for its mission. To begin, Barth asserts that it is a statement of faith. That does not mean the statement is made speculatively or based on a weak foundation. Rather, it speaks of "a particular form of God's action toward man and in and on the world for the world's salvation and His own glory."[43] In that sense, the statement that the Christian community exists for the world is true in the same sense that any statement of Christian

---

[42]Ibid., 781.
[43]Ibid., 785.

theology or belief is true: it is true as a statement of faith.[44]

From this point, Barth proceeds to say four things about the basis of his presupposition. First, "The Christian community owes its origin and continuation to a very definite power, to the constant working of which it is totally directed for its own future."[45] That is to say, the community is at first and always dependent on the Holy Spirit and can never imagine itself to exist in and by its own power. Second, everything the Christian community can do and accomplish can ultimately consist only in its confession of Jesus Christ, the truth of his person and his work. Moreover, the Jesus Christ whom the church confesses is the very God who acts in and for the world and reveals himself to it. The important implication Barth draws here is that the confession of the church must not be simply within itself. "The community called and built up by this One can confess Him only as it confesses to the world, to men, and to all men without distinction, that he is the One in whom God is their God."[46] Here again Barth is deriving the nature of the church from the nature of Christ; as Christ reveals himself to the world, so the church must attest Christ to the world.

Third, the community knows that its confession of Jesus is and can only be a grateful response to the fact that "first and supremely Jesus Christ has confessed it, does confess it, and will continually do so."[47] Christ is always the primary subject acting in and with the community. Christ is the one who gave himself for the world and whom the community follows into the world, pointing not to itself but always to its Lord. Barth is once more employing the same logic by which he argued that the community exists as a predicate of Christ: the existence of the church for the world is necessarily "imitative and ministering participation in His mission to the world."[48]

Fourth, the community can and should understand itself "in the full

---

[44]Given the postmodern turn, especially in light of the arguments by David Lose examined in chapter one, one might wonder at this point whether there is any statement that is not, finally, a statement of faith.

[45]Barth, CD IV/3.2, 786.

[46]Ibid., 789.

[47]Ibid., 790.

[48]Ibid., 792.

New Testament sense of the term as a likeness . . . of the divine-human reality distinct from itself."[49] By divine-human reality, Barth means the kingdom of God, which is revealed particularly in the resurrection of Jesus Christ and is the establishment of the absolute lordship of God in the whole sphere of creation. By likeness, Barth means on the one hand that the church is not itself the kingdom, but is a provisional representation. Yet on other hand, the community is in fact a representation and "it can and should indicate the kingdom and its revelation in its existence."[50] As it does this, and as its sees itself as this likeness, and thus as a sign, the community again understands that it exists for the world.

In these four statements Barth has laid the theological foundation for his contention that the church exists for the world and laid a theological cornerstone for a missional homiletic. To combine the four statements into one sentence: The community exists in the power of the Holy Spirit to confess Jesus Christ in response Christ's confession of it, as a provisional representation of the kingdom of God. In each of these ways one can say the community exists for the world and is compelled by the very nature of its existence to bear witness in and to the world. As the Holy Spirit is the Spirit of Christ, and as Christ gave himself for the world, and as the kingdom of God inaugurated in Jesus Christ is God's gracious rule over and for the world, so the community of Jesus Christ is intrinsically compelled to exist for the world.

The commission of the community. Moreover, the community exists for the world with a commission and is sent to fulfill that task.[51] This is the subject of Barth's third subsection. The task of the community is essential to its existence: the community exists only as it has the task, it must understand itself in light of the task, and it stands or falls in the

---

[49]Ibid.

[50]Ibid., 793.

[51]What is here translated as the "task" of the Christian community in German reads, *"der Auftrag der Gemeinde."* *Auftrag* has the sense of a task or job with which one is sent or charged. Thus, this could also be translated, especially in light of the Barth's motif of "sending" in this section, by "the mission of the community," or the "commission of the community." Indeed, in his work with Barth's ecclesiology in the context of missional theology, Darrell Guder consistently translates *der Auftrag der Gemeinde* as the "commission of the community" in order to capture the nuance and gravity of *Auftrag*, implying that there is one who commissions, one who is commissioned and a commission to be done. See ibid., 912.

expression of the task. Barth first treats the content of the task, then those to whom it is addressed, and finally the purity of the task.

The content of the community's task is to confess Jesus Christ. More specifically, it is to confess the concreteness and uniqueness of his person, work and name. The person, work and name of Christ both exhausts the possibilities of the community's confession and sets a definite limit on the community's confession. This is so because, Barth writes, enclosed within Jesus Christ is true God and true human, "their encounter, co-existence and history with its commencement, centre and goal."[52]

For Barth, the confession of Jesus Christ by the community means several things. First, it means the community is charged with a "great and comprehensive affirmation," the incomprehensible goodness of God revealed in Jesus Christ. Barth calls this the "yes" that is Jesus Christ, and it is contrasted with the "no" of the Law, sin and the wrath of God. The task of the community is to confess this "yes," and the "no" must never become a primary or even secondary theme; "no" is only an intervening or parenthetical word. Barth writes, "For to proclaim Jesus Christ is to attest the goodness of God, no more, no less, no other."[53] Among other things, this implies that the proclamation of the community is always and fundamentally a joyful proclamation.

Second, confessing Jesus Christ means proclaiming God with and for humanity, not without or against humanity. Christ signifies God who has become our friend, sibling, helper, neighbor, savior and guarantor, who has drawn near to us and redeemed us. The important implication here is that persons are part of the content of the task of the community, persons in their theological sense as "neighbors" and in their status as the ones upon whom God has conferred honor.[54] By this Barth means that the community does not understand a person primarily from the standpoint of their achievements, possessions, status or even their understanding of themselves. Rather the community understands a person theologically and most truly as the object of God's goodness. To sum-

---

[52]Ibid., 797.

[53]Ibid., 798.

[54]In German, Barth uses *Mensch* and *Menschen,* which the English translators have rendered as "man" in both cases. The German is more accurately translated as "person(s)" or "people." In this case, I have referred to persons.

marize the content of the community's task, Barth writes that it is "the good, glad tidings of Jesus Christ, of the real act and true revelation of the goodness in which God has willed to make and has in fact made himself the God of man and man His man."[55]

Having described the content of the community's task, the question now is, to whom is this proclamation made? The obvious answer is a person, as a representative of the world to which the community is sent, as the one affirmed by God and the object of God's goodness. However, in order to more clearly understand the task itself, Barth must clarify the precise nature of this person to whom the task is given. He is referring to the theological nature of the person, from the standpoint of Christ who constitutes the community and gives it its task.[56]

It is tempting, Barth begins, to define the person to whom the task of the community applies as the one who has not heard the gospel, as one who is far from God, and thus to understand the relationship between the community and that person essentially as a vacuum of unbelief. While tempting, Barth argues that this is decidedly not the first point from which to understand the people to whom the community is sent. The alienation and hostility between God and humanity is not the decisive factor in understanding humanity because in Jesus Christ God has already reconciled humanity to himself and established peace. Barth writes that God "considers [the person] already in relation to what he is in Jesus Christ, on the basis of His own Yes pronounced and applicable to him, as the object of His goodness. . . . Man's immediate being before Him is what he is on the basis of this divine will and work."[57]

Thus, as with the content of its task so in its application; the community attends first to God's great affirmation in Jesus Christ. Only then

---

[55]Barth, *CD* IV/3.2, 800.

[56]Barth notes at this point that persons are always found in particularity, conditioned by a culture and a political and economic order. However, Barth does not think that people are the sum of these cultural conditions. He writes that a person is in this situation, "but in this situation he is himself" (see ibid., 804). By this Barth means that the person is, essentially, the one to whom God has addressed God's word and is always the "subject" of any predicates that may be appended to the person. For instance, a person may be healthy or sick, child or adult, European or African, but that is not all they are. They are still who they are "in themselves." With this argument Barth means to acknowledge the cultural conditioning of the human person yet also allow himself to make a general theological assessment of the human person.

[57]Ibid., 805-6.

may the community understand the person to whom its task is addressed as the one who lacks the knowledge of the gospel and is "supremely needy." When understood from the perspective of their identity in Jesus Christ, the situation of this person is alienation from themselves and God and a profound self-misunderstanding and self-contradiction. The community must see the people to whom it is sent in two aspects of human existence: both as they are in virtue of their ignorance of the gospel and as they are in virtue of the work of God and the word God has addressed to them. This second aspect of their existence is the superior and determinative element and has at its root the "never-resting love of the living Lord, in view of which the community holds out a future of great joy for humanity."[58] In this future, the person

> will no more distort but genuinely realise his humanity before God and his neighbor. He will rejoice in it. He will be able to affirm his existence as God does. This existence itself will be a cheerful service of God, magnifying as such God's goodness to him. It will lead to existence in the community and in and with its prophetic ministry. This is the future which awaits man according to the gospel.[59]

The last question concerning the task of the community is the purity of the task, which Barth describes as the supremely critical question. It is most important because the community is constituted by its task, and thus its very existence is called into question as its task suffers distortion or impurity. Barth structures his examination according to the foregoing description of the task, considering the purity of the content and the purity of its application.

With respect to content, Barth sees two possible distortions. On the one hand is a failure to see "that the gospel is always the living Word of the living Lord of the community."[60] In other words, it is a timely and not a timeless word; it is a word that is spoken into a specific historical situation. Moreover, it calls for a response: "for a concrete decision of faith and obedience." The living word of the living Lord does not remain an

---

[58]Ibid., 809.

[59]Ibid., 811. This understanding of the person to whom the task of the community is addressed is also a neat summary of the theological basis on which Barth argues, in the soteriological doctrine preceding this section, that the vocation of every person is to be a Christian.

[60]Ibid., 813.

abstract word of knowledge but calls the person to a specific act of the will that responds here and now to the awakening Spirit of God.

Yet when the community senses this call to speak a concrete and timely word, it must be careful that it does not distort the purity of the content of the task on the other side: "The gospel is always the constant Word of its one Lord."[61] In the words of Hebrews, which Barth quotes, Jesus Christ is the same yesterday and today, and the Holy Spirit in which Christ acts and speaks is the same, and Christ's prophetic word is the same. Thus, a failure to understand the constancy of the gospel can lead a community that is otherwise open to its living quality to proclaim "another gospel." This other gospel is bereft of its power and significance and cannot achieve the prophetic witness the community intended.

So the community is commissioned to confess Jesus Christ in a timely and specific way that is also in continuity with the Church's larger proclamation of the gospel. The church is also called to consider the purity of the task in relation to the one addressed. Here Barth also sees a twofold temptation that derives from a single source. If the community withdraws from the sphere of its Lord's direction, it will either neglect or patronize the one to whom it is sent. The community neglects its addressee when the relationship of the community to that person is incidental to its existence. That is to say, the community may have some sort of relationship with the person, but the relationship can be dissolved with no harm to the community. For the community this neglect of the people to whom it is sent is critical because it undermines its very existence (again, the community necessarily exists for the world). Barth summarizes his argument with three concise statements: "1. the world would be lost without Jesus Christ and his word and work; 2. the world would not necessarily be lost if there were no church; and 3. the church would be lost if it had no counterpart in the world."[62] In Barth's theology, the church is not a necessary part of God's economy of salvation. Though the church is in Christ with the rest of humanity and thus they necessarily coexist, the rest of humanity is not there by the agency of the church. Moreover, Christ is not bound to the agency of the church and

---

[61]Ibid.
[62]Ibid., 826.

is free to declare himself to the world directly. The world is referred to the church only for a glimpse of the new reality in Christ, and then only for a partial and reflected glimpse. Thus if the church neglects the world it undermines its very existence.[63]

On the other hand, the complementary way in which the community may distort its task is to patronize the addressee. The community does this when its sees the one to whom it is sent as "the material for its own art and the object of its own deployment of power."[64] In this case the community, sure of its knowledge of the one whom it addresses, of who they are in themselves and who they are in Christ, creates a picture of a person and then addresses itself to the picture. Rather than coming alongside persons and addressing them in unity and solidarity, the community addresses them from above. It assumes that persons correspond to its picture, and thus armed with this knowledge the community has the power to execute its task. Yet by arrogating to itself this supposed power, the community falsifies its task. Barth argues that the community has no need to create its own "picture" of the human condition but only to see people in the light of the gospel as those who are in Christ and potential Christians. Moreover, the community is not sent to gather people into its own hands but to declare to them that they are already in God's hands.

This potential falsification of its task means the community must always be aware of the temptation to "create results." The community has no power over the world for which it exists and the people to whom it is sent. The task of the people of God is to confess Jesus Christ and point to him who alone is the living and constant Lord; it is to stand in unity with those for whom Christ died and rose, to proclaim their liberation and not their captivity, to serve them and not master them. Whatever success the community experiences in the exercise of this task will come as a gracious gift of the Holy Spirit.

In summary, the commission of the Christian community is to "confess" Jesus Christ, the one in whom the goodness of God is revealed and in

---

[63]In this passage we have come again to the taproot of missional theology, a theme to which we will return. The basic question is whether the mission of the church in the world is ancillary to the existence of the church or constitutive of its existence. Here Barth answers firmly that it is constitutive of its existence: no mission, no church.

[64]Barth, CD IV/3.2, 827.

whom God has accomplished the reconciliation of the world. The confession is addressed to human persons, understood fundamentally from the perspective of the gospel: as those who are the objects of God's goodness and reconciliation in Christ and who are in desperate need of that active knowledge. Finally, the purity of the work depends on the community attending both the timely and the constant quality of the proclamation and neither neglecting nor patronizing those to whom it is addressed.

The service of the community. The final subsection of "The Holy Spirit and the Sending of the Christian Community" focuses on the service of the Christian community.[65] Barth has described the people of God as they find themselves in world events; he has argued that the community exists for the world and that it has the specific commission of confessing Jesus Christ to the world. In this final section he will describe how the community fulfills its commission.

To begin, Barth elaborates on the basic nature of the community's service. It is defined in the sense that the foregoing discussion has shown that the community must exist actively for the world and must confess Jesus Christ within and to the world. The community accompanies Christ in the world bearing witness to him as the Word of God, and in this the community serves both God and humanity. Here again Barth is deriving the nature of the church from the nature of Christ. As Christ is both true God and true human, so to serve Christ is to serve both God and humanity. Moreover, only as it does this, as it follows its Lord and orients itself to him, can the community serve both God and humanity.

Furthermore, the service of the community is limited: limited because it is service and limited because it is a service of witness. First, as we discussed at the end of the last section, the service of the community is

---

[65]The English translators render this subsection as "The Ministry of the Community." The original German is *"der Dienst der Gemeinde."* The most basic meaning of *Dienst* is "service," while in a religious sense it can mean "ministry." The translation difficulty is that heretofore in this section, *Dienst* has been translated as "service." For instance, when Barth introduces the third subsection, "The Task of the Community," he writes, *"Wir fassen in diesem dritten Abschnitt ihren Auftrag als solchen ins Auge, nachher, im vierten und letzten Abschnitt, seine Ausführung: den Dienst der Gemeinde"* (*KD* IV/3.2, 911). In this sentence, the English translators render Barth's German as "the service of the community" (*CD* IV/3.2, 795). Yet when Barth comes to the fourth section, *Dienst* is translated as "ministry." The particular trouble here is that the word "ministry" is freighted with latent assumptions of a clerical paradigm. The reader may be quietly tempted to assume that everything in this subsection is meant for clergy, when in fact it is meant for the whole community.

service in the sense that the community is sent to serve and not to master and has no power to exercise over those whom it addresses. More specifically, it is a service of reconciliation, of proclaiming the goodness of God in Jesus Christ. There are many services that the people of God could render, Barth argues, but should not. The task assigned to the community is the service of reconciliation.

The service of the community is further limited because it is a service of witness. It is no less than witness in that the people of God are indeed those who have heard the divine word and cause that word to be heard in the world by their attestation of the new reality in Jesus Christ. Yet it is no more than witness, either. The reconciliation of the world to God, the new reality in Christ and the coming kingdom of God is not the community's work. The community can do no more, no less and no other than bear witness to the divine work and word in the world.

As a service of witness, the service of the community also has a promise. The promise to the community is that its cause is righteous, it is not left to its own knowledge and resources, and ultimately it does not act in vain. Sent into the world with little standing, with no power and often against great opposition, the community needs this promise to sustain, protect and renew it. The content of this promise is, simply, the content of the community's witness: the new reality revealed in the risen and living Jesus Christ. Thankfully, the promise does not always exist above and beyond the community but sometimes is revealed in specific and partial fulfillments. Occassionally the community's witness will bear fruit, which can be understood only as a gift from God and a sign of the promise. The fruit is not an ultimate end; it is only a sign of the promise. Yet the sign is an affirmation to the community of the truth of its proclamation.

Pressing deeper, Barth contends that witness is a common thread that runs through every aspect of the community's service. In any form or circumstance in which witness takes place, it always involves the declaration of the gospel.[66] The community introduces into human affairs the revelation of God in Jesus Christ, the fact of Christ's person, work and

---

[66]The word that is translated as "declaration" is *Aussage*. Yet when used with respect to legal proceedings, it has the sense of "testimony." Barth is using *Aussage* and *Proklamation* (proclamation) interchangeably.

name.[67] It does not have to replicate Christ or Christ's work but only to indicate as best it can what has already happened. Nor does the community bear responsibility for the world's reception of this news. The community cannot inspire belief; it can only announce what it has received. Yet it must announce this news. In whatever form or circumstance it bears its witness, the declaration of the gospel is the central service with which the community is concerned.

The witness of the community is also, in all its forms, an explication of the gospel. The community must not only declare the gospel but also unfold and explain it, making it intelligible to those who hear. Barth writes, "To explain the gospel is to define and describe the nature, existence and activity of God as Creator, Reconciler and Redeemer."[68] Barth is quick to note that this is not to be misunderstood as an exercise of power or independence by the community. The content of the gospel does not permit an "unfruitful acquaintance," by which Barth means that the gospel develops and explains itself in its encounter with the community. Moreover, the gospel does not permit an autonomous explanation; its interpretation must be according to its own direction and standpoint, not according to an external interpretive lens. Together, these two points mean the community must listen carefully to the gospel in order to explain it with faithfulness and obedience. Furthermore, the community can only seek to make the gospel intelligible. The knowledge of the gospel, by contrast, is a knowledge of faith and the work of the Holy Spirit. Nevertheless, the community must diligently seek to explain the gospel because, while it is not "generally knowable," it is "generally intelligible and explicable."[69]

So the witness of the community entails declaration, explanation and finally application, or "evangelical address." Here again Barth argues that the church does not live in a vacuum separate from the world but stands in a definite relation to the people whom it addresses. The community makes its declaration and explanation to them specifically, with them in mind from the beginning, in a way that allows them to see the gospel's

---

[67]By "fact," Barth means that the revelation in Jesus Christ corresponds to a concrete and definite person and event that occurred in the sphere of human history. He does not mean that it is an event available to knowledge apart from faith.

[68]Barth, *CD* IV/3.2, 849.

[69]Ibid.

crucial application to them. Now, as he has done repeatedly, Barth both circumscribes and expands the possibilities of the community's witness in this respect. On the one hand the community does not have the power to effect belief nor produce knowledge of the gospel. Yet it does have the power, with all the human skill it can muster, to summon people to make ready for knowledge, and in this sense it has the responsibility to make a loud evangelical appeal to the world. Barth writes:

> Even with the most powerful and heartfelt appeal which [the community] may make to them, it cannot change men. But with its appeal it can set before them the act of the love of God in which He has already changed them. It can make them aware that the revelation and knowledge of this act are awaiting them. It can thus make an impact in their lives and in world-occurrence . . . [and excite] a readiness which as such implies a small and provisional but real change in their being and action.[70]

This is what Barth means by the witness of the community: the declaration, explanation and application of the good news of Jesus Christ. This proclamation is essential to the commission and service of the community and must be a part of anything and everything the community undertakes. In this sense Barth sees a great unity in the witness of the community: "At every point and in all the functions of its life the Church is concerned to offer that great parable of the kingdom of God."[71] While this parable in its totality is a unified witness, Barth argues that the witness of the community must not be uniform. Rather, the witness of the community should be manifold, reflecting the various human means with which it carries out its task and the variety of ways it presents itself to the world. Moreover, the multiplicity of the community's witness is essential to its being and indispensable to its witness. This is so first because the Lord of the community is one God as Father, Son and Holy Spirit, "not with an undifferentiated, lifeless, and motionless unity, but as the eternally rich God who is the basis, source and Lord of an infinitude of different divine

---

[70]Ibid., 852.

[71]Ibid., 854. The English translation here is a "great likeness of the kingdom of God," translating *Gleichnis* as "likeness." In his discussion of the "freedom of the Christian as witness" at the end of paragraph 71, immediately preceding this paragraph, Barth specifically understands this word to mean a parable, as illumined by the ways that parables work in the Gospels. The word should thus be translated parable here also.

possibilities."[72] Second, the community God has called is not a monolithic block but lives in correspondence to the being and life of God and is gathered, called and sent by the specific callings and gifts of individuals. It is not the differentiation of individuals that gives rise to the multiplicity of witness but the differentiation of their gifts for the one service of witness.[73]

So if the community's witness is multiform, what are some specific forms of witness? Barth's delineation of these forms addresses those forms that characterize the work of the community in every age and place. On the one hand, while this approach seems far too abstract to characterize the uniqueness of ministry in various contexts, Barth intends his approach to be in the service of practical theology. He recognizes that the community will always be inspired to and gifted for new variations on the basic forms, yet he also perceives universal, basic forms that arise from the nature of the gospel itself.

Drawing on the instructions given to the disciples when Jesus sent them forth (primarily Matthew 28:18-20), Barth discerns a basic twofold form in the differentiation of the community's witness: speech (which is also always an act) and act (which is also always a form of speech). The disciples must speak and pass on that which they have received and their speech must be linked at once with distinct human action that bears witness to the same revelation. The witness of the community in following its Lord must always move along these two lines. Moreover, Barth argues, it must always maintain this sequence of speech and then action.[74] In light of this

---

[72]Ibid.

[73]Barth makes two further points with respect to this differentiation. First, it will always be the case that individual giftedness will lead some to assert their abilities in ways that are inappropriate to the witness of the community. This, however, does not undermine the legitimacy of multiplicity. Second, this multiplicity will express itself in special working fellowships within the one community; Barth argues that these fellowships must be based on rendering a particular service of witness in a particular way and not simply gatherings of like-minded people to satisfy certain needs.

[74]Barth does not insist on this sequence in order to place a relative value on either of these elements; in any given circumstance it is difficult to say which makes a greater impact on the world, the word or deed of the community. Rather, he insists on it because the call of the gospel is to active knowledge, and thus speech (conveying knowledge) must be logically prior to act. It seems, however, that there are occasions in which speech can interpret a prior act. Indeed, this is the basic scenario envisioned in 1 Peter 3:13-15: "Now who will harm you if you are eager to do what is good? But even if you do suffer for doing what is right, you are blessed. Do not fear what they fear, and do not be intimidated, but in your hearts sanctify Christ as Lord. Always be ready to make your defense to anyone who demands from you an accounting for the hope that is in you." I would argue that what is truly at stake is that speech and act go together, while the sequence is variable.

differentiation, Barth will proceed to discuss six forms of speech(act) and six forms of act(speech). The essentially dual nature of each form is what confirms that it is in fact a basic form of witness. Though Barth will discuss them separately, he sees them as an integrated, interconnected and intersecting whole where each form impinges on the others. Indeed, he comments before moving on, "This [interconnectivity] is perhaps an additional argument for the utter impossibility of a system of Church ministry constructed on analytical and synthetic lines."[75]

The first and fundamental form of oral witness is the praise of God: the affirmation, approval and extolling of God for who God is and what God has done. In one sense, the praise of God is an intrinsically worthy act that would satisfy God and the community if done in secret. Yet as part of its witness, the concern of the community is to "set up a banner, to raise a standard," in its praise of God and thus to "fill a yawning gulf in the life of the world."[76] As this is also the most fundamental act of speech, everything the community does will participate in its praise of God. Still, the community most specifically praises God when it gathers for public worship and especially as its affirmation of God wells up in song. Barth understands the praise of God in singing to be an indispensable form of the community's witness.

The second basic of form of oral witness is preaching, and since this is the major focus of our attention, Barth's discussion here deserves sustained treatment. By preaching (the German *Predigt*), a term he calls "overburdened" but unavoidable, Barth means "the explicit proclamation of the Gospel in the assembly of the community, in the midst of the divine service, where it is also heard directly or indirectly by the world."[77] What is at issue in preaching?

> Decisively that the community, and with it the world, should remind itself or be reminded explicitly of the witness with which it is charged, that it should find reassurance as to its content, that reflected in it Jesus Christ himself should speak afresh to it, that it should be summoned afresh to His service in the world.[78]

---

[75]Barth, *CD* IV/3.2, 864.
[76]Ibid., 865.
[77]Ibid., 867.
[78]Ibid.

In a sense Barth argues that preaching does in a regular and specific way what he has been doing in this section on the Holy Spirit and the sending of the Christian community: reminding the community that it exists for the world, that it is charged with a task that has a specific content, and that this task comes with a promise. To frame it in terms of the whole ecclesiology, preaching reminds and confirms the community of the vocation to which it owes "its gathering and upbuilding and indeed its very existence."[79]

Barth identifies two aspects of preaching that are essential to the task and safeguard it from distortion. First, the essential content of preaching is Jesus Christ and what has been accomplished by God in him; this content distinguishes preaching from other forms of speech or declaration. Second, the declaration of this content takes place in connection with the original witness to Christ: the Old and New Testament scriptures. In that sense preaching is a communication of the biblical message. It is not biblical studies, but it is an independent proclamation of the gospel that arises from listening to the proclamation of scripture. Nor is preaching a work of systematic theology; while it certainly includes theology, preaching "proclaims, summons, invites, and commands"; it does not "reflect, reason, dispute, or academically instruct."[80] As it fulfills this task, preaching participates in the whole witness of the community by doing explicitly what every other form of witness does more implicitly: its calls each and all to faith, obedience and active knowledge of the gospel.

The third basic form of the community's witness is the instruction given to its own members and to the world. Barth argues that every Christian must remain a catechumen throughout life. Moreover, if Christians are to give an account of the hope that is within them, they must know something of the Bible. What particularly distinguishes the witness of instruction from preaching is that there is time for questions and answers that are out of place or disruptive in worship but are essential to the work of the community.

The fourth basic form of the community's witness is for the most part directed toward the outside world, which Barth calls its "evangelization."

---

[79]Ibid., 868.

[80]To be sure, preaching is not a work of systematic theology. However, one could argue that preaching—even understood as witness or confession—does reflect, reason and dispute. Indeed, we will return to this point with respect to a criticism of confession as a mode of preaching.

For Barth, evangelization is witness directed toward a very specific group of people: those who are "nominally Christian" but who are not involved in the life of the community. Barth understands this "nominal" designation as arising from the notion of the *corpus Christianum*, which includes both the church and the world, and from the practice of infant baptism in which people belong to the community but do not yet have an active part in its knowledge or witness. Evangelization is witness that serves to awaken this "sleeping Church" and joyfully invite those who are on the edge of the community to become fully active in its life.[81]

Fifth, the community has to speak to the world in the more specific and traditional sense of "mission," in which the community extends beyond itself and its borders and proclaims the gospel to those who have never heard it. Barth expounds on this subject at length because it is a source of controversy in the contemporary church and an issue of ambivalence among many. He lays out seven criteria for "missions": (1) it is pursued in the belief that everything necessary for the salvation of these people has already been accomplished, (2) the Christian community—and not a special society—is the acting subject, (3) the purpose is to make known the gospel, not teach Western culture, (4) it must take seriously other religions while sincerely recognizing them as false gods, (5) it must be concerned with the establishment of the whole ministry of the church, (6) the goal must be to bear witness and not to save or convert, which is in the power of God alone, and (7) missionary work cannot take the form of mastering but only of serving.

The final form of speech(act) witness is the ministry of theology. What is at issue in theology is that the community tests its actions and activities, the contemporary ways in which it is seeking to bear its witness, by the standard of its commission and by the light of the word of the Lord. "In theology the community gives a critical account . . . of the appropriateness or otherwise of its praise of God, its preaching, its instruction, its evangelistic and missionary work . . . of its witness in the full and comprehensive sense."[82] Within theology, Barth identifies the branches of biblical theology, historical theology, systematic theology and practical

---

[81]Barth, CD IV/3.2, 873.
[82]Ibid., 879.

theology. The role of practical theology, he argues, is to seek what is normative for the practice of ministry arising from biblical, historical and systematic theological investigations.

Turning now to those forms of service that are predominantly action, Barth identifies as first and fundamental the service of prayer. He writes, "Prayer is the basic element in the whole action of the whole community," and as such it is the work of the community, and in and with the community it is the work of each member.[83] The prayer of the community includes an inseparable union of thanksgiving and intercession: it gives thanks for the gracious work of God in the past and it prays for the same in the future. Moreover, "In prayer the community keeps God to His Word" by expecting that God in free grace will keep God's promises and will be the same tomorrow as yesterday and today.[84] Like its service of praise, the service of prayer that the community renders is for the world and is done in the midst of the world as a witness to the work and word and God. Like praise, prayer is the fundamental act of witness and everything the community does will participate in prayer; meanwhile, prayer finds its most specific expression in the worship of the community.

The eighth form of the community's service in this schema is the cure of souls. By the cure of souls, Barth means that the community (first the community as a whole and only then individuals within it) is called to exercise the *mutua consolatio fratrum*: the mutual consolation of the fellowship. On an individual level, this means a concrete participation in the particular past, present and future of another person, in his or her burdens and afflictions, and especially in the promise and hope of this person's existence in Christ. This expresses itself in encouragement, instruction, discipline, confession, assurance of pardon and efforts toward healing. In all these ways the community serves not only the human person but God as well.

Connected with the cure of souls, the witness of the community also involves "the production and existence of definite personal examples of Christian life and action."[85] Though the life of the whole community is

---

[83]Ibid., 882.
[84]Ibid., 883.
[85]Ibid., 887.

primary, there are always members of the community who stand out in their individuality. It does not matter what function or office they have or the significance of their persons. What matters is that in their life the validity of what is common to all Christians comes through in a vibrant and exemplary way. While these persons are still only witnesses to Christ, in and by their exemplary witness they may inspire and guide the community for a time.

The tenth basic form of the community's witness is the diaconate. By diaconate Barth means simply the rendering of service, and he notes that customarily but not necessarily does this term refer to helping those who are in material or physical distress. On one hand, by stressing its more general character, Barth wants to connect the witness of service with every other act and witness of the community. Yet on the other hand, by highlighting its more specific designation, he is bringing out a special importance in this form of witness. As compared especially with the great preacher or learned theologian, in the diaconate the community renders a service that does not in any way lend itself to glory or power, and in that sense it is a unique opportunity for witness. Furthermore, in diaconate the community "explicitly accepts solidarity with the least of these little ones" and thus bears witness to the great value, in light of the gospel, of those who otherwise exist on the margins of society.[86] By this kind of service, the community has "the opportunity to reveal at least in sign the cosmic character of the reconciliation accomplished in Jesus Christ."[87]

The eleventh basic form of the community's witness is prophetic action. This is "an action based on perception into the meaning of the current events, relationships and forms both of its own history and that of the world around in their positive and negative connection to the imminent kingdom of God."[88] The community that is listening to the voice of the living Lord is moving from the present into the future under the direction of its Lord.

---

[86]Ibid., 891. Barth makes three further points with respect to areas he perceives as "hotly contested" in this form of witness: (1) the community must realize that the need of individuals is grounded in problems and disorders in the whole of human life in society, (2) the increase of welfare activities by the state does not obviate the need for a Christian diaconate and (3) the diaconate is a service of the community as such, even though the service may be performed more intensively by individuals and fellowships that are especially gifted for it.

[87]Ibid.

[88]Ibid., 895.

This means that the community is always engaged in self-examination and self-correction (*ecclesia semper reformanda*) and is also aware of the current situation in the world. Barth argues that the church should always be at least a "length or half-length" ahead of the world in understanding what is coming to pass.[89] Of course, there will be opposition to this prophetic witness; those without may oppose the community, and the community may be divided within itself. Still this opposition and division is no reason for the community to neglect this basic form of its witness.

Finally, and to conclude this whole section on the sending of the community, Barth identifies the fellowship of the community as an act of witness. The community establishes fellowship between human beings as a sign of the fellowship that God has established in Christ between God and humanity and humanity with itself. In the community people are bound more strongly to one another than in any other fellowship, and even in separation and conflict the community must aim for the unity and peace of the fellowship. This witness of the fellowship is particularly strong when it is brought into contact with the divisions that separate people. The community does not remove differences of nationality, race, culture or economics, but "it constitutes right across them a new people in which the members of all people do not merely meet but are united."[90] The specific actions by which the community establishes its fellowship are baptism, in which people enter and are received into membership in the community, and the Lord's Supper, in which the community is repeatedly and consciously unified as one people. In these acts, a visible action of the community attests to an invisible action of God, and in this sense Barth writes that these acts are "the simplest, and . . . the most eloquent, elements in the witness which the community owes to the world."[91]

Thus Barth completes his description of the twelve basic forms of the community's witness and his section on the sending of the community. Together these twelve forms constitute Barth's portrait of the ways in which the community renders its service both in acts of speech and in acts that speak. One must remember that though he discusses them

---

[89]Ibid., 896.
[90]Ibid., 899.
[91]Ibid., 901.

separately, Barth understands these twelve forms as an interconnected whole that together offers a parable of the kingdom of God. Certainly for the practical theologian or the preacher it seems impossible in practice to distinguish these discrete forms of witness. For instance, can one draw a clear line between preaching and teaching, or between mission and evangelism, or between prophetic action and the diaconate? In the next chapter, as we examine characteristics of missional congregations, we will see that the lines are blurred and these forms of witness are intermingled in the lived experience of particular communities.

Still, in each of the various forms of witness, Barth continues to bring out two themes. First, the content of the witness is none other than what God has accomplished in Jesus Christ, and this common content is a strong bond that connects the various forms of service. Second, any specific form of witness is always first in the context of and a witness of the community, even if it is done specifically by a few who are gifted and called to that work (for example, preaching, teaching, theology, diaconal service).[92] The service of these few, Barth argues repeatedly, should never be understood separately from the witness of the whole community or as a task different from that given to the whole community.

In brief summary, these are the essential elements of Barth's lengthy argument in "The Holy Spirit and the Sending of the Christian Community": (1) The vocation of a person is to be a Christian and to be united with a community of other Christians in a common mission. This doctrine leads directly into a consideration of the Christian community. (2) Barth defines the community as the people of God in the flow of human affairs, and the world is the arena both of God's providence and human confusion. (3) In this historical situation, the community necessarily exists for the world because the community exists in Christ who is himself for the world. To exist for the world means to be given insight into the world as it is, to be in solidarity with the world, and to be under obligation to the world. (4) The task of the community is to attest to the world God's goodness in Jesus Christ, the reconciliation accomplished in Christ and the new reality es-

---

[92]Even for preaching, Barth notes that if the quality of preaching in a community is poor, it is not simply the responsibility of the preacher but of the whole community to support, work toward and pray for a stronger witness of preaching. See ibid., 870.

tablished in Christ. (5) The community fulfills this commission by its witness, which is carried out in a variety of interconnected forms, all of which are united by their common witness to Jesus Christ.

MOVING TOWARD A MISSIONAL HOMILETIC

Several key features of Barth's ecclesiology raise incisive questions for the homiletical proposals considered in the previous chapter, and we will sort out these questions and their implications later as we develop a clear missional homiletic. To conclude this chapter, though, I want to highlight major homiletical issues that arise from Barth's arguments.

Relative to the homiletic proposals we discussed in the last chapter, Barth implies an important shift in perspective for homiletics in two significant ways. First, each homiletic proposal we reviewed construes witness as a way of preaching. Long contrasts the preacher as witness with the preacher as herald, pastor and storyteller. Florence presents preaching as testimony in contrast to preaching as patriarchal or foundational instruction. Lose proposes preaching as confession in response to the demise of preaching as the exposition of foundational truth. In each case, preaching is the genus and witness is the species.

Barth, however, shifts this perspective dramatically. In his understanding, witness is the genus and preaching is the species. *For Barth, witness is not a way of preaching, but preaching is a way of witness.* Barth argues that every activity in which the church is engaged is an act of witness. Moreover, each act of witness participates in the common task of the community and of every Christian, and every form of witness is united to the other forms by its common content and purpose: to confess Jesus Christ. Homiletically, when witness is a supercategory that includes every activity of the church, preaching is thus set in an interconnected relationship to those other activities.

Second, in these homiletic proposals each author implies that the individual preacher is the basic unit of witness by focusing his or her attention exclusively on the person who addresses the congregation or community and how that person makes such an address. The congregation is largely out of view in these proposals. Long's *Witness of Preaching* is a slight exception because he argues that the preacher arises from the congregation and is sent by the congregation to the text. Yet Long only mentions in passing the vocation of the whole church to proclamation and moreover does not set preaching in relationship to that broader witness. Now, even for Barth, preaching is basically a task of the individual. However, he also insists that the community is always the basic unit of Christian witness and perspective from which to understand every form of witness. The task of witness is given to the community as a whole, and any form of that witness is part of the community's discharge of its commission. Even when service is rendered by one who is specially called, that service must be understood in its connection to the whole witness of the community and not separate from it. Thus, when we consider the specific act of Christian witness that is preaching, it must be in the larger context of the community's witness.

In addition to these perspectival shifts, Barth's understanding of ecclesiology and the sending of the Christian community raises at least two other issues for homiletics. First, Barth argues that the unifying element in the variety of the community's witness is its common content, Jesus Christ. This places a premium on the content of the witness. Not only does the content ensure the connection between one form of witness and another, but it is also the criterion by which the purity of the community's fulfillment of its commission is assessed. Explicitly, each of the homiletic proposals examined is concerned with the "how" of preaching, specifically how to preach in a postmodern milieu. Consequently, the "what" of preaching, the content of the witness, is somewhat below the surface. Barth's analysis raises a question for each of these proposals: what is the proposed content of preaching? More importantly, what should the essential content be and how does that shape the preaching task?

Second, in Barth's understanding, the church exists for the world. It cannot exist otherwise because the church exists as the body of Christ and thus as a predicate of Christ. Since Christ exists for the world, so the church cannot exist in any other way than for the world. Put negatively, it cannot exist for itself and its own enjoyment and perpetuation, and it cannot exist only for Christ, because to exist for Christ is also and at the same time to exist for the world as Christ exists for the world. Thus it is not enough for the community to be simply gathered and upbuilt by the

Holy Spirit and to enjoy the benefits of Christ. For in gathering and up-building the community, in conferring Christ and all his benefits on the community, the Holy Spirit is also always sending the community out to be witnesses of what God has accomplished for the world in Jesus Christ. The issue then for homiletics is that the community is understood as for the world and sent into the world and, moreover, that preaching is an act of sending the community out into the world and reminding the community of its calling to bear witness in and to the world. For Barth this was an essential element of preaching: preaching is a "pregnant reminder and confirmation of the vocation to which [the community] owes its gathering and upbuilding and indeed its very existence."[93]

To summarize this exposition of Barth and the questions he raises, I want to offer you four assertions that arise from his ecclesiology and orient our homiletical thinking toward a missional perspective.

1. As Christian witness is fundamentally the task of the community, and the special calling of an individual or group can be understood only in the context of the task given to the whole community, then the witness of the preacher should be understood as a discrete element of the whole witness of the community.

2. To put the same point a different way: since witness is the fundamental task of the Christian community and that task is executed in a variety of forms, with preaching being one form, then it is imperative to discern the distinctive nature of preaching as differentiated from and in relation to the other forms of witness.

3. Since the unifying element in the multiplicity of the community's witness is the content of its witness, then it is also imperative to identify the essential content of preaching.

4. Since the community necessarily exists for the world, then preaching must in some way turn the community toward the world for whom it exists.

---

[93]Ibid., 868.

3

The Witness of
Missional Congregations

In chapter one we explored three homiletical models that use the concept of witness to understand the person of the preacher and the ministry of preaching. Thomas Long proposes that preaching is an act of bearing witness in which preachers go to a text seeking an encounter with God on behalf of a congregation, and the preacher then bears witness to that encounter through the sermon. Anna Carter Florence argues that preaching is testimony, and preachers testify through the sermon to an experience they have had with God. David Lose contends that preaching is a confession of faith, and that through the sermon preachers confess faith in Jesus Christ. As I noted at the end of chapter one, through their proposals each of these homileticians offers different resources for the development of a missional homiletic, and the conversation among them raises important questions that help define the contours of a missional homiletic.

In the last chapter we examined the ecclesiology of Karl Barth through a detailed analysis of section 72 of the *Church Dogmatics*, "The Holy Spirit and the Sending of the Christian Community." He characterizes the congregation as the community that is gathered and upbuilt by God and sent out into the world to bear witness to Jesus Christ. He considers in turn the situation in which the community finds itself, the calling of the community, the commission that is given to the community and the service that is rendered by the community. Barth's contention, which is also a foundational conviction of the missional theological conversation, is that the congregation is the primary unit of witness in the world and that all acts of individual witness must be understood in light of their relationship to the whole congregation. This means that preaching, along with other types of ministry, is to be understood in the context of and as it is related to the witness of the whole community.

Theologically, this means that the practice of preaching should be understood within an ecclesiological context, and Barth's ecclesiology serves as a lens through which to see preaching and the preacher in a missional perspective. Barth's argument about the vocation of the Christian community responds to some of the questions raised by the differences between the homiletical proposals, and his argument raises new questions for a missional homiletic. Before turning to that missional homiletic, however, there is one other voice to bring into the conversation: missional theology.

As I noted in the introduction, missional theology has been developed by a cluster of North American theologians who are working to reorient all Christian doctrines around the concept of *missio Dei*: the sending of God that leads to the sending of the church into the world. As Darrell Guder writes, "The doctrinal challenge is to develop every theme and subtheme relating to the theology and practices of the church from the central and foundational understanding of the church's missional vocation."[1] Hence, much of the missional literature has been ecclesiological in nature and contextually rooted, focused on the theology and practices of the church in North America. Oddly, though, there is little in the missional literature that directly addresses preaching. Even those who are actively involved in leading the missional conversation have expressed surprise at this void and see homiletics as a theological discipline that needs to be developed from a missional perspective.[2] Indeed, when read through a homiletical lens, missional theological work has important implications for the practice of preaching.[3]

---

[1]Darrell L. Guder, "Walking Worthy: Missional Leadership After Christendom," *Princeton Seminary Bulletin* 28 (2007): 271.

[2]Based on personal conversations with Darrell Guder and George Hunsberger.

[3]I have found only one other instance of mining missional literature for homiletical implications. In a paper for the Evangelical Society of Homiletics titled "Preaching in the Missional Church," Ervin R. Stutzman distills nine characteristics of missional preaching drawn from a survey of missional literature. Though he notes that his sampling of the literature is incomplete, he finds little that directly addresses preaching. Stutzman's nine characteristics share some similarities with those de-

The organizing framework by which we will explore these homiletical implications will be the book and structure of *Treasure in Clay Jars: Patterns in Missional Faithfulness*. This book is particularly well-suited because it is in itself a work of practical theology, though not self-consciously so. *Treasure in Clay Jars* is a study of "congregations that are becoming missional," an attempt to give real-life examples of congregations that are attempting to let the mission of God inform everything they do. It explicitly follows up on the ideas first presented in *Missional Church: A Vision for the Sending of the Church in North America*, and it was researched and written by the same team that wrote that book.[4] The result of their research is the identification of eight "patterns of missional faithfulness" that they found to one degree or another in the congregations they studied.

In an appendix, Walter Hobbs describes the research process the writers used to develop the book. He is clear to say that *Treasure in Clay Jars* does not constitute social scientific research in the proper sense, yet it does reflect a practical theological process in which theory was informed and critiqued by practice through field research.[5] At the beginning, two members of the research team distilled the theory in *Missional Church* into twelve indicators that could be used to identify missional congregations. These indicators were not meant to serve as measures of missional character but as pointers toward missional con-

---

scribed in this chapter, and his work serves as a resource for this chapter. Stutzman's article is brief, and his elucidation of the nine characteristics makes up less than half of the article. Moreover, in his sampling of literature he mixes missional literature with "postmodern" literature (i.e., books designed to help the church witness to a "postmodern generation"), an admixture I have intentionally avoided for the sake of conceptual clarity. There are themes of the "postmodern turn" evident in missional literature, but not everything deemed postmodern is missional and vice versa. See Ervin R. Stutzman, "Preaching in the Missional Church," Preaching.org, March 4, 2011, www.preaching .org/preaching-in-the-missional-church.

[4]Lois Y. Barrett et al., *Treasure in Clay Jars: Patterns in Missional Faithfulness* (Grand Rapids: Eerdmans, 2004), ix.

[5]This understanding of practical theological method is developed at length by Richard Osmer in Richard R. Osmer, *Practical Theology: An Introduction* (Grand Rapids: Eerdmans, 2008). Osmer understands practical theology as a four-step process comprising descriptive-empirical, interpretive, normative and pragmatic tasks. These tasks correspond to these questions: What is happening? Why is it happening? What should be happening? How can we change the situation? Osmer argues that this is the basic process pastors should use as they seek to help their congregations interpret their lives and the process practical theologians should use to craft praxis theology, in which theory is in mutual-critical dialogue with practice. In the case of *Treasure in Clay Jars*, each task of the theological process is evident to some degree but often in a complex interaction of the four "steps."

gregations. Using these twelve indicators, the research team drew on their own experience and the suggestions of others to identify a set of congregations that represented geographic, denominational and organizational diversity. They selected eight congregations and one cluster of congregations and conducted field research in the form of visits and interviews.[6] The intention of these visits and interviews was not to produce models of missional congregations, nor a step-by-step guide for how to become a missional congregation. Rather, their intention was to listen to the stories of these congregations and look for common themes that could encourage other congregations in their effort to become more missional.

In the course of their research, the team realized that the original twelve indicators were not adequate to characterize the missional nature of the congregations. Some indicators fit and others did not, and some had to be combined because of similarities. This type of revision indicates a practical theological process of revising theological assumptions in light of the actual practice and lived experience of congregations. So, over the course of the study, the twelve were reduced to eight, and the indicators became patterns. Hobbs writes that the conversations with the churches "significantly reshaped some of our earlier reasoning about the nature of missional congregations. In particular, our focus shifted away from the supposed attributes or characteristics of such churches, to *patterns* that could be detected in their lives as congregations."[7] This shift to patterns indicates the contextual complexity of the missional characteristics of these congregations, as each pattern is present in a different degree and in a different way in the congregations studied. By referring to patterns, the team also intends to emphasize that they are not listing ingredients in a missional recipe, nor are the congregations models of "missional churches." Rather, these are churches that display definite pat-

---

[6]The congregations included in the study are: Boulder Mennonite Church of Boulder, Colorado; Eastbrook Church of Milwaukee, Wisconsin; First Presbyterian Church of Bellevue, Washington; Holy Ghost Full Gospel Baptist Church of Detroit, Michigan; IMPACT Cluster, Seven Churches of the Reformed Church in America in the Synod of the Mid-Atlantics, New Jersey; Rockridge United Methodist Church of Oakland, California; Spring Garden Church of Toronto, Ontario; Transfiguration Parish of the Roman Catholic Church in Brooklyn, New York; and West Yellowstone Presbyterian Church of West Yellowstone, Montana.
[7]Barrett et al., *Treasure in Clay Jars*, 157.

terns of missional faithfulness and when taken together these patterns offer a picture of missional faithfulness in congregational life.[8]

Since these patterns have been developed through a practical theological process of theory, research and critique, they provide an excellent framework by which to explore and collate the implications for preaching found in a range of missional literature. In the discussion of the eight patterns, the authors of *Treasure in Clay Jars* rarely mention the practice of preaching explicitly, but the patterns of missional faithfulness suggest important implications for missional preaching. In this chapter we will use the eight patterns elaborated in *Treasure in Clay Jars* to tease out implications for missional preaching. In the discussion of each implication, we will bring into the conversation other missional literature that bears on that homiletical implication.

THE FIRST PATTERN: DISCERNING MISSIONAL VOCATION

The first pattern of missional faithfulness is that a congregation is actively discerning how to fulfill its calling in its particular time and place. George Hunsberger, the author of this section, writes:

> The congregation is discovering together the missional vocation of the community. It is beginning to redefine "success" and "vitality" in terms of faithfulness to God's calling and sending. It is seeking to discern God's specific missional vocation (its "charisms") for the entire community and for all of its members.[9]

As we saw through Barth's missional ecclesiology in the last chapter, every congregation has a vocation that it shares with the whole church, which is to bear witness to Jesus Christ and announce the inauguration of God's reign. However, missional theologians go one step further to say that

---

[8]The research process that the team followed is described in broad terms by Hobbs in the "Method" appendix. Once the churches for the study were identified, the team was divided into four pairs, and they visited four churches in the initial round, requesting that any relevant information be sent in advance. The visits consisted of three- or four-day weekends, including interviews with members, staff and leadership, and attendance at events such as committee meetings, Bible studies, prayer times, staff meetings, workshops and worship. After the first round of visits, the team reconvened to discuss findings and modified their approach for the remaining visits. Each pair of team members included one person who was familiar with the doctrinal heritage of the given congregation, and no pair visited more than one church. Ibid., 154-59.
[9]Ibid., 33.

not only does the church share a common vocation, each congregation is called to express its vocation in a manner specific to its context. Hunsberger writes, "When attentive to the voice of God, a congregation discerns not only that vocation that is shared across the whole church, but also its particular calling to express that vocation in its own time and place."[10]

A sense of shared identity and common calling, a belief among a congregation that it has been sent by God to a particular people at a particular time and place for a particular purpose, is central to being a missional church. Holy Ghost Baptist Church in Detroit has discerned that its vocation is to be the healing presence of Christ and to "love everybody" in the Packard community of its city.[11] The congregation discerned this calling and then moved the church to this community, and half of the congregation also moved their homes there. Likewise, the congregation of the Transfiguration Parish in Brooklyn, New York, has discerned that its calling is to be a sign of the incarnation of Jesus Christ by living in poverty with the poor of its neighborhood. In both of these cases, a clear sense of shared missional identity is present throughout the congregation.

When a congregation discerns its calling, it can also be assured of its gifting for its calling. This is what Hunsberger means by reference to "charisms," which he understands as operating on the congregational level as well as on the personal level. For instance, a congregation that is called to serve families with autistic children will also be equipped for that task. Indeed, this is not a strictly linear process; the recognition of the charism may be a part of the vocational discernment process. Furthermore, the researchers found that the shared vocation of the congregation shapes the personal vocations of its members. Recall that in the *Church Dogmatics*, Barth argued that the church is logically prior to individual Christians. Similarly, missional theologians found in their study that "*personal* vocation is shared and molded in the context of a community that has clarity about *its* vocation."[12] The discernment of a congregation's vocation can be broken into several elements, including their geographic location (where are we?), their place in the flow of history

---

[10]Ibid., 38.
[11]Ibid., 34.
[12]Ibid., 38.

(when are we?), their relationship to their traditions (who are we?), and their sense of purpose in their time and place (why are we?). Moreover, the vocations of churches in the study were discerned in a variety of ways, such as at a critical and "catalytic" moment, or over many years of slow development, or in a period of intentional and conscious reflection.

For each congregation, though, the *Treasure in Clay Jars* researchers found that pastoral leadership was vital to the discernment of the congregation's vocation. It was the founding pastor of Holy Ghost Baptist Church, Henry N. Lewis, who continually repeated to them the simple phrase "Love everybody." Father Bryan Karvelis brought the spirituality of Charles de Foucauld, characterized by a focus on the mystery of the incarnation, to the Transfiguration Parish. Marc Erickson, the pastor of Eastbrook Church in Milwaukee, was instrumental in maintaining the core identity of the congregation, which is unity with other city churches, through his stories, comments, attitudes and actions. Through his leadership, John McLaverty, pastor of the Spring Garden Church in Toronto, Ontario, helped to keep the congregation open and ready to respond to God's initiative.

By recognizing that pastoral leadership is vital to the discernment of a congregation's missional vocation, these researchers also point toward implications for missional preaching. The pastors of the congregations studied in *Treasure in Clay Jars* helped their congregations discern their vocation through many activities that characterize pastoral ministry, including the ministry of preaching. In their preaching, these pastors helped shape the vocation of the congregation through specific and repeated messages, through repeated reinforcement of the core narrative of the congregation, or by regularly calling the congregation to remain open to God's leading.

The importance of the ministry of preaching in the discernment of a congregation's vocation is a common theme in missional literature. In his book *Choosing the Kingdom: Missional Preaching for the Household of God*, John Addison Dally wonders, "What if a renewed preaching . . . could offer preachers and congregations alike the possibility of mutually empowering discernment of the activity of God in their midst?"[13] He goes on to elaborate on the kind of preaching he believes offers the pos-

---

[13]John Addison Dally, *Choosing the Kingdom: Missional Preaching for the Household of God* (Herndon, VA: The Alban Institute, 2007), 12.

sibility of such discernment, a preaching that calls the congregation to choose to live in the reign of God in tangible ways. In a lecture on leadership and ordered ministry in the missional church, Darrell Guder reflects on the offices of ministry found in Ephesians 4 and writes, "What these ministers of the Word do, in their various ways, enables the missional community in a particular place to walk worthy of its calling," or, in other words, to discern and live out its missional vocation.[14] Likewise, Cheryl Bridges Johns, in an interpretation of Acts 4 meant to elucidate missional preaching, writes that preachers must come to understand the corporate witness and "prophethood" of the church in which the identity of the church is transformed as "that of a people whose vocation and calling is mission."[15] In each of these instances, the contention is that missional preaching helps a congregation discern its missional vocation.

Catherine Gunsalus González approaches the same point from the direction of baptism, a doctrine that holds an important place in missional theology's core argument. If the church is given a common vocation in its being called and sent out by God, then baptism is the event in which each Christian is individually commissioned to that vocation. Missional theologians consistently refer to baptism as the "general ordination of all Christians to their shared calling," as Guder describes it.[16] Reflecting on the connection between scripture, baptism and preaching, González writes, "If much of scripture concerns the mission of God's people, and if preaching is dealing with such texts, then preaching to the baptized frequently includes illumination of their mission."[17] Insofar as preachers expound on scriptural texts, they necessarily help the congregation discern its missional vocation because that is in fact what the scriptures themselves do, an argument that will be expanded in discussion of the next pattern.

Many years before the missional conversation began, Lutheran homiletician Herman G. Stuempfle Jr. made a similar case for the role of

---

[14]Guder, "Walking Worthy," 274.

[15]Cheryl Bridges Johns, "Acts and the Task of Missional Preaching," *Journal for Preachers* 22 (2006): 18.

[16]Guder, "Walking Worthy," 271.

[17]Catherine Gunsalus González, "The Baptismal Lens for Missional Preaching," *Journal for Preachers* 18, no. 3 (1995): 27.

preaching in the editorial preface to a collection of sermons titled *Preaching in the Witnessing Community*. The volume was published in support of denominational evangelism efforts in 1973 (termed "Key 73"), and so Stuempfle's focus is on "evangelistic preaching." However, his basic understanding of "evangelistic preaching" is that it equips the congregation for its proclamation in the world, an understanding that is very close to what I am calling "missional preaching." Using the image of military supply and support, Stuempfle writes, "The preacher's primary task is to equip the people for this missionary outthrust into the world's life and to help with their renewal when they return from the front."[18] There are many ways in which missional preaching may thus equip a congregation, but primarily missional preaching helps the congregation discern its missional vocation.

THE SECOND PATTERN: BIBLICAL FORMATION AND DISCIPLESHIP

As Catherine Gunsalus González has noted, whenever preachers expound on biblical texts, they are equipping the congregation for its mission. Indeed, biblical formation and discipleship is the second pattern of missional faithfulness discussed in *Treasure in Clay Jars*. Darrell Guder, who penned this chapter, writes:

> The missional church is a community where all members are learning what it means to be disciples of Jesus. The Bible has a continuing, converting, formative role in the church's life.[19]

There are two dynamics at work here, biblical formation and discipleship, and they must be held together to understand this pattern. A missional congregation is both formed by the scriptural witness and is intentional about becoming disciples of Jesus Christ.

Guder notes at the outset that not all Bible study shapes a congregation to live out its vocation, and indeed it is both possible and common to study the scriptures "in such a way that its central emphasis upon

---

[18]Herman G. Stuempfle, *Preaching in the Witnessing Community* (Fortress Press, 1973), xi.
[19]Barrett et al., *Treasure in Clay Jars*, 59.

formation for mission is missed."[20] It is possible in particular to study the Bible through the lens of one's personal needs and personal salvation and miss both a personal calling and a corporate vocation. Guder suggests that one sees this type of Bible study in churches across the denominational spectrum in the West, and he specifically highlights megachurches in North America that preach a consumer-oriented version of the gospel. Guder, like Barth, sees this problem arising from the Christendom context and as a fundamental reduction of the gospel. In Christendom, so it is argued, the gospel has been reduced to the benefits of salvation, ministers dispense the benefits and the congregation is the passive recipient.[21] Thus, biblical study itself is not sufficient as a pattern of missional faithfulness because the Bible can be studied through this lens. Rather, this missional pattern is biblical study coupled with a willingness to become a disciple, to be converted in every aspect of life, "to experience the daily renewal of our inner natures."[22]

When the researchers began their work for *Treasure in Clay Jars*, one of their indicators for missional faithfulness was "a community where all members are involved in learning to become disciples of Jesus."[23] In the course of their research, they realized they needed to be much more modest than "all." In each of the churches, people displayed a range of commitment to biblical formation and discipleship. In each church, to varying degrees, were people who were resistant to the kind of biblical formation that leads to conversion and missional vocation. There were some who came to a church "to get their needs met," and in many cases intentional biblical formation and discipleship was an optional activity for those who wanted to be more committed. However, in every church

---

[20]Ibid., 60.

[21]At one point in the *Church Dogmatics* Barth ponders the question of what a person's vocation is. One classic answer is that one's vocation is to "enjoy Christ and his benefits," which is to say that one's vocation is the salvation of one's soul to the glory of Christ. While Barth affirms the importance of the personal appropriation and experience of one's calling, ultimately he argues that the *beneficia Christi* are an insufficient understanding of vocation. He writes, "But if we are not wide awake, we shall rush on to the tempting conclusion that what vocation promises and implies and effects for man personally in terms of the *beneficia Christi* is in fact the decisively and dominatingly relevant, essential and central factor in the goal of vocation." Barth, *CD* IV/3.2, 564. This, he believes, leads to significant theological problems and ultimately to something along the lines of Ludwig Feuerbach's thought.

[22]Barrett et al., *Treasure in Clay Jars*, 60.

[23]Ibid., 163.

there was at least a small group, and often the leadership, that was actively engaged in biblical study and discipleship. Moreover, they were engaged in the kind of biblical study that asks questions that lead to missional formation.

Rather than asking how a text would meet their needs, they were asking, "How does God's Word call, shape, transform, and send me . . . and us?"[24] How does a text form us for our missional vocation, for our witness? This fundamental question constitutes a missional hermeneutic that is an oft-repeated theme of missional literature.[25] The starting supposition of a missional hermeneutic is that the intention of the scriptural witness is to form the people of God for their witness. Because the missional formation of the people of God is the basic function of the scriptures, both Old and New Testaments, missional theologians argue that it should be the starting place when interpreting a scriptural text.

Guder argues that the New Testament writers are especially concerned with the missionary existence of their readers. From his perspective, the New Testament scriptures are a natural extension of the missionary strategy begun by Jesus when he called, equipped and sent his twelve disciples. Jesus called the twelve, taught them and sent them out as a community of his witnesses. Their mission was to disciple the nations, to form more communities of the baptized who also would be called and sent to bear witness. Guder writes, "[This] apostolic strategy, the formation of equipped and empowered witnessing communities, finds its continuation in these ancient documents written to such communities, which over time were collected and became the canonical New Testament."[26] When Christians study the New Testament, they are "going to school with Jesus" just as the first disciples. Guder writes:

> Like the first disciples, every Christian community is to learn from Jesus and with Jesus both his message and how it [is] to be communicated. They were

---

[24]Ibid., 70.

[25]"Missional hermeneutics" is an idea that is still under active development, and there are a range of possibilities for what constitutes a missional hermeneutic. In this chapter we are addressing the importance of a missional hermeneutic for missional congregations and the appropriateness of reading the Bible "missionally." In chapter four I more clearly define what constitutes a missional hermeneutic for homiletics.

[26]Guder, "Walking Worthy," 257.

taught to see the world through his eyes and to understand the whole course of human history from the central event that he was and is.[27]

Thus, the second pattern of missional faithfulness is Bible study that interprets the text through this missional hermeneutical lens, asking the question, "How did this text equip the missional church, then, for its vocation, and how does it do that today?"[28] For preaching, this implies that the hermeneutical lens through which the preacher interprets the text is also a hermeneutic of missional formation. The researchers of *Treasure in Clay Jars* found that all the preachers in the churches they studied were employing a missional hermeneutic in their preaching, even if that hermeneutic was not widespread throughout the church. For instance, the senior pastor at Bellevue Presbyterian was working in the pulpit and with lay leadership to wrestle with missional vocation through biblical interpretation. Not everyone at the Eastbrook Church in Milwaukee opted for intentional discipleship, but "for everyone . . . the missional challenge of the gospel is the central theme of public preaching."[29] At Transfiguration Parish, the lectionary texts used in Sunday worship are the basis for Bible studies throughout the week, so that a missional hermeneutic is carried from preaching to group study.

As we have seen, this emphasis on a missional hermeneutic, being shaped by scripture for one's witness in the world, is not unique to *Treasure in Clay Jars*. In her article "The Baptismal Lens for Missional Preaching," González interprets Luke 15:11-32 and several other Easter season lectionary passages through a missional hermeneutic. She writes that if one takes the baptism of the congregation seriously, then one cannot place the congregation in the position of the prodigal son when interpreting Jesus' parable. The baptized is no prodigal in a far-off country; he is already at home with the father. So, she argues, as the body of Christ in the world, a congregation should see itself in the position of the father, praying for and anticipating the return of prodigals. She writes, "Part of the mission of the church is to be open and receive with joy those

---

[27]Ibid., 257-58.
[28]Ibid., 258.
[29]Barrett et al., *Treasure in Clay Jars*, 65.

who have been estranged from God and who now come home."[30] Thus, a missional interpretation of the text does not simply offer the congregation the benefits of Christ and his welcome but equips them to extend that welcome to others as the body of Christ in the world.

Likewise, Lesslie Newbigin, who provided inspiration for founding the Gospel and Our Culture Network, writes at length of the need for the disciple's vision of the world to be formed by biblical study. For Newbigin, biblical formation for mission means allowing one's whole understanding of the world to be challenged and shaped by the revelation of God in Jesus Christ as found in the biblical witness. Rather than reading the Bible through the lens of secular Western culture, Newbigin argues that Christians should read the culture and themselves through the lens of the Bible.[31] This is the kind of reading for conversion that he practiced as a missionary in India, where he found it was easy for the gospel to be co-opted into the dominant Hindu hermeneutical framework, and that he believed is vitally necessary in the contemporary West.

Newbigin's experience in India points back to the two interrelated elements of this pattern of missional faithfulness: that biblical study alone is not sufficient but must be coupled with a desire to be formed as a disciple of Jesus Christ. This implies that a preacher will use a missional hermeneutic for interpreting scripture, asking how the text calls and shapes the congregation for its vocation and mission. In my view, these first two patterns, discerning missional vocation and biblical discipleship, are foundational patterns in the life of a missional congregation. The next six patterns are instructive and suggestive for a missional preacher and may be present to some degree in any missional church. However, they are all dependent on the discernment of missional vocation and biblical discipleship, and it is in these two areas that preaching has the greatest potential impact.

---

[30]González, "The Baptismal Lens," 28.

[31]See Lesslie Newbigin, *The Gospel in a Pluralist Society* (Grand Rapids: Eerdmans, 1989). On the issue of biblical formation and conversion, Newbigin has been criticized for supposing that one can step outside of one's cultural milieu to read the Bible through a different set of eyes. In other words, so critics argue, deconstructing one's cultural assumptions is not as simple as putting on a new pair of glasses. Newbigin's response, which he offers in *The Gospel in a Pluralist Society*, is that one can attempt this kind of cultural conversion only through the witness of a community, "which indwells the story the Bible tells" (p. 97). It is this community, continuous through time and crossing cultures, that provides the hermeneutical leverage needed to shift one's embedded cultural assumptions.

THE THIRD PATTERN: TAKING RISKS AS A CONTRAST COMMUNITY

Newbigin's stress on the gospel shaping one's understanding of the world leads to the third pattern of missional faithfulness identified in *Treasure in Clay Jars*: taking risks as a contrast community. Lois Barrett, the author of this chapter, writes:

> The missional church is learning to take risks for the sake of the gospel. It understands itself as different from the world because of its participation in the life, death, and resurrection of its Lord. It is raising questions, often threatening, about the church's cultural captivity and grappling with the ethical and structural implications of its missional vocation.[32]

The emphasis on taking *risks* as a contrast community is intentional on the part of the authors. Based on the indicators developed from *Missional Church*, the research team expected to find that missional churches were pointing toward God's reign through actions that displayed generosity, hospitality, reconciliation and self-sacrifice. They found that the churches they studied were performing those actions, but they discovered to their surprise that this always entailed risk. The actions these churches took to point toward God's reign routinely put their finances, their facilities, their reputation and even their lives at risk.

The Transfiguration Parish in Brooklyn was continually wrestling with how to stand in solidarity with the poor in a dominant culture characterized by materialism and conspicuous consumption. Likewise, the Boulder Mennonite Church struggled to live out an ethic of simplicity in a culture of affluence. The Rockridge United Methodist Church in Oakland, California, committed to living in small covenant communities as accountable to one another in a culture marked by individualism. And so on. In each of the churches, the congregation took risks for the sake of solidarity with the poor and marginalized and nonconformity with the dominant culture, and they displayed a willingness to suffer loss for the sake of the gospel.

In her chapter, Barrett makes no mention of how preaching may have encouraged the congregations to take the risks they took. Surely, though, the

---

[32]Barrett et al., *Treasure in Clay Jars*, 74.

imagination required to envision such countercultural alternatives and the courage to take such risks was shaped and fostered partly through preaching. Indeed, this is the kind of preaching envisioned by Dally in *Choosing the Kingdom* when he encourages preachers to call the congregation to decide to live as a contrast community. He writes, "Preachers have a unique opportunity to reach a cross-section of listeners with a vision of God's reign lived out in our neighborhoods and cities."[33] Similarly, Herman Stuempfle Jr. writes that "preaching in the witnessing community" equips the congregation "to witness through what they are and what they do in places where verbal testimony is often inappropriate, though they must be ready to 'give an account for the faith that is in them' when the occasion demands."[34]

Carlos Cardoza-Orlandi specifically emphasizes this aspect of preaching when he explores the question of missional preaching in the article "What Makes Preaching Missional?"[35] He writes that the essential aspect of missional preaching is that the gospel interacts with the congregation's "struggle with and participation in the activity of God in the world."[36] By this he means to emphasize that missional preaching does not simply help the congregation discern God's activity in the world, as if that activity were apart from them, their context and their social location. Rather, missional preaching takes up their "existential praxis," their struggle to live out their faith in their time and place, and connects it to the Christian faith with all its "historical, theological, and ministerial wealth." Cardoza-Orlandi writes eloquently of the importance of existential praxis to missional preaching:

> It is in the *existential praxis* that we relate to persons of other cultures and religions, face the injustices and incongruences of life, and are confronted with the ambiguity and fragility of our actions. It is in this vital space that we celebrate the triumphs and grieve the failures, that we listen to news that disheartens us and other news that gives us hope. In this vital space we eat and share bread or waste the food that so many need; we love passionately and hate that which

---

[33]Dally, *Choosing the Kingdom*, 18.
[34]Stuempfle, *Preaching in the Witnessing Community*, xi.
[35]Cardoza-Orlandi's full definition of missional preaching is "a ministerial, personal, and communal action in which the congregation listens and discerns the testimony of the Christian people in their struggle with and participation in the activity of God in the world." Carlos Cardoza-Orlandi, "What Makes Preaching Missional?" *Journal for Preachers* 22 (1999): 7.
[36]Ibid.

threatens us. In this vital space CEO's decide between the work of many and downsizing to increase the earnings of their corporations; blue-collar workers decide between maintaining their salaries or going on strike to gain greater benefits. This space of *existential praxis* is the resource of missional preaching.[37]

The difficult decisions to which Cardoza-Orlandi points are the kinds of risky endeavors that characterize this practice of missional faithfulness. To put it in the language of *Treasure in Clay Jars*, existential praxis is where the missional congregation takes risks as a contrast community. For a missional homiletic, this implies that missional preaching equips and calls the congregation to take those risks.

THE FOURTH PATTERN: PRACTICES THAT DEMONSTRATE GOD'S INTENT FOR THE WORLD

The fourth pattern of missional faithfulness focuses on the internal life and relationships of the community. Dale Ziemer, author of this chapter, describes the pattern this way:

> The church's life as a community is a demonstration of what God intends for the life of the whole world. The practices of the church embody mutual care, reconciliation, loving accountability, and hospitality. A missional church is indicated by how Christians behave toward one another.[38]

The life of the Christian community is itself an act of public witness and a proclamation of the gospel to the watching world. The relationships and interactions among the congregation are not ancillary to the witness of the church but communicate, at least in a provisional way, God's redemptive purpose for the world.

Ziemer notes that this understanding of the church is quite different from a vision of the church as a collection of programs and services administered by religious professionals and offered to a consumer congregation. In the case of missional congregations, Ziemer quotes Dietrich Bonhoeffer in *Life Together*: "The church and ministry are becoming understood as 'redemptive relationships in community.'"[39] In

---

[37]Ibid.
[38]Barrett et al., *Treasure in Clay Jars*, 84.
[39]Ibid., 85.

each of the congregations visited, the researchers noticed patterns of redemptive relationships that reflected simple yet profound communal practices. In none of the congregations did they find the fullness of the new creation, but in each they found glimpses of God's reign.[40]

One fundamental characteristic of these churches was the practice of listening to one another, which corresponds to the practice of listening to God. Both acts of listening involve quieting the self, and both are challenged by the heavily scheduled and frantic pace of the dominant culture. Indeed, researchers found that the pace of the surrounding culture was one of the primary obstacles to genuine listening, and the leaders had to raise and reinforce the expectation that members of the congregation would spend significant time together. At Transfiguration Parish, the weekly small groups (called fraternities) spend the whole evening together, each week listening to a different member's testimony about the aspect of the Christian life he or she is struggling with at the time. During these times, "The general climate of the fraternity is characterized by nonjudgmental, compassionate, and accepting interaction with one another."[41]

Another pattern of communal life in the churches was active helpfulness toward one another. Members were consistently willing to change their plans and sacrifice their time or possessions in order to help another member of the congregation. Ziemer sees this in sharp contrast to "the pattern of individualism that is so common in the dominant North American culture."[42] The conviction "I can do it myself" is challenged by and contrasted with the practice of helping each other. For instance, members of one of the covenant groups at Rockridge Church joined

---

[40]In his dissertation, Benjamin T. Conner brings missional theology into dialogue with the Christian practices discussion in practical theology. Conner's basic argument is that Christian practices need a deeper purpose than simply Christian formation, a critique that corresponds roughly to Barth's criticism of the appropriation and experience of the *beneficia Christi* as one's vocation. Conner's response is to suggest, using the work of missional theology, that Christian practices are formation for witness. He writes in conclusion, "Participation in the practices is the way that we can participate in God's self-witness through our witness." Benjamin T. Conner, "Practicing Witness: A Contribution to the Theology of Christian Practices Issuing From a Conversation Between Missional Theology and Craig Dykstra's Theology of Christian Practices" (PhD diss., Princeton Theological Seminary, 2009). This work has been published as *Practicing Witness: A Missional Vision of Christian Practices* (Grand Rapids: Eerdmans, 2011).

[41]Barrett et al., *Treasure in Clay Jars*, 87.

[42]Barrett et al., *Treasure in Clay Jars*, 89.

together to help pay the salary of another member after he took a job at a needy school near the church and subsequently learned the school didn't have the money for the position. It was a small act of helpfulness but also a sign that pointed to God's new creation.

Another sign of God's kingdom in the congregations studied in *Treasure in Clay Jars* was that they bore one another's burdens and shared their sorrows. For example, in Boulder, half the congregation helped to make a music tape for a family whose child, just born, was dying from complicating birth defects. The churches also displayed a pattern of crossing boundaries and welcoming the "other." This hospitality often took the form of welcoming the visitor, not in order to recruit a new member but to show the welcome of Christ, of fostering multicultural and intergenerational interactions, and of raising the expectation of confession, forgiveness and reconciliation when one person wronged another.

Ziemer writes that these practices of community life "are taught, and reciprocally, they teach those who participate in them what it means to be the church. These social patterns are cultivated intentionally by the attention given to them by leaders, by the structures that ensure their continued growth and development."[43] Though he does not directly connect the teaching of these practices to the ministry of preaching, preaching is surely one of the ways in which the leaders of these congregations teach new patterns of social interaction that reflect the missional vocation of the congregation. Indeed, this pattern implies that missional preaching cultivates practices of communal life that demonstrate God's intention for the life of the whole world.

Catherine Gunsalus González offers an example of how a preacher might cultivate such a practice. She writes that those who are baptized are called to love, and to love one another is part of the mission of the church. As Jesus says in John 13, it is by love that the world knows that the disciples belong to him. González notes that there are some congregations that are committed to social mission or love for the outsider in an exemplary way while love within the congregation has grown cold. John's Gospel, she argues, challenges such a condition by connecting love for those outside

---

[43]Ibid., 98-99.

the congregation with the practice of love within the congregation. She writes, "The love within the congregation is a sign to those outside. Love is to some degree for the sake of mission. It is part of the mission."[44] A sermon based on this interpretation would be missional preaching in the sense that it would seek to cultivate the intramural practice of love as a public witness to the world of God's intention for all human life.

THE FIFTH PATTERN: THE PUBLIC WITNESS OF WORSHIP

Since the community's life together is a public witness to a watching world, the core of that life, which is their worship of God, is also public witness. The fifth pattern of missional faithfulness explored in *Treasure in Clay Jars* is the public witness of worship. Linford L. Stutzman and George R. Hunsberger describe the pattern this way:

> Worship is the central act by which the community celebrates with joy and thanksgiving both God's presence and God's promised future. Flowing out of its worship, the community has a vital public witness.[45]

Worship in the missional church requires careful definition because it can be easily misunderstood. On the one hand, it is often characterized as worship that equips and empowers the congregation to take up its mission in the world. The difficulty with this definition is that worship becomes a tool to serve mission. On the other hand, worship is described as a strategy for church growth or social activism, a venue to either win converts or rally troops. In this case, worship is more strongly instrumental than in the first instance. Thomas Schattauer, a Lutheran professor of worship, examines these two approaches and suggests a third approach that he argues is more faithfully missional. Stutzman and Hunsberger write:

> This approach locates worship within the larger scope of God's reconciling mission toward the whole world, a mission into which the church is immersed by baptism. So then, "the visible act of assembly (in Christ by the power of the Spirit) and the forms of this assembly—what we call liturgy—enact and signify this mission. From this perspective there is no separation between liturgy and mission.[46]

---

[44]González, "The Baptismal Lens," 29.
[45]Barrett et al., *Treasure in Clay Jars*, 100.
[46]Ibid., 103.

Essentially, missional worship is focused on God and does not use worship as a means to another end. Worship may indeed accomplish many other aims, but the primary purpose of public worship in the missional church is the worship of God.[47]

How is missional worship specifically focused on God? Schattauer argues that Christian worship is oriented around the retelling of and ritual participation in the death and resurrection of Jesus Christ, most specifically in the liturgy of the Lord's Supper, but also in other elements of the liturgy. The praise of the people is praise to God for God's saving act in Jesus Christ. The ministry of the word is a public proclamation of the significance of his death and resurrection. The confession of sins and assurance of pardon is the appropriation of the good news of salvation. And baptism and the Lord's Supper are tangible signs that God's reign and new creation are at hand. Through all of these acts, the gospel is proclaimed and the community is formed in its new identity as the people of God. By rehearsing the salvific mission of God in the world, the congregation is formed for its mission in the world. This is, Stutzman and Hunsberger write, a wonderful paradox: while the focus of worship is what the people give to God, through worship God forms his people.

The authors argue that in contrast to the worship of other religions at the time, early Christians understood their worship to be part of their public witness. The words they chose to describe worship point to this public nature. To describe their gathering, they took the word *ekklēsia*, which means a public assembly gathered for decision making. To describe their proclamation, they took *kērygma*, which is the announcement of a herald in the name of one who has ultimate authority. To describe their activities, they used *leitourgia*, which is the word for a public works project done on behalf of the people and for their good. Each of these words brings into view the public horizon of Christian worship.

Missional worship publicly declares the reign of God, and in worship the congregation declares its allegiance to God's reign. In this sense,

---

[47]Clayton J. Schmit has explored the liturgical implications of missional theology at length in Clayton J. Schmit, *Sent and Gathered: A Worship Manual for the Missional Church,* Engaging Worship (Grand Rapids: Baker Academic, 2009). Schmidt, himself a Lutheran, draws on Schattauer's definition of missional worship and other missional theological resources to propose how each element of Christian worship can identify more closely with the *missio Dei.*

public worship blends into other areas of public witness in which the congregation points toward God's reign and contends for the lordship of Jesus Christ. In describing the worship at Transfiguration Parish, Stutzman and Hunsberger write:

> We began to see that their worship is public witness and their public witness is worship. If worship is a kind of public intervention, an acknowledgment of God's purposes, so also is the church's public witness. Worship motivates and permeates public action, for it is an encounter with the God who both calls his people out of the world and sends them into it.[48]

In the missional congregation, worship motivates and sustains other forms of public witness.

The discussion of public worship in the missional congregation leads immediately to implications for missional preaching. Although preaching is not discussed in this chapter of *Treasure in Clay Jars*, two basic implications are apparent. First, preaching in missional worship will be a clear declaration and interpretation of the good news of God's revelation in Jesus Christ. Second, missional preaching flows out of and into the other forms of the congregation's witness. Every form of the congregation's witness is in some way a declaration of the gospel, and preaching is a specific kind of verbal declaration in public worship. Preaching is not separate from but is in continuity with every other form of witness. The proclamation of preaching flows from, interprets and feeds into the other forms of proclamation.

In his article for *The New Interpreter's Handbook of Preaching*, Pablo Jiménez captures both of these implications succinctly in his definition of missional preaching. Jiménez understands preaching to be one of the many forms in which the church proclaims the gospel and calls the world to be converted to Christ and be reconciled to God. He writes, "Missional preaching is . . . the proclamation of God's love for the world and of the divine offer of salvation for humanity. Such proclamation of love and salvation necessarily leads to the promotion of holistic liberation and human rights, through word and deed."[49] In other words, public acts of witness

---

[48]Barrett et al., *Treasure in Clay Jars*, 113.
[49]Pablo Jiménez, "Missional Preaching," in *The New Interpreter's Handbook of Preaching*, ed. Paul Scott Wilson (Nashville: Abingdon Press, 2008).

flow from missional preaching. Moreover, one could also say that reverse is true: public acts of witness flow into and fuel missional preaching.

Lesslie Newbigin speaks of this mutual relationship in lectures he gave to young ministers in India. As a missionary in India, Newbigin was a pastor and frequent preacher, and as a bishop of the Church of South India he instructed ministers on the practice of ministry. In *Good Shepherd—Meditations on Christian Ministry in Today's World*, a printed collection of talks originally given to clergy in Madras, Newbigin writes eloquently of this relationship:

> True preaching of Christ springs out of action and leads into action. The word which we preach was made flesh, became part of history. If you and your congregation are really involved together in tackling the trouble and pain and sin in the world around you, in the slums around your church, in the lives of your members; if you are standing beside your members in their battles with the world and in their trials and problems, then the words you speak in the pulpit will not be empty words. They will be part of the obedience of you and your congregation to the living Lord. And they will lead your people into further action.[50]

The implication of the public witness of worship in the missional church is that missional preaching is a clear declaration of the gospel made in public worship that flows from and into the congregation's other acts of public witness.

THE SIXTH PATTERN: DEPENDENCE ON THE HOLY SPIRIT

The sixth pattern of missional faithfulness identified in *Treasure in Clay Jars* is dependence on the Holy Spirit, a characteristic that is especially displayed when congregations are enthusiastic about prayer. Walter Hobbs writes in this chapter, "The missional community confesses its dependence upon the Holy Spirit, shown particularly in its practices of corporate prayer."[51] By prayer, Hobbs does not mean a privatized activity, an emergency practice or a ceremonialized and routine exercise. This, as he understands it, is the common view of prayer in the twenty-

---

[50]Lesslie Newbigin, *The Good Shepherd: Meditations on Christian Ministry in Today's World* (Leighton Buzzard, UK: Faith Press, 1977), 26-27.
[51]Barrett et al., *Treasure in Clay Jars*, 117.

first-century West. Rather, by prayer Hobbs means "serious, carefully framed petitions brought by needy, powerless people to the all-powerful God of the universe for disposition as God sees fit."[52] This is prayer that is essential to the people of God in their mission, a mission they have no hope of fulfilling without the guidance and empowerment of God's Spirit. It is not surprising, argues Hobbs, given the scope of the task of bearing witness to the reign of God, that missional churches are actively dependent on the Holy Spirit through prayer. Their mission requires it.[53]

Each of the congregations visited by the researchers in this study displayed an enthusiastic commitment to corporate prayer and dependence on the Holy Spirit, though they practiced it in different ways. Forty to fifty members of Holy Ghost Full Gospel Baptist Church met every Monday through Thursday for prayer; people in Transfiguration Parish met every Saturday morning for prayer, a meal and Bible study; the Spring Garden congregation engaged in prayer walks through their neighborhood; and members of the Eastbrook Church met Monday through Friday at six a.m. for Bible study and prayer. Hobbs writes, "In a world where even small groups find it difficult to get together regularly with everyone showing up, most congregations consider the practice of corporate collective prayer virtually impossible."[54] Yet these congregations, which take seriously their missional vocation, are consistently committed to the corporate practice of prayer and dependence on the Holy Spirit. It is not dependence on the Holy Spirit as a concept that sets these congregations apart; it is dependence on the Holy Spirit as a costly and countercultural practice that marks them as missional churches. Few would disagree that prayer and dependence on God's Spirit are appropriate church practices. Yet as these authors repeatedly stress, in a culture that is heavily scheduled and prone to independent self-reliance, there are few who seriously engage in the practice.

---

[52]Ibid., 118.

[53]Craig Van Gelder construes his entire understanding of what it means to be a missional congregation as "Spirit led." He writes that the primary role of a missional church is "discerning and responding to the leading of the Spirit." Craig Van Gelder, *The Ministry of the Missional Church: A Community Led By the Spirit* (Grand Rapids: Baker Books, 2007), 19. In this pattern of missional faithfulness, the authors of *Treasure in Clay Jars* understand the intentional practice of prayer as the primary church practice through which this leading occurs.

[54]Barrett et al., *Treasure in Clay Jars*, 124.

The implications of this pattern of missional faithfulness for preaching are twofold. First, just as the congregation relies on God's Spirit to empower their other acts of witness, so the missional preacher relies on God's Spirit to enliven the word that is spoken and heard. Without the quickening Spirit of God, the words of the preacher have no power to accomplish the purpose for which they are spoken. Second, the missional preacher calls the congregation to depend on the Holy Spirit and engage in the practice of prayer. In each of these patterns, we have seen that the ministry of preaching helps to embed the missional pattern in the life of the congregation, and the same is true here. Missional preaching helps to cultivate active dependence on the Holy Spirit in the life of the congregation.

Missional theologians understand the challenge facing the church in the West as one of renewal, or conversion. They understand the challenge as the recovery of a sense of vocation and mission in a church that has reduced the gospel to the private salvation of the individual, or reduced mission to the management and implementation of programs for social improvement. This renewal, writes Guder, "is a work of God's Spirit that we cannot manage or program. 'Revival' is a not a program we can put on a calendar and post on a banner hung out in front of a church."[55] Missional preaching, therefore, is not ultimately about a strategy for congregational renewal because no strategy can accomplish the renewal envisioned. The renewal of which missional theologians speak is nothing short of conversion to Jesus Christ, a turning toward God that is ultimately only accomplished by God. Conversion is a work of God's Spirit, and thus missional preaching depends on God's Spirit and calls on the congregation to do the same.

In his lectures on preaching to the ministers in Madras, Lesslie Newbigin speaks eloquently of relying on God's Spirit to give life to the words of preaching. Newbigin writes that Jesus gives to the church the word of life, spoken in the reading and interpretation of scripture and enacted in the sacraments. In both instances, the word must be made active by the Spirit. Without the Spirit, bread is simply bread and words are only words, but by the power of the Spirit, "the words of Jesus, which are spirit and life, are the source of continually renewed life in the Church."[56]

---

[55]Darrell L. Guder, *The Continuing Conversion of the Church* (Grand Rapids: Eerdmans, 2000), 151.
[56]Newbigin, *The Good Shepherd*, 23.

Newbigin concludes his lecture to the young clergy on preaching by assuring them of the promise that "the Holy Spirit can take even our words and make them the vehicles of God's eternal life."[57]

The homiletical implication of dependence on the Holy Spirit in the missional church is that missional preaching must rely on the Holy Spirit to enliven the words of the preacher even as it calls the congregation to actively depend on the Spirit.

THE SEVENTH PATTERN: POINTING TOWARD THE REIGN OF GOD

In a sense, this seventh pattern of missional faithfulness characterizes a certain perspective that underlies the practices that make up the other patterns. It relates to a self-understanding that is infused in the various acts of public witness in which the missional congregation is engaged. Darrell Guder writes:

> The missional church understands its calling as witness to the gospel of the inbreaking reign of God and strives to be an instrument, agent, and sign of that reign. As it makes its witness through its identity, activity, and communication, it is aware of the provisional character of all that it is and does. It points toward the reign of God which God will certainly bring about, but knows that its own response is incomplete and that its own conversion is a continuing necessity.[58]

The primary point here is that the missional church *understands* that its acts of witness do in fact bear witness to the reign of God. The reign of God is not understood as a social program or restricted to the personal sphere or a matter left to the end of the age. Rather, the missional church understands, at least in part, that through its activities and efforts it undertakes to offer provisional signs of Christ's lordship and God's reign in the time and place to which it is sent.

In the course of their research, the *Treasure in Clay Jars* team became increasingly convinced that while this self-understanding is essential to missional faithfulness, it is fraught with difficulty. It is easy for a congregation's understanding of God's reign to be captive to the surrounding culture in ways the congregation does not see, and it is tempting for a congregation

---

[57]Ibid., 27.
[58]Barrett et al., *Treasure in Clay Jars*, 126.

to define God's kingdom by the vision it has of and for itself. Moreover, there is no method for initiating awareness of the kingdom of God in a congregation. Nevertheless, in their study of these churches the researchers discerned what they believe are signs that point to this dawning awareness.

First, they discerned in the congregations both conviction and modesty in their self-understanding. In various ways and with different language, the churches display a vision of the reign of God in their midst and a desire to become more like Christ. The kingdom of God is a defining feature of their preaching and teaching and has become an emphasis in the way they understand and speak of themselves. Yet at the same time, they have profound questions about how to move toward that vision and deep awareness about their own incompleteness and deeper need for conversion. For instance, the pastor at First Presbyterian in Bellevue knows that many leaders sense that the church is on a journey with God but wonders if that journey is confused with its own version of progress. The Rockridge Church recognizes that its commitment to mission covenant groups is a sign of God's reign, and yet its members are honest about the disturbing pride they feel when they compare themselves to others who have not made the same commitment. In each of the congregations studied, there is a sense of humility when they compare themselves and their practices to God's calling for their church and the missional vision they see. Guder writes, "All of these churches appear, in varying degrees, to know that their definitions and assumptions about the lordship of Christ in their midst are too small."[59] Paradoxically, far from being a weakness, this understanding is a profound strength in a congregation that seeks to be continually formed by God for witness.

Preaching is clearly important in helping a congregation to understand itself as a provisional sign of the kingdom of God. This is true in the Boulder Mennonite Church where, Guder writes, "the preaching of the kingdom of God forms the intentional center of [the church]. The biblical language of God's reign is an essential dimension of their formation."[60] Likewise, the biblical images of the kingdom of God, the household of God and the body of Christ have been crucial to the formation of the IMPACT congregations. In *Choosing the Kingdom: Mis-*

---

[59]Ibid., 132.
[60]Ibid.

sional Preaching for the Household of God, Dally points to the importance of preaching in the formation of a congregation that sees itself in terms of the biblical images of God's kingdom. He writes:

> The degree to which preachers can hold up images of the reign of God made flesh in local places, names, and activities . . . will be the degree to which such images can function proleptically, allowing listeners to experience God's future now, and thus begin to make concrete choices that move them toward that future in hope and anticipation.[61]

Thus, the first implication of this pattern for missional preaching is that using the language of God's reign and biblical images of God's kingdom can help a congregation understand itself as a provisional sign of the kingdom of God.

However, missional preaching must not forget the provisional nature of that sign and the accompanying humility that is found in this pattern of missional faithfulness. Carlos Cardoza-Orlandi connects this charac-teristic of missional preaching to the testimonial nature of missional preaching. He argues that missional preaching is found when the con-vergence of the Christian faith and the participation of the people of God in the activity of God produce a testimony that is then submitted to the scrutiny of the congregation. This scrutiny is crucial. Missional preaching is provisional and tentative, dependent on faith and upon God, and subject to the discernment of the community of faith. Cardoza-Orlandi writes, "This peculiarity of the contingency of missional preaching is born out of the knowledge and experience that all that is preached is not the gospel. Therefore, missional preaching is tentative, yet assertive."[62] In the words of *Treasure in Clay Jars*, missional preaching is done with con-viction and modesty, using the biblical language of God's reign to help a congregation understand its life as a provisional sign of God's kingdom.

THE EIGHTH PATTERN: MISSIONAL AUTHORITY

The last pattern of missional faithfulness raises an issue that the re-searchers did not expect, and yet it is one we have already encountered

---

[61]Dally, *Choosing the Kingdom*, 65.
[62]Cardoza-Orlandi, "What Makes Preaching Missional?" 8.

in the development of a missional homiletic: authority. Lois Barrett writes that in their initial indicators, the team did not anticipate this aspect of missional identity, but when they compiled their research it emerged as a clear pattern.

The Holy Spirit gives the missional church a community of persons who, in a variety of ways and with a diversity of functional roles and titles, together practice the missional authority that cultivates within the community the discernment of missional vocation and are intentional about the practices that embed that vocation in the community's life.[63] By authority, the authors do not mean the kind of leadership found in business books or the "consent of the governed" culturally common to a democratic society. Rather, they mean a biblical vision of authority that is understood in terms of ministry, servanthood and even slavery, under the authority of Jesus as Lord and for the sake of the reign of God.[64]

In the communities they visited, the team discerned three clear aspects of the missional authority being practiced. First, those in authority form missional community, which is to say there are always multiple leaders and they themselves form a sent community. Some of the leaders are ordained and some are not, and they all engage in various ways and practices of study, prayer and discernment. Second, those in authority focus on vocation, which means that whether or not they help discern the missional vocation of the community, they have always carried the vision and "helped hold people accountable to the vocation to which God had called the congregation." In meetings, leaders focus not on better management techniques but on centering the congregation in its missional vocation. These leaders both help the congregation discern God's call and fully participate in the discernment of that call. Finally, those in authority foster missional practices, which is to say, "It is not enough for them to lead the congregation in good projects. If the congregation by its life together is to be a sign of the reign of God, leaders will encourage missional practices and hold people accountable for them."[65] At Rockridge Church, leaders

---

[63]Barrett et al., *Treasure in Clay Jars*, 139.
[64]Here Barrett is drawing from 2 Corinthians 4:1 and 4:5, where Paul refers to authority in terms of "ministry" (*diakonian*, service) and "servants" (*doulos*, slaves).
[65]Ibid., 146.

model and promote a covenant lifestyle, and at Transfiguration Parish, Father Karvelis identifies with the poor in his dress and lifestyle. Through practices such as these, missional leaders foster missional identity.

How do these aspects of missional authority reflect on preaching, and what do they imply for a missional homiletic? In the discussion of other patterns, we have already pointed to some of the implications for preaching found here. As missional leaders focus on missional vocation, so missional preaching helps the congregation to discern and be shaped by its vocation. As missional leaders foster missional practices, so missional preaching helps cultivate in the congregation practices that help it become a sign of the reign of God. Perhaps the most challenging implication of this pattern of missional faithfulness, however, is found in the communal character of missional leadership.

Darrell Guder directly addresses the question of communal authority in relation to the ministry of the word in a discussion of ordered offices in *The Continuing Conversion of the Church*. He expounds on the gifts of ministry listed in Ephesians 4:11-12, each of which is a gift given to the church for the "equipping of the saints," and each of which involves a different aspect of the ministry of the word. He asserts that, though ordered offices will change as the particular missional vocation of the church changes, the ministry of the Word will always bear the following characteristics: it will be apostolic, in the sense that it will continue the basic apostolic ministry of gospel proclamation; it will be prophetic, in that it will unfold the implications of the gospel in a particular place and time; it will be evangelistic, in the sense that it will call all Christians to "continuing conversion, to growth and healing in the life of faith"; and it will be pastoral and instructive, as it will teach the faith compassionately and provide the community "the understandings of the gospel and the world which are needed for faithful witness."[66]

Guder concludes his exposition of these gifts of the ministry of the word by saying:

> If this five-dimensional ministry of the Word is necessary for the equipping of the church for its mission, then it is immediately clear that no one person

---

[66]Guder, *The Continuing Conversion of the Church*, 163.

can ever do it all. The concept of the "solo minister" is foreign to the missionary congregation.[67]

Indeed, Guder calls for ministry to be performed in teams and for congregations to discern those whom God has placed in their community
to help carry out the ministry of the word. For preaching this is a radi-
cally different vision, especially when seen from a context in which the
ministry of the word is exercised exclusively by one who is ordained to
the office, often a "solo minister."

This call to a communal preaching ministry is not found with the
same clarity in other missional literature, but others point toward it. We
have already seen how Carlos Cardoza-Orlandi emphasizes the role of
the community in discerning the gospel that has been preached. In her
discussion connecting baptism to the royal priesthood of the baptized
and hence the congregation, Catherine Gunsalus González points toward
the communal authority granted in the general ordination of baptism.
Pablo Jiménez picks up on this point and takes it even further in his
discussion of missional preaching: "Baptism marks not only a person's
initiation in the faith; it is also a call to share the message of the gospel
with those who still have not heard. . . . Those baptized become a 'royal
priesthood' (see 1 Pet 2:9). They not only preach the gospel but also in-
tercede for the world."[68] For each of these homileticians, there is an emphasis on the agency of the community within a discussion of missional
preaching. Guder's proposal can be seen as an extension of that emphasis,
arguing that there are gifts for the ministry of the word present in the
congregation among the laity and thus a community of people who can
be brought into the ordered ministry of preaching for the equipping of
that congregation.[69] This is the most clear and challenging implication
for missional preaching that arises from this pattern of missional faithfulness: the vision of a communal preaching ministry.

---

[67]Ibid., 164.

[68]Jiménez, "Missional Preaching."

[69]Here it is important to note how Guder understands the ordering of ministry as found in Ephesians 4:11-12. He writes that it is not the office that is important here, but the calling and gifting
by the Spirit in the common service of the word. Thus, it is possible in this understanding that if
one is identified as called and gifted to the ministry of the word, one could participate in that ordered office even if one were not "ordained."

MOVING TOWARD A MISSIONAL HOMILETIC

One striking characteristic of missional theological literature, and the work of the Gospel and Our Culture Network, is the degree to which it is grounded in the lived experience and practices of the churches in North America. The initial positive response to *Missional Church: A Vision for the Sending of the Church in North America* and the proliferation of the "missional" terminology speak to the identification people perceive between the challenges and questions posed in this literature and those of their own context. This strength is extended and deepened through *Treasure in Clay Jars*, which takes the initial work of *Missional Church* and revises it in light of research into the lived experience of missional congregations.

The patterns of missional faithfulness developed in *Treasure in Clay Jars* reflect a practical theological process in which normative theological suppositions are revised in dialogue with concrete church practices in order to produce more critically held theological convictions. Because of its practical theological strength, *Treasure in Clay Jars* has enduring value in the missional conversation, and these eight patterns offer rich suggestions for the ways in which missional preaching may equip a congregation for its witness.

In summary, these are the implications for missional preaching from the missional literature. I am reordering them slightly to highlight the ones I see as most significant for missional preaching:

1. Missional preaching helps a congregation discern its missional vocation, which is its unique giftedness for witness in its time and place.

2. Missional preaching interprets scripture using a missional hermeneutic, leading the community in biblical discipleship and in discerning how God is shaping the community through the witness of scripture.

3. Missional preaching is a clear declaration of the gospel that flows from and into the congregation's other acts of witness, centering the multiform witness of the community in the good news of Jesus Christ.

4. Missional preaching uses the biblical language of God's kingdom to help the congregation understand itself as a provisional sign of God's reign and imagine how it can participate in the coming kingdom.

In my view these first four implications form the essence of what mission-al preaching is about and the work that missional preachers do. Still, the implications of the following four patterns are instructive for mission-al preaching and point to the kind of community that missional preaching can cultivate:

5. Missional preaching calls and equips the congregation to take risks as a contrast community, demonstrating life in the kingdom of God in counter-cultural and costly ways.

6. Missional preaching cultivates communal practices that demonstrate God's gracious intention for all human life, as the life of the community becomes a parable of the reign of God.

7. Missional preaching intentionally depends upon the Holy Spirit and calls on the congregation to do the same, especially through a corporate and intentional prayer life.

8. Missional preaching practices communal authority by sharing the ministry of the word with others in the community who are gifted for it.

These implications, which resonate across the missional literature with respect to preaching, point toward a missional homiletic that is rooted in and conversant with the North American ecclesial context. Moreover, as you can see clearly, there are strong connections among these implications, a homiletics of witness and Barth's missional ecclesiology. Taken together, these three conversation partners lead us into a theologically and contextually faithful missional homiletic.

4

A Missional Homiletic of Witness

W e now come to the moment where the voices in this conversation come together to move toward a missional homiletic. This does not mean that these voices will now speak in unison, nor that they will speak in perfect harmony. While there is much commonality among them, there is also strong disagreement. In this chapter I will take up some arguments and leave others behind, and I will argue that some of the voices in this conversation are more useful to a missional homiletic than others.

The best way to understand this work is as ironic discourse. As I mentioned in the introduction, I understand practical theology as a form of ironic discourse, using the terminology of the rhetorician Kenneth Burke. This means, first, that practical theological reflection proceeds as discourse; it is an interdisciplinary and mutually critical conversation about a practice of Christian ministry. In this discourse, each conversation partner approaches the subject from a different perspective, and no perspective is privileged above the others. Indeed, it is mutually critical because each perspective is open to critique and revision.

However, at some point the conversation must come to a tentative conclusion, a conclusion held with full recognition of its own perspectival nature. Burke uses the rhetorical trope of irony to describe the way a discourse of multiple perspectives is brought to a tentative conclusion. He writes, "Irony arises when one tries, by the interaction of terms upon one another, to produce a development which uses all the terms."[1] From the standpoint of an observer who considers the participation of all the terms, irony offers a

---

[1] Kenneth Burke, "Four Master Tropes," *Kenyon Review* 3 (1941): 431.

"perspective of perspectives," which is then able to produce a "resultant certainty." This certainty is necessarily ironic because it requires that "all the
sub-certainties be considered as neither true nor false, but contributory."[2]

Thus, we are now at the point when the conversation must come to a
tentative conclusion, as we now embark on the development of a "perspective of perspectives." To organize this discussion logically, we will
carefully work through the following assertion, which describes succinctly my understanding of a missional homiletic: *Preaching confesses
Jesus Christ, through a missional interpretation of scripture, in order to
equip the congregation for its witness to the world.* Here is a brief summary
in advance of how this argument will unfold:

Preaching is a discrete form of the church's witness, and the normative
paradigm for preaching is proclamation of the gospel in response to the
reading of scripture in Christian worship. Here I will address the crucial
questions of authority and ordination that have arisen in this conversation and the proposal of a communal preaching ministry that is a distinctive contribution of missional theologians.

Confession is the most appropriate mode of testimony for preaching;
moreover, the essential content of the confession is Jesus Christ. This
contention is not at all clear or universally held in the homiletical literature, but it is essential for preaching to take its place as one form of
Christian witness and to have coherence with other forms of witness.

Third, preaching arises from a missional interpretation of scripture. It
is commonly held in homiletics that a sermon arises from the interpretation of scripture and the preacher uses some hermeneutical lens
through which to read scripture. In a missional homiletic, the hermeneutical lens is a missional interpretation that understands scripture as
equipping the reader and hearer for participation in God's mission.

Finally, the witness of preaching equips the congregation for its
witness to the world. The congregation is the basic unit of Christian
witness, and preaching has a particular centering, contextualizing and
kindling function within the congregation, as preaching arises from and
moves into the whole witness of the community.

---

[2]Ibid., 432.

PREACHING

The first move of this missional homiletic is to understand preaching in light of the questions, challenges and insights raised by the homiletical proposals we have considered, by Barth's ecclesiology and by research into missional congregations in North America. Specifically, we need to answer two questions: First, what is preaching? Second, who preaches and on what basis is that person authorized to preach?

Let's begin by defining preaching as a specific form of proclamation. The general call to proclamation is the vocation of witness that is given to the whole church and to the individual members of the church through their baptism. Thus, within the category of general proclamation, there is a wide variety of activities, acts and forms of speech that are considered Christian witness. The specific form of proclamation that we refer to as "preaching" is the proclamation that occurs in the liturgy of public worship in response to the reading of scripture.[3] Homiletically, this is an important distinction since both Florence and Lose argue for what I earlier called a "general theory of proclamation." That is to say, especially seen from a missional perspective, both of their homiletical proposals argue for the epistemological and theological basis on which every baptized Christian is able and authorized to testify or confess.

For instance, Florence argues that preaching arises from an experience with God through the study of a biblical text, and anyone who has such an experience is authorized to testify about it. She does not assign any special characteristics or categorical differences to one form of testimony or another. This would indicate that testimony given in a group Bible study or in a conversation with a friend is categorically the same as testimony given in regular public worship in response to the reading of scripture. Similarly, Lose argues strongly that confession is the proper epistemological category for making statements of Christian belief in the postmodern world. Yet his argument applies to confession generally, whether made to a coworker in the office or to a spouse over dinner. The only sense in which Lose assigns special characteristics to preaching is

---

[3]Barth references in passing the confusion that arises when the term *preaching* is used to refer both to the specific form of proclamation and more generally to a variety of forms of proclamation. For that reason he reluctantly uses the German *"Predigt,"* citing it as unavoidable. Barth, *CD* IV/3.2, 867.

as nurturing or catalytic confession within the larger "conversation of the faithful."[4] Yet even this characteristic might be applied to forms of confession other than preaching in public worship, such as teaching or writing.

By developing these general theories of proclamation, Lose and Florence have offered valuable resources for understanding the vocation of proclamation that is given to the whole church and every baptized Christian, specifically how that vocation can be faithfully pursued in the postmodern context. Nevertheless, by ignoring special characteristics that pertain to preaching in public worship as a response to the reading of scripture (what one might consider "paradigmatic preaching"), Lose and Florence do little to illuminate how preaching as a discrete practice may nurture and encourage the wider proclamation of the gospel.

It is hard to draw bright lines between one form of proclamation and another, both theologically and rhetorically. As an example, when is preaching more like teaching, and when is teaching more like preaching? The definitional boundaries overlap, and it is nearly impossible to answer that question analytically. Sometimes a preacher in the pulpit "sounds" like she is teaching, and sometimes a teacher in a classroom "sounds" like he is preaching. It is hard to say what gives rise to these "sounds," to the distinctive characteristics and qualities that lead the listener to feel he or she is experiencing teaching or preaching. It is as much in-the-moment intuition as reflective reasoning. Thus, I am not advocating a bright line between preaching and other forms of proclamation. Still, when we reflect homiletically, there is something like a basic paradigm of preaching that we have in mind. This basic paradigm is the preaching that occurs in public worship as a response to the reading of scripture. Quite simply, it is the Sunday morning preacher in the pulpit delivering a sermon.

This is the person Florence envisions as her audience in the introduction to *Testimony*, though she never directly addresses such specific pulpit preaching. This is the person Lose envisions as he attends to a preacher's engagement with the text in the latter part of *Confessing Jesus Christ*, though he never specifically addresses the distinctiveness of

---

[4]David J. Lose, *Confessing Jesus Christ: Preaching in a Postmodern World* (Grand Rapids: Eerdmans, 2003), 145.

"pulpit proclamation." I am contending that there are specific and essential characteristics that pertain to this form of proclamation that do
not pertain in the same degree to other forms. Preaching is a specialized
form of proclamation that must be treated as a discrete practice if we are
to understand how it relates to and influences other forms of proclamation. Thus, in this missional homiletic I am referring to preaching as
that form of proclamation that occurs in response to the reading of
scripture in the public worship of a Christian congregation.

Now, turning to the second question in this section, who is allowed
to preach? Among the homileticians we have encountered, Long answers
this question most clearly, and his argument represents the dominant
paradigm in the church in North America. In his imaginative introduction to *The Witness of Preaching*, he writes that, theologically speaking,
the preacher comes from the pew to the pulpit, having been sent by the
congregation to the text in order to have an encounter with God and
return to bear witness to that encounter. Thus, those who may preach are
those who have been called and sent by the congregation for that purpose.
Moreover, in Long's view this sending is formalized through licensing
and ordination, which is often predicated on special education and examination of the one who is called.[5]

At this point we must consider two objections to this argument, the
first of which comes from the feminist perspective offered by Florence.
She begins her project by "waking up" the dormant knowledge of a
women's preaching tradition, arguing, "Preaching is not a right or privilege reserved for those who locate themselves at the power center."[6] For
most of the church's history, the ministry of preaching has been largely
restricted to men, and the procedures for licensure and ordination have
been embedded in a male-dominated hierarchical system that has reflected both the cultures in which the church has existed and the church's
interpretation of the biblical witness. Florence argues that this patriarchal
system has reflected systemic sin and oppression in both the culture and

---

[5]There is great variety among Christian churches in North America as to how the special calling of
preaching is recognized and the necessary requirements for that calling are to be validated by the
church. In most cases this process is one of licensure or ordination, and sometimes both, and in
many cases it requires extended education and examination.

[6]Anna Carter Florence, *Preaching as Testimony* (Louisville: Westminster John Knox, 2007), 3-4.

the church. In speaking of the personification of wider forces that oppose the gospel, what one might theologically categorize as "sin," "evil" or the "devil," Florence uses the term "system." She writes, "I have come to believe that the fear that holds us preachers captive is an invention of the System, the Deceiver, the Powers and Principalities—whatever we choose to call that force . . . [that intends] to keep us and the Word apart."[7] The historical and contemporary exclusion of women from the ministry of preaching represents a captivity of the church to the "system," to the power of sin, that is present in the church and in the world.

In her historical research Florence discovered that the history of women's preaching is rich with examples of powerful and effective preachers, though they necessarily operated outside of and often in opposition to the official structure of the church. This history both validates the authority of women's preaching and points to the problems inherent in the structure of ordination. Her concern about the tendency of the official structure to be captive to sin and oppression leads her to ground preaching in an authority entirely outside the process of education and ordination. For Florence, the only true authority for testimony is an experience of God.

Nevertheless, the classic concern with this position is that it opens the door to fanaticism.[8] For example, from the Reformed perspective, the requirements of education and ordination for clergy arise from an ecclesiological conviction that the true church exists wherever the word is truly preached and heard and the sacraments are rightly administered.[9] The true preaching of the word and the right administration of the sacraments, so the argument goes, requires education and a process of communal discernment, which is formalized in ordination. Thus, at least in part, the integrity of the church depends on an ordered ministry. Florence's critiques notwithstanding, it is not enough to say that because the

---

[7]Ibid., 120.

[8]See James F. Kay, *Preaching and Theology: Preaching and Its Partners* (St. Louis: Chalice Press, 2007), 16-19.

[9]Calvin wrote, "Wherever we see the word of God purely preached and heard, and the sacraments administered according to Christ's institution, there, it is not to be doubted, a church of God exists." John Calvin, *Institutes of the Christian Religion* (Philadelphia: Westminster Press, 1960), 1023. To move earlier than Calvin and into the Lutheran tradition, the Augsburg Confession in Article VII.1 reads, "The Church is the congregation of saints, in which the Gospel is rightly taught and the Sacraments are rightly administered."

church is captive to systemic sin and has a history of oppression, ordination itself, involving both training and communal discernment, should be discarded. The irony is that in her critique Florence is aiming for the same goal served by ordered offices: a sanctified church. The fact that the process of ordination has historically been corrupted by patriarchal sin does not necessarily invalidate ordination as a practice. Rather, it indicates that the theology and practice of ordination is in need of reform.

The reform of ordered ministry is exactly what missional theologians have proposed, and this brings us to the second objection we must consider with respect to ordination as authorization for preaching. Whereas the feminist critique is that ordered ministry has traditionally excluded women from the practice of preaching, the missional critique is that ordered ministry has traditionally excluded those who are not ordained from the ministry of proclamation, restricting proclamation to the clergy rather than equipping the laity for its proclamation to the world. In *Missional Church*, the authors describe a three-iteration shift in the historical models of ecclesial leadership.

The first iteration is the leader as priest, a role that emerged as the church was united with the Roman Empire; became a community oriented around worship, sacrament and spiritual care; and saw its clergy become a separate social order. A priest in this era "was a shepherd to a static people and the provider of the focused and limited mission of caring for the church's members by ordering and dispensing the means of grace in a geographic locale."[10] The next iteration came with the Protestant Reformations, as ecclesial leadership in Protestant churches shifted from priest to pedagogue. In this case, the qualifications for leadership were more closely associated with academic achievement, and the emphasis of ministry was on teaching right doctrine and the right administration of sacraments. Still, however, pedagogues, like priests, belonged to a special social class and served an institution that was understood as a "static people."[11]

Finally, there was a shift from pedagogues to professionals, a shift that

---

[10]Darrell L. Guder et al., *Missional Church: A Vision for the Sending of the Church in North America* (Grand Rapids: Eerdmans, 1998), 192.

[11]*Missional Church* authors recognize that the Radical Reformers, the Free Church and their followers went much further than Reformed, Lutheran and Anglican leaders in reforming ecclesiology and ordered offices. Ibid., 193.

Missional Church authors argue began in nineteenth-century Europe as theologians such as Schleiermacher sought to secure a place for theological study in the post-Enlightenment academy. These theologians argued that "scientific study showed religion to be an irreducible dimension of human activity and one essential for the proper functioning of a culture."[12] Thus, the training of religious leaders was as necessary for society as the training of leaders in law and medicine. Continuing into the twentieth century, using the seminal work of Edward Farley in *Theologia: The Fragmentation and Unity of Theological Education*, missional authors argue that seminaries have perpetuated this understanding of ministry by focusing on "preparing a professional clergy for a set of tasks considered to be 'ministry.'"[13] Moreover, this concept of a "professional clergy" cuts across the various models of ministry found in contemporary churches, from "social activist, to mega-church entrepreneur, to therapist-pastor."[14]

In essence, the authors of *Missional Church* contend that, whether the ecclesial leader is understood as priest, pedagogue or professional, the existence of a specialized social class of "clergy" within the church has effectively divided the church into those who minister and those to whom they minister. The authors conclude their argument about the three iterations of this "clerical paradigm" with a paragraph that eloquently summarizes their objection to the historic and current patterns of ordered ministry and connects us back to Florence's objection:

> This view effectively eclipses the gifts for leadership in the non-ordained contingent of God's sent people, those known in Christendom as the laity. Ministry remains identified with the static roles of clergy as priest, pedagogue, or professional, all dispensers of spiritual resources. . . . In most denominational structures, leadership in the church involves a series of clearly marked requirements that mean few can give leadership without some form of seminary education that prepares them for ordination to the professional ministry. Therefore the priesthood of all believers is continually undermined by the practices of ordination.[15]

---

[12]Ibid., 194.
[13]Ibid., 195.
[14]Ibid.
[15]Ibid.

With these two objections in mind, we now return to the question, who is allowed to preach? On the one hand, we have Long's argument that the traditional process of ordination, and the education and communal discernment it entails, is an expression of the calling and sending of the community. Moreover, we have the classic contention that ordered ministry safeguards the integrity of the church, its ministry and witness. On the other hand, we have the argument that the practice of ordination continually undermines the ministry of non-ordained Christians and is corrupted by patterns of exclusion that ultimately can be characterized as captivity to sin. Underneath the arguments of both advocates and critics of ordination, there is an animating concern for the integrity of the church and its witness.

In chapter two, I noted that Karl Barth offers a rationale for ordered ministry that, while certainly not novel, provides a helpfully constructive answer to the question "Who is allowed to preach?" while taking into account the critiques mentioned above. His argument is, essentially, that the authority to exercise specialized office within the church is grounded in calling and giftedness for that office. Barth discusses this when he comes to the "service of the community," his explanation of how the community fulfills its task of witness. He argues that the witness of the community must be multiform and not uniform, because it must reflect the richness of the triune God, the various human means with which the community carries out its task, and the variety of ways it presents itself to the world.

However, the diversity of the church's witness does not correspond to race, gender, nationality, social status or the differentiation of individuals in any way. Rather, the diversity of the church's witness reflects the differentiation of the specific callings and gifts of individuals. Some are called and gifted for preaching, some are called and gifted for prayer, some are called and gifted for evangelism and so forth. This diversity reflects the diverse ways that God calls and gifts the church for its one unified task of witness. Moreover, Barth also recognizes that there will be within the community special working fellowships. These fellowships, he argues, must not reflect like-mindedness, common interests or personal characteristics but common gifting and calling for ministry. They should be ordered around the shared calling and gifting of individuals for a particular service of witness.

Now one might ask, is not Barth reintroducing a clerical class within the church by providing a place for "fellowships" within the community? The crucial difference between the clerical order that Florence and missional theologians have criticized and Barth's proposal is that the fellowships he proposes are not based on gender, special training, educational attainment or a certain standing in human society. Rather, these fellowships are determined by God's calling and gifting of individuals. Women such as Anne Marbury Hutchinson would indeed find their place in this company of preachers, as would many non-ordained Christians who are gifted for the work of preaching.

By locating the authority to preach in God's calling and gifting of persons within the community, and by ordering their fellowship according to their calling and giftedness and not any personal characteristics or achievements, Barth has gone a long way toward addressing the concerns raised by Florence and missional theologians. The question of whether one is allowed to preach would not be determined by gender, or education or even membership is a separate class known as "ordained clergy." The only and decisive question would be, is this person called and gifted to preach? If so, then he or she is authorized—by God's decision made through God's gifting and calling—to preach and thus belong to the fellowship of preachers.

While that goes a long way toward addressing the concerns raised, there is still the question of how an individual's calling and gifting is discerned and whether that process itself might not be captive to sin. On the one hand, one might suggest that calling and gifting is self-determined; if a person says she is gifted for preaching, then that settles it. Essentially, this is the position that Florence takes as she rests the authority to preach exclusively on an individual's experience with God. On the other hand, I would argue that communal discernment of gift and calling is important for at least two reasons. First, as Barth argued, individual Christians are understood first not as atomized units but as members of the visible fellowship into which they have been gathered, upbuilt and called. Any special gifts or callings that an individual may have are not for the individual alone but are part of the multiform way the community performs its vocation. The vocation of witness is primarily and ultimately given to the community; it is given to individuals only within the communal context. Thus the community has an essential role in the discernment and confirmation of special gifts that are to given its members.

Second, communal discernment is necessary for testing and confirming an individual's discernment. An individualistic view of discernment is no less immune from sin than a communal understanding. Sin, or the "system," is at work in the individual as well as the community, and the individual may be discerning the Spirit of God or "another spirit." This is the essence of the exhortation in 1 John 4:1: "Beloved, do not believe every spirit, but test the spirits to see whether they are from God; for many false prophets have gone out into the world." The community, the plural "beloved," is instructed to test and discern to see whether a call and gift is from God.

Thus, communal discernment is integral to the process of identifying those who are called and gifted to preaching. Of course, this poses another problem: if the community consists of those who discern God's call and gift, what is to stop the community from saying that only men are gifted and called to the service of preaching, or only those who can pass certain educational requirements? This is the heart of the challenge of reforming ordered offices because every process of discernment, whether in the individual or the community, is open to sin and error, insofar as the Spirit's sanctification of the community is not yet fully realized. Ultimately, the only theological answer to the problem of captivity to sin is the ongoing reformation of the church as part of the continuing sanctifying work of God's Spirit.

Nevertheless, there are ecclesiological reforms that have been proposed by missional theologians, and which bear striking resemblance to proposals by some homileticians, that would help address this challenge and guard against error in the exercise of preaching. The proposals, essentially, have been to move away from a hierarchical understanding of preaching in which one person discerns God's voice and preaches for the whole community and toward a more communal understanding of the ministry of preaching in which it is shared by the community. We will first consider the proposals of missional theologians and then compare those to proposals made by homileticians.

In *Treasure in Clay Jars*, the researchers noticed that there was a particular characteristic of leadership in missional churches that formed a distinct pattern. The first aspect of this pattern was that authority comes from God, a point that is echoed in the foregoing arguments from Barth. The second aspect of the pattern, they argue, is that those in authority form missional community. They write, "A central theme of the Gospels is Jesus' choosing, calling, preparing, and commissioning a *company* of people."[16] This is the thrust of Paul's analogy of the church to a body in 1 Corinthians 12, and it becomes more explicit in the list of various gifts for ministry found in Ephesians 4, which together "equip the saints for the work of ministry" (Eph 4:12). Moreover, in the churches the team researched they found that the missional leadership community consisted of a mix of pastors, elders, staff and committed laity. Participation in the community of leaders was less a result of ordination than of gift and calling.

Up to this point, I think missional theologians are simply discerning the kind of shared leadership that is widely recognized and practiced in many local churches. However, the radical nature of this concept becomes apparent when we apply the notion of communal leadership to the work of preaching specifically. Here I envision not one person in a congregation bearing the primary preaching responsibility, but a community of people who share the work. Over recent decades a variety of homiletical proposals have gestured in this direction, particularly as homiletics has "turned to the listener" in various ways.[17] By far the most common proposal for actively engaging the laity in the sermon has been what Ronald Allen calls "feed-forward" groups, in which a small group of parishioners meet during the week before the sermon to discuss the interpretation of

---

[16]Barrett et al., *Treasure in Clay Jars*, 142 (italics mine).

[17]This "turn to the listener" is largely associated with the New Homiletic, which views the listener as an active partner in the preaching moment, and attempts to craft the sermon in view of how the listener will hear the sermon. See Thomas G. Long, "And How Shall They Hear? The Listener in Contemporary Preaching," in *Listening to the Word: Studies in Honor of Fred B. Craddock*, ed. Gail R. O'Day (Nashville: Abingdon Press, 1993). While some aspects of the turn to the listener dovetail with the interests of this proposal, many do not. There is a great difference between, on the one hand, engaging laity on the basis of a common vocation of proclamation and, on the other hand, engaging laity in order to preach a sermon that is more "on-target" for their context, listening styles, needs, experiences and so on. Indeed, the terminology of "turn to the listener" itself implies that the laity are listening to the clergy who are speaking.

the text for the coming service and how it intersects with their experiences. The most seminal and sustained version of this proposal is John McClure's *The Roundtable Pulpit: Where Leadership and Preaching Meet.*[18]

In this book, published in 1995, McClure argues that the preparation of the sermon should be a genuine collaboration between the preacher and the congregation. Gleaning from the Jewish tradition of hospitality, McClure proposes that the pastor "host" the congregation in preparation for the sermon. This collaboration is not in the oft-recommended metaphorical sense of "taking the congregation into the study with you" but is an actual conversation with a small group of people. Those who are invited, he proposes, take up their vocation as interpreters and proclaimers of the word. They share their interpretation of the text and their experiences with God, and their testimonies then inform and give shape to the preacher's sermon.[19]

This approach to sermon preparation is a concrete expression of what Carlos Cardoza-Orlandi describes as the importance of existential praxis to missional preaching. Cardoza-Orlandi argues that missional preaching does not simply help the congregation discern God's activity in the world but takes up their struggle to live out their faith in their place and time and connects to the Christian faith in all its "historical, theological, and ministerial wealth."[20] In a feed-forward group such as these homileticians propose, the lived experience and struggle of the congregation can be connected to the Christian tradition, and those connections can be tested, challenged and affirmed in actual dialogue.

---

[18]Ronald Allen helpfully catalogs a variety of these "feed-forward" proposals in "The Turn to the Listener: A Selective Review of a Recent Trend in Preaching," *Encounter* 64 (2003): 167-96. He surveys major works and articles in homiletics and, in addition to McClure's work, finds proposals along the feed-forward lines from Dietrich Ritschl, Browne Barr, Reuel Howe, Jerry Carter, Les Hughes and Dow Edgerton. Feed-forward is only the first of Allen's five categories of work in the "turn to the listener." The others are proposals that rely heavily on (1) communication theory, (2) philosophy of language, literary criticism and rhetoric, (3) congregational studies and (4) efforts to listen directly to listeners. This last category has been extended most recently with a large funded study conducted from 2000 to 2004 called "Listening to the Listeners," the results of which have been published in a series of books called *Channels of Listening* by Chalice Press.

[19]A more recent homiletical contribution in this same vein is O. Wesley Allen, *The Homiletic of All Believers: A Conversational Approach to Proclamation and Preaching* (Louisville: Westminster John Knox, 2005). Allen proposes a practical method by which a preacher could regularly engage with parishioners in sermon preparation over the course of several sermons in series.

[20]Carlos Cardoza-Orlandi, "What Makes Preaching Missional?" *Journal for Preachers* 22 (1999): 7.

So how should the preacher approach the feed-forward group? Does the group gather simply so the preacher can learn more about listeners' lives and better discern their hermeneutical frameworks so he or she can relate the sermon more closely to their experience and be more clearly understood? Or is the preacher seeking to understand how listeners struggle to live out their faith in order to interpret that struggle in conversation with the gospel in a mutually critical dialogue? If the approach is the former, I would argue that a feed-forward group is essentially an exercise in the rhetorical maxim "Know your audience." On the other hand, if the approach is the latter, then a feed-forward group can be a true exercise in praxis theology, in which an understanding of the gospel is brought into genuine dialogue with lived experience and struggle. The resulting sermon would be, essentially, a work of practical theology that proclaims the gospel in the context of the lived experience of the community.

While feed-forward homiletical proposals are a strong gesture toward a communal preaching ministry, it is a leap to move from weekly feed-forward groups to a community of laity who are actually preaching on Sunday morning.[21] As we noted in the last chapter, this leap is proposed specifically by Darrell Guder in *The Continuing Conversion of the Church*, in which he interprets Ephesians 4:11-12 as calling for a five-dimensional ministry of the word, which will "equip the saints for the work of ministry." In any given congregation, he argues, it would require a team of people to carry out the apostolic, prophetic, evangelistic and pastoral-instructive dimensions of verbal proclamation. Whereas McClure and others envision feed-forward groups as a gathering of the "average listener," Guder envisions a gathering of those in a congregation who are specifically gifted for the ministry of the word. Moreover, whereas feed-forward groups offer insights and experiences that eventually help shape the sermon that the clergyperson preaches, Guder envisions a group of people who actually share the weekly preaching responsibilities.

---

[21]Allen notes one example in his review of literature where a preacher was experimenting with "laity actually preaching." It is found in Nancy Taylor, "The Work of the People: From Silence to Faithful Proclamation," *Chicago Seminary Register* 87 (1997): 10-42. Taylor's proposal, however, is for preacher and laypersons to work together to craft a sermon that is a multivoice event.

In *Preaching in the Context of Worship*, pastor and homiletician Douglas Gwyn writes of his experience training members of his congregation to preach in a chapter titled "A School of the Prophets: Teaching Congregational Members to Preach." It should come as no surprise that Gwyn is a Quaker pastor and his Quaker theological framework shapes his experience. Even as a Quaker, though, when it comes to preaching, Gwyn writes, "we enter a realm where the rule of expertise and the franchise of the academy, which are so strong in our society, begin to take over."[22] In the course of two pastorates in Berkeley, California, Gwyn worked to develop a company of preachers who would themselves preach and share the ministry of the word in that congregation. He began with something like a midweek feed-forward group, and the participants of that group began to speak up during the period of silent worship in the Quaker service. Gwyn also removed the pulpit, began preaching from the floor level, left his manuscript in the study and preached without notes, all in order to help make preaching more "imaginable" for members of the congregation. In his second pastorate of this same church, Gwyn worked with a small group of four or five "volunteers" to teach them how to preach, offering consultations and printed resources. The group met monthly and shared the preaching responsibilities for a period of about six months. After each person had a chance to preach and receive feedback, the group would dissolve and another group of four or five would form.

Looking back, Gwyn counts the two-part experiment as a great success, though he is honest about the difficulties. There were some in the congregation who were uneasy with multiple preaching voices and would have preferred the "pastor" to preach each week. There were some who felt that only more "experienced members" should preach and others who wanted to hear from everyone. (It appears that Gwyn was inviting anyone who would be interested in preaching to participate in a preaching group rather than restricting it to those who were called or gifted to the work.) He concludes his account of the experiment with an affirmation that addresses exactly the issues raised in this discussion of who is authorized to preach:

---

[22]Douglas Gwyn, "A School of the Prophets: Teaching Congregational Members to Preach," in *Preaching in the Context of Worship*, ed. David M. Greenhaw and Ronald J. Allen (St. Louis: Chalice Press, 2000), 100.

Teaching congregants to preach undermines the larger-than-life profile of the pastoral ministry. It reduces the "professional distance" between the individual and the people he or she serves. It distributes power and authority more broadly in the congregation, allowing the church to demonstrate "the wisdom of God in its rich variety" (Eph 3:10) through a multiplicity of preaching voices. It allows the gospel to be heard through the varying textures of gender, ethnicity, economic class, and general life experience.[23]

In summary, a communal preaching ministry is a helpful response to two homiletical affirmations and two homiletical concerns. The affirmations are: (1) the congregation as a whole is engaged in the struggle and joy of living out their faith, which means they have insights and experiences that are essential to the faithful proclamation of the gospel in their context, and (2) in any given congregation, God has gifted multiple people for the ministry of the word, gifts that should be used for the equipping of the whole community. Developing a communal preaching ministry is thus essential for the practical theological work of preaching and for the faithful exercise of the gifts God has given to the community. The concerns are: (1) the process of discerning the gift and call of a preacher is intertwined with sin and is thus subject to patriarchalism and other errors, and (2) abuse of authority and totalizing of perspective is virtually unavoidable when one person alone exercises a preaching ministry for a community. Developing a communal preaching ministry in a congregation addresses these problems directly and guards against abuse.

How a preacher implements a communal preaching ministry will necessarily vary by context and community. There are a variety of options, one of which is a praxis-oriented feed-forward group that brings the gospel into dialogue with the lived experience of the community and out of this dialogue the preacher develops a sermon. Another option is a community of people who are gathered according to their giftedness for the ministry of the word and who develop sermons as a team each week, but the sermons are then delivered by the same person week after week. This option might be more practical in a congregation that strongly expects to hear primarily one speaker. A third option is a team of people gifted for

---

[23]Ibid., 106-7.

the ministry of the word who share the responsibilities of weekly preaching on a rotating basis. One congregation could try all of these approaches in different ways and times. What is most at stake in the communal ministry I propose is that those who are invited into it are not just those who are seminary-educated or ordained but those who are gifted and called for the ministry of the word.

Thus far we have answered the two questions that have structured this initial section. To the question what is preaching, the answer is the form of proclamation that occurs in response to the reading of scripture in the public worship of a congregation. To the question of who preaches and on what basis is that person authorized to do so, the answer is the community of persons whom God has gifted and called to preach on the authority of their gifting and calling, as it is confirmed by the larger community.

PREACHING CONFESSES JESUS CHRIST

We turn now to consider the essential activity in which preachers are engaged: confessing Jesus Christ. The homiletical proposals we explored earlier all operate within the general framework of "testimony" and consider preaching a form of that activity. Long proposes preaching as bearing witness, connecting to Old and New Testament precedents and the hermeneutical work of Paul Ricoeur. However, he argues that the witness testifies and what the witness offers is a testimony. Thus, going back to Ricoeur's courtroom analogy, Long appears to combine witness and testimony. Likewise, Anna Carter Florence describes "preaching as testimony" and draws on the same material in Ricoeur. Influenced by Walter Brueggemann, she has much of the same Old Testament precedent in the background. Although she appears to prefer the term "testimony" to "witness," like Long, Florence combines the two. By contrast, David Lose purposefully characterizes preaching as confession rather than witness or testimony, and the bulk of his work in *Confessing Jesus Christ* aims to develop "confession" as a distinct concept for homiletical use. In my view, confession is the more appropriate category for missional preaching for several reasons.

First, there are the reasons Lose himself offers. While he does not compare "confession" to other testimonial terms used in homiletics, he does argue that it is a useful term for at least four distinct reasons. First,

"'Confession' designates a summary of the church's essential assertions concerning God's decisive activity in Jesus of Nazareth, the one crucified and raised from the dead."[24] Lose finds this aspect of confession important both in contemporary theology and in New Testament usage, especially in the post-Pauline documents, where *homologein* had evolved to signify both a doctrinal summary of the gospel and the essential tenets that distinguish orthodox from heterodox teaching.

Second, "'Confession' denotes articulating faith as a living response both to this proclaimed word and to the current situation and crisis of the world."[25] It is important here that confession is the articulation of faith in response to the challenge and crisis of the world because by this dimension of confession Lose draws a thin distinction in biblical usage between *homologein* (to confess) and *martyrein* (to bear witness). He writes, "For whereas 'witnessing' is most often self-consciously evangelistic in purpose, 'confessing' reflects a stalwart declaring of what one believes, not simply toward the end of evangelistic persuasion, but also and especially because the circumstances demand it."[26]

Third, confession is central to the life of faith and the life of the church. This insight is present in the New Testament usage and even more strongly in the work of theologians Miroslav Volf, Brian Gerrish and Douglas Hall, upon whom Lose relies.[27] It is by confession, which is the essential summary and articulation of faith, that the community maintains its identity, learns its distinctive way of making meaning in the world, confers identity on individuals and responds to the questions and challenges posed by competing confessions. Finally and fourth, drawing on the speech-act theory of John Searle, Lose argues that confession is an assertive speech act, which means that it does not coerce a response from the hearer but invites a response of belief or disbelief from those who hear.

In addition to Lose's reasons, I believe confession is appropriate to

[24]David J. Lose, *Confessing Jesus Christ: Preaching in a Postmodern World* (Grand Rapids: Eerdmans, 2003), 102.

[25]Ibid.

[26]Ibid., 108.

[27]See Miroslav Volf, *After Our Likeness: The Church as the Image of the Trinity,* Sacra Doctrina (Grand Rapids: Eerdmans, 1997); B. A. Gerrish, *Saving and Secular Faith: An Invitation to Systematic Theology* (Philadelphia: Fortress, 1999); and Douglas John Hall, *Confessing the Faith: Christian Theology in a North American Context* (Philadelphia: Fortress, 1998).

missional homiletics because it has two distinct advantages in relation to the proposals of testimony and witness put forward by Long and Florence. First, confession provides an essential and definite content and criterion for proclamation that is absent in the proposed usages of testimony. For Long and Florence, the content or "object" of the preacher's witness is ultimately the preacher's subjective experience. Florence argues that the preacher's testimony bears witness to the preacher's experience of God through the text. Long argues that the preacher bears witness to an encounter with the living presence and voice of God, an event that happens through the study of the biblical witness. In both cases the preacher bears witness to his or her own experience. In confession the preacher confesses the essential summary of the faith, which both defines the essential content of the sermon and provides criteria by which to determine the sermon's faithfulness as gospel proclamation.

In addition, confession provides a robust though circumscribed place for the experience of the preacher in the sermon. Long and Florence both argue effectively for the importance of the experiential engagement of the preacher; a sermon is not a lecture about ideas but a testimony to an event, an event that makes a claim first on the life of the preacher. However, preaching must not be reduced simply to the personal experience of the preacher with God, especially apart from any normative relation to the historic Christian witness. Confession provides a place for the preacher's personal experience while also stressing the common faith that the preacher speaks "for and with the community."[28] Miroslav Volf understands this twofold aspect of confession as cognitive specification and personal identification. Confession "proffers the content of the church's understanding of who Jesus is and what significance he holds . . . and allows believers to identify with this content and, indeed, claim it as their own."[29]

Moreover, confession is most appropriate to this missional homiletic because the twofold dynamic of confession just described by Volf works very well in the framework of Barth's ecclesiology and theology. In his ecclesiology, Barth uses the term "witness" when he argues that witness is the sum of the service the Christian community offers in any form.

---

[28]Lose, *Confessing Jesus Christ*, 109.
[29]Ibid., 85.

Witness, he argues, in any form is always "proclamation, explication, and application of the Gospel of the Word of God."[30] The German noun that Barth uses, which is translated "witness," is *das Zeugnis*, which means a report of something or an attestation of something. It is often translated "testimony."

Unlike Long and Florence, however, Barth does not argue that proclamation bears witness to an encounter with God but that it bears witness to "the Gospel of the Word of God." Thus, the object of witness is in one sense objectively outside the experience of the preacher, yet in another sense it is subjectively appropriated by the preacher. The reader may recall that in the metastructure of the *Doctrine of Reconciliation*, justification, sanctification and vocation refer to objective acts of God in Jesus Christ, while gathering, upbuilding and sending refer to the community's, and within that the individual's, subjective appropriation of those acts. That is to say, Barth does not discount the subjective experience of the individual but circumscribes it within the context of the decisive and prior action of God in Jesus Christ. As a homiletical concept, confession makes a similar move by joining the personal identification of the preacher to the proclamation of the essential content of the Christian confession, which is made first to the preacher as a hearer.[31]

Finally, confession is the most the appropriate category by which to understand missional preaching because it provides a homiletical way of framing the formation of communal identity that is accomplished by preaching in missional congregations. The first pattern of missional faithfulness discerned in *Treasure in Clay Jars*, and one of the most important for preaching, is the discernment of missional vocation. Hunsberger writes, "The congregation . . . is seeking to discern God's specific missional vocation (its 'charisms') for the entire community and for all its members."[32] This is understood in a twofold sense. First, the congregation shares its vocation with the whole church, which is to bear witness to Jesus Christ

---

[30]Barth, *CD* IV/3.2, 843.

[31]A important question can be raised here in comparing Barth and Lose, though it is not germane to the usefulness of Lose in this project. One wonders if the confession of the hearer is eschatologically decisive for justification. Lose seems to tend toward a positive answer to that question, while Barth—the Reformed theologian—would tend toward a negative answer.

[32]Barrett et al., *Treasure in Clay Jars*, 33.

and announce the inauguration of God's reign. Second, this general vocation is given to a congregation in a particular sense, relative to a congregation's particular gifts and particular location and time. Missional preaching helps the community discern its particular vocation through specific and repeated messages that form and reinforce a core identity.

This is the very work that Lose argues is done in and by confession. He argues that when a person or a community confesses faith in Jesus Christ, the tradition is activated and actualized into a living tradition. Miroslav Volf goes further, arguing that confession is declarative (stating what the community believes), performative (transforming the cognitive element of faith into active commitment) and social and public (inviting a response from others and binding the confessor to the larger community). Likewise, Gerrish argues that confession preserves and sustains a church's identity and provides the community with a pattern to make sense of the world.

Moreover, Lose argues, confession is a better way of understanding the formation of identity through preaching than narrative. Charles Campbell's *Preaching Jesus* is an excellent example of a homiletic attempt to understand preaching as forming congregational identity through narrative. Using the work of Hans Frei, Campbell argues that the story of Jesus Christ narrated by the Gospels builds up the church and constitutes the people of God.[33] Preaching in this sense seeks to "create a universe of discourse" and put the hearer in the middle of that world so that the hearer is "absorbed" by the text.[34] While he clearly appreciates Campbell's intention to shape the church in a core identity, Lose expresses several concerns that stem from his work with confession. It is worth quoting Lose at length because his critique both strengthens the argument for the use of confession in a missional homiletic and raises a serious question about metanarrative formation in other missional theological discussions:[35]

---

[33]The reader may notice a theological difficulty here, noted by Lose and by James F. Kay in *Preaching and Theology*, that Campbell ascribes to narrative powers ordinarily reserved for the Holy Spirit: to wit, the upbuilding of the church.

[34]Charles L. Campbell, *Preaching Jesus: New Directions for Homiletics in Hans Frei's Postliberal Theology* (Grand Rapids: Eerdmans, 1997), 234.

[35]As a prime example, see Christopher J. H. Wright, *The Mission of God: Unlocking the Bible's Grand*

The hearer that is absorbed by the text has no ability to engage in critical
conversation by which to appropriate the biblical narratives for him or herself.
This lack of space in which to appropriate the text limits, as Ricoeur pointed
out, the ability of the hearer really to be encountered by the narrative, to enter
into the text, or be changed by it. Confession, recall, is decidedly assertive—
making claims about the nature of reality—and therefore demands a response
from the listener. Nevertheless, it is not coercive, as its integrity does not
depend upon the affirmation of the hearer.[36]

Confession, Lose argues, provides the critical distance necessary for
the hearer to participate in the narrative with integrity and to respond
genuinely to its claims. As he develops his proposal, Lose offers three
further clarifications of the way identity and distance work in preaching
as confession. First, Lose bolsters his argument for the critical distance
provided by confession by pointing to work in biblical studies suggesting
that gaps and indirection in the biblical narratives provide the reader
with critical distance to engage and appropriate the story; he also points
to the work of other homileticians who have worked with the importance of critical distance in preaching from perspectives informed by
both performative and communications theory perspectives. Second,
drawing on Brueggemann's understanding of the nature of the biblical
texts, Lose argues that confession simultaneously grounds the community in an identity and offers the hearer critical space in a dynamic
interplay. Finally, the critical distance provided by confession is not
simply the distance for the hearer to "choose" but is primarily the space
in which the Holy Spirit can effect faith.

Michael Brothers, who also deals substantially with the concept of
critical distance in preaching in his dissertation, "The Role of Distance
in Preaching: A Critical Dialogue with Fred Craddock and Post-Liberal
Homiletics," further illuminates how preaching as confession can help
the community discern its particular vocation through simultaneously
grounding in narrative and providing critical distance. He notes, like
Lose, that Campbell's homiletic depends on absorbing the hearer into
the world of the text and further that Campbell, Frei, Lindbeck and other

---

Narrative (Downers Grove, IL: InterVarsity Press, 2006).
[36]Lose, *Confessing Jesus Christ*, 126.

"postliberals" borrow this concept of absorption from Eric Auerbach's *Mimesis*. In *Mimesis*, Auerbach writes that it does not matter whether Homer's epic relates to a historical reality; "his reality is powerful enough in itself; it ensnares us, weaving its web around us, and that suffices him."[37] Brothers notes, however, drawing on the work of Alfred Lord in *The Singer of Tales*, that Auerbach is working with Homer as a finished text, reading him as a completed work. As an epic and oral poem, however, Homer's work was composed in performance, not prior to performance. Brothers writes:

> An oral performance is not composed *for* but *in* performance through the audience's response. This mutual response between both performer and audience includes interplay between distance and participation. The story is always altered and created according to the hearers who participate. Contrary to Auerbach's *reading* of Homer, there is no absorption into the world of a text. The text is created through the participation of the hearer in the performance.[38]

To extend this insight into the present discussion of missional preaching and discernment of missional vocation, the discernment of a congregation's particular missional vocation occurs in the interplay between the essential confession and the congregation and between the preacher and the congregation in any given sermon, with the inspiring activity of the Holy Spirit present throughout. Moreover, the preacher's confession is always altered and created according to the hearers who participate. That is not to say that the essential content changes but that the confession as preached and heard is contextual and particular to the congregation, responsive to the present activity of God in that community, and interacting with community members' struggle to live out the faith in their time and place.

All of this is to say that the preacher's role in the discernment of a congregation's missional vocation is not as simple as "telling the story of God." Nor does it consist in absorbing the congregation into that story (as a linguistic universe) such that they see their lives and world as par-

---

[37]Erich Auerbach, *Mimesis: The Representation of Reality in Western Literature* (Princeton, NJ: Princeton University Press, 1953), 13.

[38]Michael Brothers, "The Role of Distance in Preaching: A Critical Dialogue With Fred Craddock and Post-Liberal Homiletics" (PhD diss., Princeton Theological Seminary, 2003), 229-30.

ticipating in the biblical narrative. Rather, the preacher's role in a congregation's missional discernment is to confess the essential core of Christian faith in response to the proclamation of the word through the reading of scripture and in light of the particular lived experience of the community, providing the community with critical distance to hear the confession, to attend to the work of the Holy Spirit within and among them, and to respond in faith. The discernment of missional vocation that arises from such preaching is the result of a complex interplay of participation and distance, of the historic confession, lived experience and the present working of the Holy Spirit.

Because of the way the concept holds this complex interplay in tension, confession offers an excellent way to understand homiletically what missional researchers mean by the discernment of missional vocation in a congregation. Missional research makes clear that one of the most important patterns of missional faithfulness is that a church is discerning its missional vocation. To the extent that this discernment occurs in the preaching moment, the question is, how does it happen homiletically? The concept of confession suggests that it happens as the preacher centers the community in a core identity while simultaneously offering the hearer the critical distance to test, question, affirm and appropriate that identity with integrity.

To summarize briefly, confession is the most appropriate category for a missional homiletic in light of David Lose's arguments, in comparison to the concepts of witness and testimony, in the framework of Barth's ecclesiology and in the context of research into missional congregations. Before examining what the essential content of the confession is, we should first take up and respond to two significant concerns about the use of confession in homiletics and then raise a final caution. The first objection can be summarized thus: Does the category of confession provide room for the reasoned argumentation of the gospel, including the use of rhetoric?

At least two scholars who have reviewed Lose's work raise this question. Susan Bond writes, "There are some weaknesses [in Lose's proposal] and most of them are related to the initial premise that the Christian faith must be confessed instead of argued. This moves Lose away from the rhetorical tradition in general and homiletical rhetoricians specifically."[39] Moreover, she suggests that Lose mischaracterizes Paul by suggesting that Paul is "confessing his faith," if by that he means to gloss over Paul's sophisticated rhetorical and rational argumentation. Likewise, Richard Lischer suggests that Lose's opposition to cognitive sermons that rely on proofs is attacking a "straw" sermon, writing, "I have to wonder if tightly written sermons and closely argued defenses of the faith really pose a problem to the church today."[40] The question here is, can, and perhaps should not, the gospel be argued on rational terms, and does "confession" preclude such argumentation?

Indeed, there is room for the gospel to be argued on rational terms within the framework of "confession," but one must employ the concept carefully and ignore the fact that Lose does not specifically envision such reasoned, rhetorical argumentation. In one sense, Lose speaks of confession in reference to "critical fideism," which means confession as an epistemological category. As an epistemological category, confession does not preclude reasoned and rhetorical argumentation. Confession in this sense simply refers to our inability to claim unquestionable, self-evident epistemological premises and thus points to the fideistic basis of all our knowledge. In the critical fideism for which Lose has argued, knowledge rests on essential confessional premises, not blindly, but open to challenge and critique by others who may speak on the basis of other confessional claims.

The other sense in which Lose uses confession is as a speech act, particularly drawing on the work of J. L. Austin and John R. Searle. As a speech act, the concerns of Bond and Lischer would seem to have more merit, yet Lose carefully addresses their concerns by virtue of the theorist on whom he relies. He notes that the theologians who follow Austin typically describe confession as a commissive speech act, meaning it "first, commits the speaker to a particular existential stance; second, makes a pledge to the hearer that the speaker does indeed believe what she says; and, third, seeks to engage the hearer by making a commitment, rather than by ordering or commanding."[41] Now, if that were the sense

---

[39] L. Susan Bond, review of *Confessing Jesus Christ: Preaching in a Postmodern World*, by David J. Lose, *Homiletic* 28 (2003): 28.

[40] Richard Lischer, review of *Confessing Jesus Christ: Preaching in a Postmodern World*, by David J. Lose, *Theology Today* 60 (2004): 584.

[41] Lose, *Confessing Jesus Christ*, 105.

in which Lose employed confession, then perhaps rational argumentation would not be possible in the context of confession. However, Lose purposefully turns to John Searle's taxonomy of speech acts, where confession is described as assertive rather than commissive. He writes, "Describing confession as assertive rather than commissive not only highlights the promissory nature of confession (as assertives and commissives overlap at several points) but also addresses the question of truth more directly."[42] Assertives, according to Searle, "commit the speaker to something's being the case, to the truth of the expressed proposition."[43] Moreover, an assertive speech act invites a speech act in response and in kind, which is to say a confession that aims to say something true invites the hearer to affirm, challenge, question or reject the confession in response. Thus, the door is open to rational argumentation.

This is not to suggest that Lose understands preaching as confession as a reasoned defense of the gospel. He never indicates that it is such, and moreover his understanding of confession does not envision a "coercive" persuasion. He intentionally envisions an "invitational" model of persuasion that allows ample critical distance for the hearer. One might seriously question whether this invitational model can account for the skilled rhetorical arts one finds in Paul's letters, never mind the broader history of Christian preaching and a host of other contemporary homiletical proposals. Nevertheless, the category of confession as such, as Lose has articulated it in relation to critical fideism and John Searle's work, does not preclude, and in some cases may conceivably entail, reasoned argumentation in Christian preaching.

The second objection to the homiletical use of confession is arguably the more difficult, and it is this: By construing preaching as confession, is the sermon too dependent on the preacher and the preacher's capacity to believe? Susan Bond suggests this concern when she notes that in describing the status of scripture, Lose argues for a functional rather than ontological status for the word of God. That is to say, scripture is the word of God because we believe and act as though it is. Roy Harrisville raises this issue when he quotes Lose, who writes, "The words of the Bible only

---

[42]Ibid.
[43]Ibid., 104.

take on meaning when they are viewed *both* in relation to the narratives in which they are used *and* in relation to the common words of the hearers as they go about their daily lives." Harrisville wonders if Lose, even in spite of himself, is not arguing that the preacher validates the message.[44] Thomas Long in his review of *Confessing Jesus Christ* raises the question most pointedly when he writes, "Is there room . . . for the preacher to point to and announce, with fear and trembling, a gospel that is larger and deeper than the preacher's fragile capacity to believe?"[45]

I am inclined to give Lose the benefit of the doubt on the question of whether the efficacy of the sermon is dependent on the preacher's confession because he stresses the agency of the Holy Spirit in at least two instances. He does so when he argues for the hearer to have critical distance, for both the integrity of the hearer and to provide room for the work of the Holy Spirit, and as part of his critique of Charles Campbell's post-liberal homiletic that appears to ascribe to narrative the agency properly belonging to the Holy Spirit.[46] It is unclear to me, though, whether there is room within Lose's work for the preacher to confess that which he or she may not believe, or believe confidently.

For instance, can the preacher preside at a funeral and in the sermon bear witness to the resurrection of Jesus Christ when she can hardly believe it herself, or perhaps does not believe it at all? This is a similar question to the one I posed in discussing Florence's *Preaching as Testimony*, wondering whether the preacher's proclamation was constrained to what he or she had personally experienced. The response, I contend, is that the preacher does not confess merely or mostly his or her own confession, and thus the confession of preaching is not bound to the preacher's capacity to believe. This is so in at least four ways.

---

[44]Roy A. Harrisville, review of *Confessing Jesus Christ: Preaching in a Postmodern World*, by David J. Lose, *Word and World* 25 (2005): 354.

[45]Thomas G. Long, review of *Confessing Jesus Christ: Preaching in a Postmodern World*, by David J. Lose, *Interpretation* 58 (2004): 218.

[46]With reference to whether the sermon is dependent on the preacher's confession, James Kay notes, "While divine accommodation to the human linguistic condition pertains to the freedom of God to accompany the creature, that God has elected human language (or bread and wine) does not mean that God is *bound* or subject to these media in the event of revelation." James F. Kay, "Preacher as Messenger of Hope," in *Slow of Speech and Unclean Lips: Contemporary Images of Preaching Identity*, ed. Robert Stephen Reid (Eugene, OR: Cascade Books, 2010), 32.

First, in the sermon the preacher articulates the confession of the text as well as his or her own confession in response to the text. The voice of the text, in the reading of scripture prior to the sermon and the interpretation of that scripture in the sermon, has its own confession that is not subsumed or overwhelmed in the confession of the preacher. Second, the preacher is shaped and nourished by a Christian tradition that has its own confessional voice, speaking to and through the preacher. Even if a preacher has doubts about his or her own personal beliefs, he or she rises to preach as a steward of a living tradition of belief. Third, as Long stresses in *The Witness of Preaching*, the preacher comes from the congregation and goes to the text on behalf of the congregation. To that I would add, as I argued earlier in speaking of a missional community of preachers, the preacher speaks on behalf of the congregation. The preacher's confession is not simply his or her own confession but is also the confession of the community, of their experience of the gospel, distilled in the sermon. Only a fraction of a sermon is a confession of what a preacher personally has experienced. Sometimes that fraction is greater than others, but never is the preacher left without the confession of scripture, the living tradition and the community of God's people. Most importantly, never is the preaching moment without the speaking—the confessing—of God's Holy Spirit. Ultimately, it is by God's Spirit is that the gospel is spoken and heard. The gospel always exceeds the preacher's capacity to believe or to confess. The preacher is but a witness, partial and often unsure, to the living Christ who by the power of the Spirit awakens faith and builds the church.[47] Thus, just because preaching is confession, the proclamation of the gospel is not necessarily restricted to the preacher's capacity to believe.

Finally, I want to raise a caution with respect to the use of confession particularly in the sense of a response "both to the word of faith and to the external circumstances necessitating it."[48] For Lose confession as response is an attractive aspect of this concept vis-à-vis witness or testimony, and I share his affinity. However, while Lose writes that confession is a response

---

[47] As we noted in the discussion of Barth's ecclesiology, Barth writes that the community knows that its confession of Jesus Christ is and can only be a grateful response to the fact that "first and supremely Jesus Christ has confessed it, does confess it, and will continually do so." See Barth, *CD* IV/3.2, 790.

[48] Lose, *Confessing Jesus Christ*, 78.

both to the proclaimed word and the crisis of the world, it appears that he focuses first on the crisis of the world and then on the proclaimed word. For instance, in describing the movement of the sermon he writes, "Confessional preaching implies not simply movement, but a consistent movement from the truth of our condition to the new truth of God's merciful response to our condition."[49] Now this fundamental movement is perhaps a reflection of Lose's Lutheran heritage and the tradition of law-gospel preaching. Moreover, I recognize that I am a Reformed person in primary dialogue with a Reformed theologian. Nevertheless, I do want to raise a caution that arises from the discussion of Barth's argument that the preaching of the gospel is never occasioned primarily or fundamentally in response to the need of the world. The primary impetus and basis for the preaching of the gospel is God's gracious activity in Jesus Christ. The gospel is certainly addressed to the crisis of the world, but the proclamation of the gospel does not arise from that crisis; the proclamation of the gospel arises from the speaking of God's own word.

Moreover, the preacher should not address the world primarily on the basis of its need and crisis but primarily on the basis of God's election of humanity in Christ. In speaking of the commission of the Christian community, Barth writes that it is tempting to define the person to whom the community is sent as the one who has not heard the gospel, who is far from God, who is alienated and confused. Yet the alienation of God and humanity is not the decisive factor in how the community (or the preacher) views the person to whom it is sent. Rather, the community must first attend to humanity as it is in Christ, reconciled to God. Only on the basis of this great affirmation and in the context of this accomplished fact do the community and the preacher then move to consider the crisis and need of humanity. Speaking confessionally, what Lose calls the "truth of our condition" is not the truth at all but is confusion, and the "new truth" is in fact the only truth: humanity is already reconciled to God in Christ. In short, while confession is made in response to the crisis of the world, we must not let that overshadow the fact that confession is first and primarily a response to God's gracious activity in Jesus Christ.

---

[49]Ibid., 216.

THE PREACHER CONFESSES JESUS CHRIST

So confession is the most appropriate mode of preaching, but what is the confession? The essential content of the Christian confession is Jesus Christ, and more specifically it is the reconciling work that God has accomplished in the cross and resurrection of Jesus Christ. To unpack this, we will begin by examining the core confession developed in David Lose's biblical research and then flesh out the meaning of the core confession in relationship to Barth's understanding of the content of the community's task as it is sent by the Holy Spirit. Finally, I will set this understanding of confession in relationship to other proposals in the area of missional preaching.

As Lose reviews New Testament writings and scholarship relative to confession, he concludes that the essential early Christian proclamation is the cross-resurrection kerygma: Jesus Christ, who was crucified, has been raised.[50] This essential content is sounded strongly in Pauline writings, becomes an essential summary and test in post-Pauline literature, and is the hermeneutical lens through which the Gospel writers narrate Jesus' life. Lose writes:

> When the early Christians reduced the faith to its bare essentials . . . they focused neither on Jesus' teaching nor his miracles, but rather on his crucifixion "under Pontius Pilate" and God's raising him up from the dead "on the third day . . . in accordance with the Scriptures."[51]

Moreover, Lose finds that making this confession not only entails a cognitive acknowledgment but functions in a binding, contractual way. First, the confession proves to be eschatologically decisive, uniting the confessor to Jesus Christ, and in that sense becomes an actualization of baptism. Second, confession unites a person to Jesus publicly in a way that often brings the animosity of his opponents. Indeed, the essential confession of the crucifixion and resurrection of Jesus Christ is the basis

---

[50]Lose engages many sources in this discussion, but his primary conversation partners in New Testament theology are Otto Michel, C. K. Barrett, Günther Bornkamm, Rudolf Bultmann and Oscar Cullman. He draws most heavily on Pauline literature and particularly Romans. L. Susan Bond notes that Lose follows J. Christiaan Beker in assuming that Paul's letters are both contingent and coherent. See Bond, "Confessing Jesus Christ," 28.

[51]Lose, Confessing Jesus Christ, 73.

on which the early Christian community made its confession that Jesus is Lord. Through these twin events, the early Christians perceived that Jesus of Nazareth shares the "name and nature" of the God of Israel and is set over every other ruler and power as the supreme Lord, at whose name every knee should bend.

In *Confessing Jesus Christ*, Lose does not go further with his own understanding of the essential summary of the Christian confession.[52] Scattered throughout his work are allusions to his own understanding of the essential summary of the confession, but nothing is sustained. For instance, he writes, "The Christian gospel makes an ultimate claim: in the cross and resurrection of Jesus Christ God has acted decisively for the redemption of all humanity and the whole cosmos."[53] The theologians with which Lose engages in his discussion of confession have other conceptions of the essential confession. For instance, Volf emphasizes simply that the church gathers in Christ's name and confesses the name of Jesus Christ, while Gerrish argues the church is the community that confesses faith in "the risen Christ," and Hall focuses on "God's activity in Jesus Christ." Lose never assesses these statements, either to flesh out their meaning or compare them to early Christian confession and to his understanding.

The differences between the early Christian confession, the three contemporary theologians Lose references and his own silence on the issue point to the necessity for pressing further into the content of the essential summary of the Christian confession. Moreover, the diversity among the other homiletical proposals considered so far, including those for missional preaching, highlight the need for careful attention on this point. In one sense this far exceeds the scope of this or any book—defining the essential summary of the Christian confession was, in essence, the major four-hundred-year project of the early church. Thus, our goal from this point is a modest unpacking of the meaning of the essential Christian confession. First, we will rely on Barth's understanding of the essential content of the confession, drawing first on the interpretation of Eberhard Busch as he

---

[52]In her review of *Confessing Jesus Christ*, L. Susan Bond notes, "At the end of Lose's work, we have an idea about confessional shape (moving from cross to resurrection) but maybe less of an idea about confessional content than we wanted." Bond, review of *Confessing Jesus Christ*, 28.

[53]Lose, *Confessing Jesus Christ*, 221-22.

offers a helpful introduction, and then connecting to Barth's discussion in "The Holy Spirit and the Sending of the Christian Community."

The essential kerygmatic confession of the early Christian community was, as we find it in Mark 16:6, "You are looking for Jesus of Nazareth, who was crucified. He has been raised." Of the crucifixion of Jesus, Busch writes that for Barth, "His death on the cross was and is the [perfected consummation] of the incarnation of the Word and therefore [of] the humiliation of the Son of God and [of the] exaltation of the Son of Man."[54] It is important to understand how Barth relates the "incarnation of God" to Jesus' fulfillment of the covenant God made with Israel, that God would be their God and Israel would be God's people. Barth argues that Jesus Christ is the fulfillment of God's covenant with Israel by grace, and in Christ the covenant with Israel is opened to those outside Israel. In the incarnation, God himself becomes the covenant partner who can keep the covenant and preserve the relationship. Busch writes, "The incarnation of God is the fulfillment of the covenant as a radical form of the relationship between God and Israel, Israel and God."[55] God has assumed human form as the one Jewish man, Jesus, and "in this one man humanity as a whole is *assumed* and *accepted* by God, and yes, accepts God Himself."[56]

Busch writes that two things happen in the crucifixion. First, "God has shown his deity in his acceptance of the sinner and her misery." Second, "The human, liberated from her Godforsakenness . . . accepted by God and transferred into indissoluble unity with God, is the 'exalted' human."[57] Thus, the decisive "glad tidings" of God's goodness in Jesus Christ, as the incarnation of God and the embodiment of the fulfillment of the covenant by grace, comes to white-hot focus in the event of the cross. Here is true God, submitting himself to the rejection and humiliation of a cross in order to be God with and for his people. Here is true human, faithful to God "precisely at the place where the covenant was

---

[54]Eberhard Busch, *The Great Passion: An Introduction to Karl Barth's Theology* (Grand Rapids: Eerdmans, 2010), 102.

[55]Ibid., 103. This is important because it means that the church that confesses Jesus Christ also confesses its unity with Israel.

[56]Ibid., 100.

[57]Ibid., 103.

and is broken. For by a 'free choice' he became obedient to God, 'unto death, even death on a cross.'"[58]

What then of the resurrection? Busch argues that for Barth the resurrection is not simply the intellectual realization of the truth of the crucifixion and the one who was crucified, though it is that. First and foremost, the resurrection is a "new act of God" in which God confirms and acknowledges that God has accepted the truly human one, and the truly human one has accepted God. Busch quotes Barth at length:

> His resurrection . . . *confirmed* His death. It was God's *answer* to it. . . . It was God's acknowledgement of Jesus Christ, of His life and death . . . his judicial sentence that the action and passion of Jesus Christ were not apart from or against Him, but according to His good and holy will, and especially that his dying in our place was not futile but *effective*, that it was not to our destruction but to our *salvation*.[59]

In the resurrection, Jesus Christ himself "reaches out to us" and proclaims that the separation of humanity and God has been overcome and that in him "we are the new and true humanity," humanity that accepts God and is accepted by God.[60] Moreover, this is a work that is fulfilled and accomplished in Christ. The human person who hears this proclamation and accepts God does not make herself the true human but bears witness to what has been done for her in Christ, "that in Christ we have first been accepted by him and are truly human as such."[61] Indeed, the visible Christian community is those who have been gathered by and through him in order to bear to witness to this new reality that God has accepted us in Jesus Christ.

In "The Holy Spirit and the Sending of the Christian Community," Barth discusses the commission that is given to the community, treating its content first. Much of this discussion elaborates and expands on the core understanding of cross and resurrection articulated by Busch. Barth writes that the task of the Christian community is to confess Jesus Christ, who gives himself to be known by the community in order that the com-

---

[58]Ibid.
[59]Ibid.
[60]Ibid.
[61]Ibid.

munity may and should confess him. Moreover, the task of the community is to confess Jesus Christ in the concreteness and uniqueness of his person, work and revealed name. The restriction of the confession to the concrete and unique person, work and name of Jesus Christ is in no way to diminish the magnitude of the confession's implications. Indeed, Barth writes that in Jesus Christ, we are dealing with "the true and living God and true and living man; their encounter, co-existence and history with its commencement, centre and goal; the grace of God triumphant in judgment, His life triumphant in death and His light in darkness."[62] Yet all of this is enclosed and revealed in Jesus Christ "supremely and decisively." Jesus Christ gives the community its commission, and the totality of its task is to confess him.

Now, what does it mean to confess Jesus Christ? Barth continues by expounding two basic elements. First, and fundamentally, Jesus Christ is God's revealed goodness, and in that sense Barth writes famously that he is God's great and comprehensive "yes." Note that Jesus Christ is himself this yes and not merely one who speaks this affirmation or signifies it. He himself is the affirmation in his person, work and name. Moreover, Barth argues that if the affirmation of God's goodness is abstracted from Jesus Christ, "it can only be powerless, even though sung with the tongues of angels."[63] The content of the community's confession is the goodness of God in Jesus Christ, the unique and concrete person. Barth elaborates on this, practically preaching through his writing:

> Jesus Christ is in person the faithfulness of God which draws near to the unfaithfulness of man and overpowers it as God Himself not only confirms and maintains His covenant with His creature but once and for all leads it to its goal and secures it against every threat. He is the reconciliation of the world to God which does not merely look and go beyond the sin of man but sets it aside. He is the effective justification and sanctification of sinful man, and indeed his honourable vocation to the service of God. He is the kingdom of God which with its comfort and healing has approached and invaded torn humanity suffering from a thousand wounds, and put an end to its misery. He is in the deepest sense the reformation, i.e., not merely the restoration but the

---

[62]Barth, *CD* IV/3.2, 798.
[63]Ibid.

disclosure or manifestation of the purpose and glory of all creation. He is the gift of what it has not merited, its liberation by the free love, the free grace and the free mercy of God in the purity of His will and with the superiority of His power. In a word, He is the goodness of God.[64]

Thus, when the community seeks to confess the goodness of God, it proclaims first and fundamentally Jesus Christ in his person, work and name.

The second element Barth highlights is that the confession of the goodness of God in Jesus Christ also implies the confession of humanity. As Barth describes it, it implies "man in all the forms and at all the stages of his general and individual development."[65] This is not humanity in light of any achievements, products or possessions, nor in view of any moral, political or economic principles. All these are important, but they have limited validity. The human person herself, on the other hand, is always of value and interest. This is because "God sets value on him, and God in all His power is interested on his behalf."[66] Again, the human person is not of perpetual value because of some quality in the person's specific or general existence. Rather, the person is always of value because God has chosen the human person to be the object of his goodness; God has chosen in Jesus Christ to be for him and to be his God. Thus, Barth contends that the Christian community fails in its task, fails even to be the Christian community, "if all the emphasis does not fall on man, on man only in relation to God, yet also on God only in relation to man."[67]

Thus, for Barth, the essential summary of the Christian confession is the goodness of God toward humanity in Jesus Christ, decisively consummated and revealed in the cross and resurrection. This summary statement is in some contrast to what we found in *The Witness of Preaching* and *Preaching as Testimony*, and the comparison helps to clarify the essential content of the confession. In Long's work it is difficult to determine what he understands to be the essential content of Christian preaching. The clearest answer he gives is that "Christian preaching bears witness to Christ" and that the Christian community bears witness to Christ through

---

[64]Ibid., 799-800.
[65]Ibid., 800.
[66]Ibid.
[67]Ibid., 801.

every aspect of its life.[68] Indeed, the presence of Christ in the assembly of the faithful is basic to how he understands preaching. He writes, "To preach is to join our human words with the word that God in Christ in the power of the Spirit is already speaking to the church and to the world."[69] Yet beyond "bearing witness to Christ," Long is hesitant to say more definitely what the content of preaching is. Moreover, he indicates that it is decidedly not a set of facts about God or the faith but is witness to "God's voice speaking to us ever anew, calling us in the midst of the situations in which we find ourselves to be God's faithful people."[70] This is not necessarily at odds with the understanding of Christian confession articulated above, but without asserting the unmerited grace of God in Jesus Christ that constitutes God's faithful people, it can hardly stand alone.[71]

Florence, on the other hand, is both more clear about her understanding of the essential summary of the Christian confession and further removed from an apparent connection to the early Christian confession. For Florence, an encounter with God through the study of a text is a sine qua non of any sermon. She recognizes, however, that this encounter cannot simply be open-ended; in order to be faithful proclamation it needs to conform to some criteria. The criteria she chooses comes from Rebecca Chopp's feminist theology of proclamation. Chopp argues that the word is a perfectly open sign that is not bound in any cultural system, and by its very openness it always challenges and disrupts the present order. Moreover, the perfectly open sign always signifies freedom and liberation. Thus, Florence argues that a faithful sermon is a sermon that is an open sign, insofar as it testifies

---

[68]Thomas G. Long, *The Witness of Preaching*, 1st ed. (Louisville: Westminster John Knox, 1989), 51.
[69]Ibid., 17.
[70]Ibid.
[71]If I had one quibble, it would be that God does not call us to be God's faithful people as much as to accept and acknowledge that we already are God's faithful people in Christ. On the whole, my sense is that Long's understanding of the essential summary of Christian faith is not open-ended or untethered from the Christian tradition. I do not think he believes that whatever a preacher thinks he or she hears from God is the gospel. Rather, my sense is that Long is writing a textbook for a diverse audience of preachers. In *The Witness of Preaching*, he argues that whatever claim the preacher makes in the sermon must develop directly from exegesis of the text (108-12) and that preachers should reflect on their own theological heritage and core affirmations before going to a text (59-63). Thus, I imagine that Long does have for himself an understanding of the essential content of the gospel, but he does not find it appropriate or necessary to incorporate that into his homiletical textbook.

to the word that is a perfectly open sign, comes from the margins and always speaks a word of liberation to those oppressed by the "system."

While this is a helpfully clear criterion for faithful proclamation in preaching, it is disconnected from the theological and historical specificity of the early Christian kerygma. Florence and Chopp have substituted a quality of Jesus Christ for Jesus Christ himself. In Barth's terms, they have abstracted an idea from the unique and concrete Jesus Christ. An open sign not bound to a cultural system that always challenges and disrupts the present order is indeed a characteristic of Jesus Christ and very much what the early church meant when it confessed, "Jesus is Lord." However, a characteristic of Christ is not a substitute for the incarnate Word of God, Jesus of Nazareth. Moreover, the liberation and freedom that comes through Christ is not open-ended or undefined freedom but freedom to be truly human *in Christ*. The essential content of Christian preaching is the goodness of God in Jesus Christ, and any freedom the preacher may proclaim is both made possible by and circumscribed by his concrete and unique person, work and name.

Indeed, it is ironic that the very goal Florence seeks is undercut by the criteria she uses. Florence seeks the disruption of systemic sin and cultural oppression by a perfectly open sign that liberates the oppressed and that is not subject to a cultural system. Yet her criteria come down to abstractions, the idea of liberation and the idea of an open sign. Ideas, in contrast to free persons, are ultimately subject to the control and manipulation of those who think them and wield them. Ideas are shaped and molded by the human subject and thus distorted by sin. Jesus Christ, by contrast, is not only an idea but a living person, a subject, an agent, a true "Other," who in his perfect otherness stands outside of any system, person or group that would seek to control him. As a living Lord, Jesus Christ speaks a living word that always challenges and disrupts the present age, a living word that liberates the oppressed and sets the captives free. Yet his living word, spoken as it is by a living subject, cannot be replaced by concepts such as liberation or freedom or even "an open sign." These concepts are tentative ways of describing the living word we hear Christ speak, but they can never be substituted for the one who speaks.

Thus in Long we a have very undefined essential content of proclamation, and in Florence we have an essential content that serves as a kind of reinterpretation of the essential summary yet that falls far short of the essential confession. When we come to other proposals for missional preaching, we have similar theological substitutions but in different terms. Dally argues that the essential content of Christian preaching is the kingdom of God, a move common in missional literature. He writes, tongue-in-cheek, "Unfortunately, Jesus did not send the Twelve or the Seventy to offer sermons that people would enjoy or find meaningful. 'He sent them out to proclaim the kingdom of God and to heal' (Luke 9:2)."[72] Dally then arranges his proposal around this understanding of the essential summary of preaching. He explores the kingdom of God by examination of the synoptic Gospels, cataloging its features and characteristics in Mark, Matthew and Luke, and then gives the preacher practical helps for imagining the kingdom of God in their context.

In a sense Dally replaces Jesus Christ with the kingdom of God, essentially saying that the preacher proclaims what Christ preached, not Christ himself. Many people have made this move and it has a long theological and homiletical history, but it stands in stark contrast to the early Christian witness. As David Lose notes in his review of confession in New Testament literature, the essential summary of the Christian confession was the crucifixion-resurrection of Jesus Christ. For instance, Paul came preaching Christ, not the kingdom as such, and everything that is recorded about Jesus' life and teachings about the kingdom was written and understood in light of this central confession. It was the cross-resurrection that caused the disciples to scour the scriptures and their experiences with Jesus to both understand this central event and discern how to live in response to it. Moreover, as Barth argues, it is the cross-resurrection that is the perfect consummation of the incarnation of God and that makes it possible for humanity to live under God's gracious rule and reign. Understood in the framework of missional theology, the record of the life and teachings of Jesus instructs his followers how to live in the reign he embodies, inaugurates and accomplishes in the cross and resurrection. The kingdom of God is a reality that flows from

---

[72]Dally, *Choosing the Kingdom*, 14.

the cross-resurrection of Jesus Christ and cannot take the place of it.

In my view, Dally and others who focus on missional preaching as "preaching the kingdom" fundamentally misunderstand the basis of missional preaching. Preaching is missional not because it sends the congregation out on good works but because it participates in God's mission, which is a mission of redemption and new creation in Christ. In Jesus Christ, God begins a new creation in which the kingdom of God and life under God's rule are made possible. Unless the preacher points to this new creation, preaching "the kingdom" and calling hearers to "choose the kingdom" constitute yet another impossible burden for the human person whom God has liberated in Christ. The new humanity in Christ makes life in the kingdom of God possible and is indispensable to the proclamation of the gospel or an invitation to live under God's reign.

To compare another proposal for missional preaching, Al Tizon discusses the essential content of the Christian confession in the first three chapters of *Missional Preaching: Engage, Embrace, Transform*. More than anything else, Tizon returns to the idea that "because of the *missio Dei*, we preach the centrality of God in all things. . . . All of life revolves around God and God's desires for the world."[73] In his understanding, God's "desires for the world" are his mission and purpose in the world. Moreover, he writes, "Jesus Christ of the Gospels [is] at the very center of that mission."[74] Yet in what sense? Tizon writes that Jesus Christ "was the kingdom of God incarnate" and that though "the forces of darkness tried to snuff out the kingdom by killing Jesus . . . Christ rose on the third day."[75] Now by Christ's risen presence the kingdom of God continues, and by the power of the Holy Spirit it continues to be embodied in the community of Jesus' disciples. Therefore God's desires for the world, which are embodied in God's reign and rule, continue to work themselves out until they are eschatologically completed. On the basis of this broad framework, Tizon turns the remainder of his book to considering marks of the kingdom of God as they are found in the community of disciples.

---

[73] Al Tizon, *Missional Preaching: Engage, Embrace, Transform* (King of Prussia, PA: Judson Press, 2012), 8.

[74] Ibid., 6.

[75] Ibid., 18.

While I would have framed it differently, I can affirm Tizon's basic characterization of the mission of God, of God's purposes in the world, of the presence of the Holy Spirit empowering the church to demonstrate the reign of God to the world, and God's ultimate promise of the final transformation of creation. Nevertheless, I think Tizon's characterization of Jesus Christ raises two cautions and further clarifies what I mean by confessing Jesus Christ. Tizon describes Jesus Christ as the "incarnation of the kingdom of God," and this is presumably different than the "incarnation of God." As the incarnation of God, in Jesus Christ God himself becomes the human partner to fulfill God's covenant with Israel. Thus, the incarnation establishes the relationship of humanity to God and God to humanity in an "indissoluble unity." Relationship here is a key concept as a personal God assumes the form of a personal human becoming both true God and true human. By saying that Jesus Christ is the incarnation of the kingdom of God, does one walk back from this radical understanding of incarnation? The phrase could indicate that Christ is the incarnation of God's will and way but not of God himself. Thus, I believe we need to be more careful in our talk about the kingdom of God that Jesus Christ is the incarnation of God and thus also of God's will and way.

Second, Tizon describes Jesus Christ as the living, inaugurative embodiment of the kingdom of God, writing, "God's Rule in Christ is the crux of the kingdom story, as the birth, life, teaching, death, and resurrection of Christ inaugurate the fulfillment of the hope of the kingdom."[76] The trouble here is the focus on inauguration. Yes, Christ inaugurates God's reign and rule, but he is also its fulfillment and completion. In Christ, God has begun redeeming the world and has already redeemed the world; in Christ, God is beginning to bring all things into subjection to Christ and has already done so. Tizon writes that we preach "the future victory of God in Christ," and yet I would argue that we also preach the accomplished victory of God in Christ, which we now only partially realize.[77] Recall Barth's dual understanding of justification discussed in the second chapter. In Christ one is already justified objectively, and one subjectively experiences that justification as one is gathered into

[76]Ibid., 17.
[77]Ibid., 20.

the community of God's people. Just because the subjective appropriation and experience are not complete does not mean that justification
has not been completed objectively from God's side.

In part, we are dealing with the difficult task of thinking theologically
on the one hand from a temporal perspective and on the other hand from
an eternal perspective. However, if we do not keep the accomplished, objective work of Christ in view, we will be tempted, or perhaps compelled,
to look at the redeeming work of God as we experience it as a progressive
journey on the upward way. Tizon encapsulates this view when he writes,
"The Spirit-empowered church today continues to advance God's rule in
its life, deeds, and words." The language of continuing advance does not
take seriously the places where the evidence indicates that God's reign is
not advancing both globally and personally. Warfare, violence, hatred,
greed and injustice continue to mark the world, and Christians are often
complicit. At the most, the life of the Spirit-empowered church is a provisional sign—an often dim representation, but a representation and
likeness nonetheless—of the new creation that is begun and has already
been completed in Jesus Christ. Moreover, the sign that the church provides is often *tectum sub cruce*, hidden under the sign of the cross, in
weakness and suffering and not in apparent power and victory.

Thus, to summarize this argument, the essential content of missional
preaching must be to confess Jesus Christ in his person, work and name.
It is Jesus Christ in his concreteness as the incarnation of God and in his
fullness as the accomplishment of God's redemption and reign. Moreover,
confession is the most appropriate mode of preaching, especially in contrast to witness or testimony, because confession captures the strengths
of the witness motif while providing a stronger sense of the definite
object of Christian witness. Having said this, I sense keenly that much
more could be said. Nevertheless I believe it is important to lay down
some sense—even if only a sketch—of the essential content of Christian
preaching for at least two reasons. First, for the integrity of the catholic
and apostolic witness of the church, there must be some criteria for as-
sessing what is and is not faithful Christian preaching. As a Reformed
Christian, I believe that what unites the church across time and space is
its common confession of Jesus Christ. If the church fails in this con-

fession, then it fails to be the church. Second, and this is especially important from a missional theological perspective, the confession of Jesus Christ is the common thread that weaves together all the varied and multiform witness of the Christian community. What stitches together a pastor's sermon, a deacon's service in a soup kitchen, a scholar's research, a musician's composition and a host of other words and deeds from members of the Christian community? It is their common witness, that all the words and deeds of the Christian community in some form seek to confess God's goodness to humanity in Jesus Christ.

PREACHING CONFESSES JESUS CHRIST THROUGH A MISSIONAL INTERPRETATION OF SCRIPTURE

When missional preaching confesses Jesus Christ, it should do so through a missional interpretation of scripture. It has never seemed self-evident to me that preaching proceeds as an interpretation of a biblical text. It is certainly paradigmatically so, and almost any homiletical theory assumes that the preacher's sermon arises from the interpretation of a text. Moreover, for some it is dogmatically necessary on the basis of their theological tradition that preaching proceed from an interpretation of scripture. Still, I think one could imagine faithful preaching that does not involve a sustained interpretation of a text.[78] Nevertheless, I am arguing that the interpretation of scripture is a crucial element in a missional homiletic for two reasons.

First, as I argued at the beginning of this chapter, we are developing a homiletic that understands preaching specifically as a form of proclamation that occurs in the liturgy of public worship in response to the reading of scripture.[79] The characterization of the sermon as a response

---

[78]As one excellent example of such preaching, see Austin Farrer, *Austin Farrer: The Essential Sermons* (London: SPCK, 1991). This is a moving and intellectually stimulating collection of sermons preached by Austin Farrer to university students. Farrer was an Anglo-Catholic priest and theologian, and in no sermon of this collection does he reference any specific scripture that he is interpreting, though I am certain the assigned texts for the day were read as part of the service of worship.

[79]I am aware that there are some traditions where the scripture is not read as a separate element prior to the sermon but is interspersed throughout the sermon. In this case is the sermon still a response? Yes, because even here the sermon has arisen from the preacher's engagement with that text prior to the moment of preaching.

is important. The sermon is a continuation of the proclamation already begun in the reading of scripture and as such is an interpretation that directs the text specifically into the living context of the gathered community. Moreover, as Lose argues, the scripture is itself a confession of faith, asserting a claim to truth, and as such elicits a response, which in the case of the preacher is the sermon. Second, as we saw in the exploration of the patterns of missional faithfulness developed in the research for *Treasure in Clay Jars*, biblical formation and discipleship are essential patterns in the life of a missional congregation. Guder writes, "The missional church is a community where all members are learning what it means to be disciples of Jesus. The Bible has a continuing, converting, formative role in the church's life."[80] The two dynamics at work in this pattern, both of which are necessary, are biblical formation and discipleship. The community does not reserve biblical study for educated clergy, nor does it study scripture simply to meet personal needs for inspiration or edification. Rather, the community is intentional about being formed and transformed by the biblical witness, asking how God's word is shaping, calling and sending them personally and corporately.

Moreover, the researchers found that all the preachers in the churches they studied were employing a missional hermeneutic in their preaching. This was crucially important because it ensured that the "missional challenge of the gospel" was put before the whole community, even if the members were not engaged in other biblical study.[81] Indeed, the researchers found that they had to adjust their initial expectations that "all" members of the church would be involved in formational bible study, finding that in some cases it was only a small group. Yet through preaching in public worship, the whole community was being shaped by a missional interpretation of scripture.

Thus, a missional interpretation of scripture is an essential element of a missional homiletic. What is a missional interpretation? A missional interpretation of scripture is an interpretation that employs a missional hermeneutic. That is, it uses a hermeneutic shaped by missional theological convictions. As George Hunsberger describes it, a missional hermeneutic

---

[80]Barrett et al., *Treasure in Clay Jars*, 59.
[81]Ibid., 65.

implies that the reader approaches the Bible from the perspective "of the mission of God and the missionary nature of the church."[82] As of now, in the missional theological conversation the very concept of a missional hermeneutic is in the early stages of development. David Bosch articulated such a view of scripture in the 1980s, and James Brownson coined the term "missional hermeneutic" in 1992. Yet the conversation did not begin in earnest until a decade later, in 2002, as a series of meetings and later as a forum at the annual meetings of the Society for Biblical Literature.[83]

For this analysis, we will draw on various contributors to the missional hermeneutic conversation to sketch the outlines of a missional hermeneutic for homiletics, but as the missional hermeneutical conversation is in its infancy this will only be a sketch. Nevertheless, I want to develop this hermeneutic along three assertions: (1) that the confession of Jesus Christ, which we just examined, is the interpretive matrix through which the preacher reads scripture, (2) that the aim of the biblical witness, as well as the interpretation of it, is to form the community for participation in God's mission and (3) that the text must be read from the location of the Christian community in its unique place and time.

As we just saw, missional preaching confesses Jesus Christ, who is in himself the goodness of God toward humanity, consummated in the cross and resurrection event. This confession is also the interpretive matrix that guides the preacher in an engagement with and interpretation of the text. The term "interpretive matrix" comes from James Brownson's *Speaking the Truth in Love: New Testament Resources for a Missional Hermeneutic*. The origins of this book trace to a 1992 presentation Brownson gave to the Gospel and Our Culture Network, which was then published in 1994 in the *International Review of Mission* and then expanded into this slim volume in 1998.[84] Brownson argues that the gospel is a hermeneutical framework, or basic matrix, that allows the

---

[82]George Hunsberger, "Proposals for a Missionary Hermeneutic: Mapping a Conversation," *Missiology: An International Review* 39 (2011): 309.

[83]See David J. Bosch, *Witness to the World: The Christian Mission in Theological Perspective* (Eugene, OR: Wipf & Stock Publishers, 2006), and *Transforming Mission: Paradigm Shifts in Theology of Mission*, American Society of Missiology 16 (Mary Knoll, NY: Orbis Books, 2011). As for the history of the missional hermeneutic conversation, see Hunsberger, "Proposals for a Missionary Hermeneutic."

[84]Hunsberger offers this lineage in "Proposals for a Missionary Hermeneutic."

interpreter to bring the tradition (including scripture) and the contemporary context into dynamic interaction.

In the background of Brownson's work are many of the cultural and postmodern concerns that were raised by Lose. In particular, he wonders how Christians can profess beliefs that are cosmic in scope in an era when "religion in general, and Christian faith in particular, has been relegated to the private realm, where truth claims are immaterial and where disputes are not resolved but simply massaged into docility by psychological and sociological analysis."[85] Moreover, he argues, the question is not simply how the church can reenter the public sphere, because the public sphere is fractured into a variety of competing interest groups where claims to truth are characterized as "yet another bid for power." Resonating strongly with the concerns so lucidly discussed by Lose, Brownson writes, "What does it mean to be called to speak the gospel as truth in a culture that declares that religious speech can never be true, but only 'true-for-you'?"[86]

By sketching the outlines of a missional hermeneutic oriented around the interpretive matrix of the gospel, Brownson aims to address two crucial issues. First, he seeks to develop a model that accounts for diverse interpretations of scripture, both within the canon and among contemporary interpreters, and a plurality of expressions of faith. From a hermeneutical perspective, he argues that diverse interpretations of scripture are both unavoidable and a sign of faithful interpretation, as every reading of scripture is influenced by the individual, historical and cultural particularity of the interpreter and the community for which the text is interpreted. From a theological standpoint, Brownson argues that his missional hermeneutic "begins with the assumption that the mode in which God is present among the faithful is irreducibly multicultural."[87] That is to say, the reality of God's presence is available to every culture, and the "Christian experience of salvation" both challenges and enriches one's distinctive cultural identity; it also "deepens the awareness that one participates with all of humanity in a multicultural worship of God that transcends any par-

---

[85]James V. Brownson, *Speaking the Truth in Love: New Testament Resources for a Missional Hermeneutic,* Christian Mission and Modern Culture (Edinburgh: T & T Clark, 1998), 6.
[86]Ibid., 7.
[87]Ibid., 22.

ticular context."[88] Thus, by arguing for a hermeneutic of diversity, Brownson seeks to embrace diverse interpretations and expressions of faith.

The second issue he addresses in his model lies in the other direction: without a sense of coherence or center of scripture and Christian faith, diverse interpretations and expressions threaten to dissolve into the kind of "true-for-you" relativism with which he is wrestling. At this point Brownson argues for a hermeneutic of coherence, which is to say that diverse interpretations still maintain "a sense of coherence surrounding core assumptions regarding the character and purpose of God."[89] In this argument, Brownson is relying on his own New Testament scholarship and the work of his teacher J. Christiaan Beker to argue that the New Testament writers used an "interpretive matrix," a set of implicit interpretive rules to guide their appropriation of Jewish and Christian traditions for their specific contexts. Quite simply, the interpretive matrix is the gospel. By gospel, Brownson means "the proclamation of God's soteriological purpose and claim on this world, a purpose and claim extended paradigmatically through the crucified and risen Christ."[90] Furthermore, the gospel implies several basic structural features that guide interpretation. It: (1) "makes a claim that summons to allegiance and decision," (2) "presupposes a public horizon of interpretation" and (3) presents its claim "in the context of the religious realities disclosed by the death and resurrection of Christ."[91]

Furthermore, Brownson does not primarily mean that this simple statement of the gospel is the content of what is preached but rather that this structure "delineates how the entire tradition is to be preached and interpreted."[92] The matrix of the gospel provides parameters by which specific texts may be read and understood, as he demonstrates through interpretations of passages from Romans, Luke, John and Revelation. More broadly, this matrix offers a central metaphor by which Christians interpret the tradition, themselves and their situation in the world. Brownson writes, "The root images implicit in the gospel, when juxtaposed against the Christian tradition and against a specific situation,

---

[88]Ibid., 25.
[89]Ibid., 27.
[90]Ibid., 51.
[91]Ibid., 50.
[92]Ibid., 51.

disclose a new and all-encompassing mode of self-understanding and orientation."[93] Indeed, Brownson perceives that the New Testament writers have done the same basic interpretive work that Christians do daily: bring the tradition into dynamic interplay with one's context in light of the gospel. This interplay leads to deeper questioning about which expressions of faith one has received from tradition, which are shaped by culture and how these interactions shape the understanding of the gospel. This questioning leads to deeper understanding of the tradition, of one's culture and, most importantly, of the gospel.

Before leaving this discussion of the interpretive matrix of the gospel, it is important to see this way of construing a missional hermeneutic as distinct from another common way of understanding a missional interpretive framework, which is the "story of the mission of God and the formation of a community sent to participate in it."[94] In his article "Proposals for a Missional Hermeneutic: Mapping the Conversation," George Hunsberger describes this approach as one in which the narrative of the *missio Dei* provides the framework for biblical interpretation. The chief exemplar of this approach is Christopher Wright, who in his book *The Mission of God* "offers a detailed rationale for interpreting the Bible in light of the mission of God as the heart and core of the biblical narrative."[95] Wright acknowledges that the Bible is multivocal and presents many often conflicting narratives, yet he asserts that underneath the canon is a narrative of God's mission. He writes, "A missional hermeneutic proceeds from the assumption that the whole Bible renders to us the story of God's mission through God's people in their engagement with God's world for the sake of the whole of God's creation."[96]

There is much that I appreciate about this approach to defining a missional interpretive framework, and indeed it is attractive. It connects well with the origins of missional theology in its attention to the *missio Dei*, in ordering mission in relation to the mission of God, and in not adding it as

---

[93]Ibid., 54. James F. Kay has articulated a similar interpretive matrix for use in homiletics in his article "The Word of the Cross at the Turn of the Ages," *Interpretation* 53 (1999): 44-56.

[94]George Hunsberger, "Proposals for a Missionary Hermeneutic," Gospel and Our Culture Network, Jan. 28, 2009, gocn.org/resources/articles/proposals-missional/hermeneutic-mapping-conversation.

[95]Wright, *The Mission of God,* 310.

[96]Ibid., 122.

an addendum to the church's activities. Moreover, its emphasis on story connects well with narrative studies in terms of how we understand the Bible, God and how human beings make meaning. Nevertheless, this approach has deep problems. Many have already been discussed in this chapter, so I will name them only briefly here. First, there is the problem that usually attends metanarrative claims, which is the suppression of difference and the totalizing of perspective. This is especially troubling when one is dealing with multivocal biblical texts enclosed in a diverse canon.[97] Second, and this is a related problem that is particularly important for preaching, when the interpretive matrix is a metanarrative, all the texts that are not narrative—for instance wisdom sayings, prayers and ethical instructions—seem awkward and are subsequently marginalized. Third, as we saw in Lose's critique of Charles Campbell's postliberal homiletic, narrative theory works by absorption. The reader is "absorbed" into the world of the story and thus "participates" in the narrative. However, as Lose and Brothers have helpfully argued, this understanding of narrative does not provide critical distance that preserves the integrity of the hearer or reader, nor does it honor the particularity of the hearer or reader's social location.

Finally, from a theological standpoint, when one reads descriptions of "the mission of God," are we not dealing with what Barth would call an abstraction from Jesus Christ? That is to say, does not the "mission of God" as an interpretive framework perhaps function the same way as Anna Carter Florence's "perfectly open sign," a concept that has been abstracted from the person and work of Jesus Christ and then substituted in his place? In *The Mission of God*, Wright notes that we already recognize the christological focus of the Bible and understand that Jesus Christ is the "hermeneutical key" by which we interpret scripture. Then he proposes that we consider the missiological focus of the Bible in the same way and "take mission as a hermeneutical matrix for understanding the Bible as a whole."[98] This is suggestive and interesting but also risky and unnecessary. By substituting mission for Christ, one risks (1) subsuming the decisive self-

---

[97]Richard Bauckham has tried to work out of this problem by suggesting that the metanarrative of God's mission privileges the poor and expects multicultural expressions to thrive. See Richard Bauckham, *Bible and Mission: Christian Witness in a Postmodern World* (Grand Rapids: Baker Academic, 2004).

[98]Wright, *The Mission of God*, 32.

disclosure of God in Christ into a broader metanarrative of God's activity that has been teased from a multivocal canon and (2) reducing Jesus Christ to a character in the story of God.[99] When we interpret scripture through the framework of God's goodness toward humanity in Jesus Christ, we are at the same time interpreting it in the framework of God's mission. Jesus Christ is in his person the mission of God, and no substitution is necessary.

Thus, I am arguing that a missional interpretation of scripture begins with approaching the text through the interpretive matrix of Jesus Christ. The second element of a missional hermeneutic is to recognize the formational purpose of the biblical witness and carry that purpose through the interpretation of the text. Recognizing the formational purpose of the biblical witness involves two central premises. The first is that the New Testament, and in some sense the whole canon when read through the interpretive matrix of Jesus Christ, is a missionary document. David Bosch makes this argument most forcefully in *Transforming Mission* with respect to the New Testament. As he traces historical shifts in paradigms of Christian mission, he argues that the first and "cardinal" shift is the event of Jesus of Nazareth and what follows him. Moreover, he argues, the documents written and transmitted as the New Testament are not primarily a record of intramural doctrinal struggle among early Christians, though there is that aspect in them and for a long time it was customary to read them that way.[100] Rather, he argues, the New Testament writings first and foremost bear witness to the missionary encounter between the early Christians and their surrounding culture. Moreover, these docu-

---

[99]James Brownson raises this concern about the metanarrative of the "mission of God" in a response to George Hunsberger's "Mapping a Conversation." Brownson notes the importance of cross-cultural encounter in missional engagement and draws on Derrida's notion of *différance* to suggest that the metanarrative of the "mission of God" may simply be another instance of a group of people crafting a totalizing narrative and suppressing différance. He does not say that it is but raises this as a concern to which missional theologians must attend. He says he is working toward a missional hermeneutic that "engages the reality of difference as deeply as the post-modern world does" but that presses deeper to draw these differences into the body of Christ. See James V. Brownson, "A Response at SBL to Hunsberger's 'Proposals . . .' Essay" (paper presented at the Gospel and Our Culture Network, 2009). For a creative and incisive analysis of the potential problems inherent in "story theology," particularly with respect to making Christ a monological character in the story, see Francesca Aran Murphy, *God Is Not a Story: Realism Revisited* (New York: Oxford University Press, 2007).

[100]Bosch, *Transforming Mission*, 15.

ments were intended to equip their communities for the mission of living in light of the gospel in their place and time. This mission is rooted in God's revelation in Jesus Christ and determined by the knowledge that in him God has decisively intervened in history, that in him the eschatological hour has come. Bosch writes:

> The New Testament witnesses assume the possibility of a community of people, who, in the face of the tribulations they encounter, keep their eyes steadfastly on the reign of God by praying for its coming, by being its disciples, by proclaiming its presence, by working for peace and justice in the midst of hatred and oppression, and by looking and working toward God's liberating future.[101]

Indeed, the intention of the written record of the New Testament is to form and equip a community of people to live in just this way. In this sense, Bosch argues, the New Testament must be read as a missionary document.

The second premise is a dogmatic extension of the first, and that is that these documents written to form the Christian community for its mission perform the same formational function, by the empowering of God's Spirit, when interpreted in the Christian community now. This argument has been advanced most forcefully by Darrell Guder, who shares Bosch's conviction that the New Testament is essentially a missionary document written for the formation of "missional communities." In a lecture published as "Missional Hermeneutics: The Missional Authority of Scripture," Guder elaborates on how the formational function of scripture continues in the church. Working as a Reformed theologian, he argues that this is in fact what we mean when we confess the authority of scripture, that God's Spirit works through scripture to form the people of God. He writes:

> Scripture's authority resides in the ongoing event in which Christ is encountered in scriptural testimony as God's word; that Word can be heard and listened to, and by virtue of the Holy Spirit's empowering, responded to and obeyed. Faith and discipleship emerge as the Scriptures work with their distinctive authority.[102]

Understood from the missional perspective, especially as Guder proceeds on the basis of Barth's doctrines of vocation and sending, "faith and disci-

---

[101]Ibid., 54.
[102]Darrell L. Guder, "Missional Hermeneutics: The Missional Authority of Scripture," *Mission Focus: Annual Review* 15 (2007): 119.

pleship" entail being called and sent as witness to Jesus Christ. The authority of scripture, therefore, lies in its capacity "to be the Spirit's instrument for the continuing calling, conversion, equipping, and sending of the saints into the world as Christ's witnesses."[103] Thus Guder elaborates on the equipping capacity of scripture in light of the empowering of God's Spirit.

In *Confessing Jesus Christ*, David Lose performs a similar move linguistically, describing the Bible as confession and then utilizing the linguistic and hermeneutical features of confession to describe how scripture can function as God's dynamic word. He argues that when understood as confession, the biblical authors are engaging in assertive discourse and they "self-consciously intend that their writing corresponds to [an extra-textual] reality."[104] This does not establish that the biblical writings are the word of God but rather how they might function as such. Lose writes that if the biblical text itself purports to speak for God, "even if we do not believe their claims, we can at least admit that they still might speak for God, however unlikely that seems to us."[105] Thus the possibility has been introduced that the biblical text is not just words about God but is God's dynamic word.[106]

In terms of a missional hermeneutic, this means that the act of biblical interpretation is something Guder calls "going to school with Jesus." In the Gospels we see how the disciples' thinking and conduct are affirmed, challenged and shaped through their interactions with Jesus; these records are written in light of the cross and resurrection in order to form Christian communities. In the Epistles, we see how the challenges and situations of the various communities are brought into dialogue with the revelation of God in Christ and result in ethical exhortations toward lived discipleship. As the contemporary interpreter comes to the text, a double-barreled question guides the interpretation: "How did this text equip and shape God's people for their missional witness then, and how

---

[103]Ibid., 120.

[104]Lose, *Confessing Jesus Christ*, 166.

[105]Ibid., 167.

[106]In Lose's discussion of this aspect of the Bible as confession, we see again the risks of leaning too heavily on the narrative of God's mission as the basic framework of a missional hermeneutic. In response to Brueggemann, Thiemann and Frei, Lose argues that construing the biblical texts as a self-referential narrative gravely misunderstands their fundamental nature as assertive discourse that clearly purports to refer to reality outside of the text.

does it shape us today?"[107] The question of how it shapes us today moves into the locatedness of the contemporary community, which is the third element we will treat in this missional hermeneutic. Before doing so, though, we need to look at one potential challenge to Bosch's and Guder's understanding of the formative purpose of the biblical witness.

What of the Old Testament? How does the Old Testament form the Christian community to live in light of the cross and resurrection of Jesus Christ? Michael Goheen, a missional theologian who shares these perspectives of Bosch and Guder, affirms explicitly that the Old Testament scriptures were written to equip God's people for mission.[108] Yet it is clear that the interpretation of a Hebrew text in light of its formative purpose for Christian witness will require more nuance and imagination than might be required when interpreting an Pauline epistle. For this reason, Hunsberger has suggested that it may help to "soften or widen the way the missional purpose of the biblical materials is characterized."[109] He notes that Brownson, himself a New Testament scholar, has suggested that perhaps it is best to cast the formative purpose of scripture in a wider frame than equipping for witness. For instance, Brownson suggests that one might understand the purpose of scripture as forming a shared identity as the people of God who are called to participate in God's mission.

Indeed, the theme of the formation of God's people is pervasive in the Old Testament. Yet this formation is not apart from witness. Israel's call is to be a light to the nations, to share its covenant blessings with all peoples of the earth. God elects Israel to be God's covenant people, not so the rest of the world can wander in darkness but so Israel can bear witness to the nations. Moreover, as one finds in the theology of Isaiah 42 and 49, Yahweh will help Israel accomplish this task. Israel's formation as God's people is for witness, and in that sense the vocation of the people of God begins not with the early Christian witnesses but with the Abrahamic covenant.[110] To

---

[107]Darrell L. Guder, *Unlikely Ambassadors: Clay Jar Christians in God's Service* (Louisville: Office of the General Assembly, Presbyterian Church [U.S.A.], 2002), 5.

[108]See Michael W. Goheen, "Continuing Steps Towards a Missional Hermeneutic," *Fidelis: A Journal of Redeemer Pacific College* (3): 49-99.

[109]Hunsberger, "Proposals for a Missional Hermeneutic."

[110]See Walter C. Kaiser Jr., *Mission in the Old Testament: Israel as a Light to the Nations*, 2nd ed. (Grand Rapids: Baker Academic, 2012).

be sure, the Old Testament poses interpretive challenges to the Christian preacher not presented by, for instance, the epistles. Nevertheless, the formation of God's people for witness is appropriate in a hermeneutical framework for reading the Old Testament.

To summarize what we've discussed to this point, in a missional hermeneutic the preacher engages with the text through the interpretive matrix of Jesus Christ, foregrounding the formational purpose of the biblical witness and carrying that purpose through the interpretation. The final element of a missional hermeneutic is the locatedness of the community of interpreters, their particularity in space and time. The locatedness or particularity to which I refer, however, is not understood first in terms of culture, race, gender, socioeconomic status, education or any other aspect of human life that distinguishes one group from another. Recalling Barth's assertion noted earlier, when the Christian community considers human persons, it considers them first and decisively in light of God's revelation in Jesus Christ. This means that when we consider the social locatedness of a particular Christian community in a missional hermeneutic, we must first and primarily consider the particularity of that community in light of its identity as the people of God, whom God has gathered, upbuilt and sent to bear witness to Jesus Christ. To be sure, other aspects of their existence come to bear in their interpretation of scripture. But the fundamental orientation of their social locatedness is as a community of witness to Jesus Christ in and to a particular place and time.

Michael Barram has done the most to advance this understanding of social locatedness in relation to the interpretation of scripture. The bulk of his work has been to build connections between biblical and missiological studies, attempting to press each discipline with questions from the other, and he has engaged a range of hermeneutical issues.[111] Barram helpfully elucidates the importance of social location in a missional hermeneutic in the proceedings of a talk given to the Gospel and Our Culture Network.

He begins by highlighting the importance of questions. He recognizes that, as a concept, "missional hermeneutic" is very much in development and there is much elasticity and ambiguity in the conversation, and

---

[111]He has done this most notably in Michael Barram, *Mission and Moral Reflection in Paul* (New York: Peter Lang, 2006).

indeed there are many questions. This, he argues, is healthy. He writes, "I suggest that it would be difficult to overestimate the significance of good questions for a viable missional hermeneutic."[112] He cautions against reducing a missional hermeneutic to a method, which could easily become a "faddish method" and be reduced to a set of assumptions and tools. Moreover, he highlights the importance of asking questions that are self-critical, that examine our own assumptions and call attention to our blind spots. Furthermore, he notes the importance of questions in the biblical literature for deepening understanding of God's character and mission. He writes, "Questions punctuate critical turning points in Scripture, in many cases providing the opportunity for a deeper understanding and appropriation of God's purposes and intentions."[113]

Thus he argues that a missional hermeneutic should primarily be a set of questions brought to the text from the located position of the Christian community, questions we ask the text and questions the text may ask us. By this Barram means that a missional hermeneutic should not be associated with a particular exegetical methodology but should comprise questions that are brought to bear in the use of any method. He writes, "The uniqueness of a missional hermeneutic will be found in its relentless commitment to articulating critical questions aimed at faithfully articulating the *missio Dei* and the community's role within the purposes of God."[114] Moreover, these critical questions arise from the located position of the community of God's people who are sent to bear witness to Jesus Christ in a particular place and time.

Barram concludes his argument by listing several questions he regularly asks himself in the interpretation of scripture. He poses questions such as "In what ways are we tempted to 'spiritualize' the concrete implications of the gospel as articulated in this text?" and "In what ways does the text challenge us to rethink our often-cozy relationships with power and privilege?" These questions are not meant to be universal but reflect his own particular location and especially the blind spots and oft-overlooked

---

[112]Michael Barram, "'Located' Questions for a Missional Hermeneutic," The Gospel and Our Culture Network, Nov. 6, 2006, gocn.org/resources/articles/located-questions-missional-hermeneutic.
[113]Ibid.
[114]Ibid.

assumptions of his context. He suggests that the questions may be the same for another context or may be very different. Interestingly, as George Hunsberger notes in commenting on these questions, Barram's questions both read the text and the interpreter simultaneously.[115]

Barram argues convincingly that a missional hermeneutic brings focused and critical questions to the interpretations of a text that arise from the locatedness of the Christian community as the people of God and that aim to deepen the community's discernment of its calling and task as a sent witness. He has not proposed universal questions but argues that these questions must arise from the context. One might wonder at this point, however, how one develops such questions. This appears particularly vexing if the questions Barram envisions are ones that challenge assumptions, highlight cultural captivities and reductions of the gospel, and call attention to blind spots. For instance, a reviewer of *Foolishness to the Greeks* by Lesslie Newbigin remarked that trying to criticize one's own culture is like "trying to push a bus while sitting in it." Newbigin picks up on this critique and continues:

> Can I get off the bus? Can I stand outside myself and look at my way of thinking as a critic of it? More specifically, can this book . . . the Bible, call into question the whole way in which I, as a member of this society, understand the world? . . . Where can we find that Archimedean point outside our culture? Are we compelled to sit tight in the bus, even if it is headed over the precipice? Or can we appeal to the Bible to call our culture in question?[116]

Where can we find a point from outside our culture from which to approach our culture with new critical awareness? In brief, the answer is through crosscultural engagement. This is the experience of Newbigin himself as a foreign missionary who gained a critical awareness of his own Western presuppositions through immersion in an Indian, and specifically Hindu, context. Moreover, the importance of crosscultural engagement is rightly stressed by James Brownson in his response to George Hunsberger's "Proposals for a Missional Hermeneutic." He writes, "A missional hermeneutic envisions a three-way conversation between

---

[115]Hunsberger, "Proposals for a Missional Hermeneutic."
[116]Newbigin, *The Gospel in a Pluralist Society*, 96.

the reader, an 'other' who hears the text differently, and the text itself. It is this notion of otherness, implicit in reading the text in the midst of crosscultural encounters, which is vital to a missional hermeneutic."[117]

Who is this "other"? I would argue that at a most basic level the "other" can be another person in the local Christian community. Though two people may share the same basic cultural context, there is still much difference—much "otherness"—between them. As a pastor leading Bible studies, I am always amazed at the diverse interpretations that arise when a few seemingly homogenous people have a free-ranging discussion about the meaning of a text. This leads back to the importance of a community of interpreters, the communal preaching ministry that I stressed earlier in this chapter. More dramatically, the "other" can be a person who is located in a completely different social context. Darrell Guder notes in this vein the kind of crosscultural experiences that regularly occur in "mission trips" from North America to the developing world. He writes, "Experiences with Christian communities in the non-Western world are profoundly converting for culturally captive North Americans. Seeing ourselves and our culture through the lenses of other cultures sensitizes us to our cultural captivity."[118] When a reader encounters an "other" interpretation of a text, that interpretation illumines the hidden assumptions and blind spots that shaped the reader's initial interpretation.

As we conclude this discussion of the importance of crosscultural encounter in the development of missional hermeneutical questions, it may be helpful to place this in dialogue with Anna Carter Florence's homiletical use of Mary McClintock Fulkerson's investigations into the differing interpretations of text according to social location. Recall that Fulkerson found that a middle class Presbyterian woman and a poor Pentecostal woman would interpret the same text in very different yet faithful ways because of different "subject positions, purposes, and interpretation methods."[119] Moreover, Fulkerson argued, they shift the interpretation of a text to quietly or publicly confront sin in the community's dominant reading. You

---

[117]Brownson, "A Response at SBL to Hunsberger's 'Proposals . . .'"
[118]Darrell L. Guder, "Missional Hermeneutics: The Missional Vocation of the Congregation—and How Scripture Shapes That Calling," *Mission Focus: Annual Review* 15 (2007), 135-36.
[119]Florence, *Preaching as Testimony*, 84.

will recall that a reading of a text is a "graft," an interpretation of that text from that community's particular place. Sometimes one person or group of people shift the interpretation slightly to create a new interpretation, a "graf(ph)t." This graf(ph)t is a signal that something is wrong with the "graft." Florence writes that, theologically, this graf(ph)t is confronting sin hidden in the normative interpretation.

The point of making this connection is to note that we have already encountered a specific instance of the homiletical use of social locatedness in the interpretation of biblical texts. Florence's concern for multiple interpretations and interpretations that arise from the margins finds a place in this aspect of a missional homiletic, but it is important to recognize that this missional hermeneutic is different in at least two respects: (1) "locatedness" in a missional hermeneutic is primarily oriented around the community's identity as the sent people of God in a given culture, and only secondarily around various other aspects of individual or corporate identity such as race or gender, and (2) the whole community is called to a continual, ongoing "graf(ph)ting," what Guder has called a "continual conversion," of the way it interprets scripture. Graf(ph)ting, the task of continually revising interpretations of texts in response to the ongoing activity of God's Spirit, is not simply the work of some within the community but the work of the whole community that finds itself bearing witness to the new reality disclosed and being disclosed in Jesus Christ.

As we turn to consider specifically the equipping nature of the preacher's witness, here is a summary of the missional hermeneutic just sketched: (1) the confession of Jesus Christ is the interpretive matrix through which the preacher reads the text; (2) the primary purpose of scripture is the formation of the community for witness as the people of God; (3) the preacher reads the text with questions that arise from the particular locatedness of the community, questions that especially challenge cultural blind spots and point to areas for continued conversion.

PREACHING CONFESSES JESUS CHRIST THROUGH A MISSIONAL INTERPRETATION OF SCRIPTURE . . . TO EQUIP THE COMMUNITY FOR WITNESS TO THE WORLD

In a sense, this whole homiletical proposal has been leading to this last aspect of missional preaching: preaching confesses Jesus Christ, through a missional interpretation of scripture, in order to *equip the community for witness to the world*. Throughout our conversation, the "community" that gathers before the preacher in public worship has been in view: as those who nurture, confirm and test one's call to and gift for preaching; as those who help shape, hear and respond to the preacher's confession; as those who have been gathered by Jesus Christ and commissioned to bear witness to him; and as those who have a particular location in place and time from which they approach the interpretation of scripture. It is now important, however, to press more deeply into the nature of this community and how preaching is in service to it.

In relation to wider conversations in the area of homiletics, it is here that missional preaching can be most distinctive. A missional homiletic foregrounds the theological, and specifically vocational, identity of the congregation as it relates to preaching. Though many homiletical proposals, especially of the past fifty years, give close attention to the listeners, we are considering the listeners from an ecclesiological standpoint. Who are they who listen to the preacher, not simply as atomized individuals, but as a community? And furthermore, what is the nature of this community, not from a hermeneutical, phenomenological, anthropological or sociological perspective, but from a theological perspective?

In other words, we are inquiring into the theological, and more precisely the ecclesiological, identity of the audience the preacher addresses. In chapter two, we examined Barth's "Holy Spirit and the Sending of the Christian Community" in detail in order to lay the groundwork for understanding the Christian community in a missional homiletic. This was appropriate in two ways: (1) David Bosch argues that Karl Barth is the twentieth-century theologian who most fully developed an understanding of a "missional" God and thus a "missional" church. Indeed, as Darrell Guder has noted, if one does a digital search of the *Church Dogmatics*, one finds that the language of mission is pervasive in Barth's theology, both in German and in English.[120] (2) Barth writes in a spiral sort of way, circling back to themes he has developed earlier as he builds his theological ar-

---

[120]Guder, "Missional Hermeneutics: The Missional Authority of Scripture," 118.

gument. Thus, in "The Holy Spirit and the Sending of the Christian Community," he presupposes and explicitly draws on the arguments he has developed earlier in the *Doctrine of Reconciliation*. Now, as we seek to understand the Christian community in the framework of a missional homiletic, we will draw heavily from that exploration of Barth and also from the findings of research into missional congregations.

This final piece of the missional homiletical puzzle will have three distinct parts. First, the congregation is the basic unit of Christian witness. This is axiomatic in missional theological conversations, but we need to unpack what that means, especially here in this missional homiletic. Second, preaching is a distinct form of witness that centers, contextualizes and kindles the multiform witness of the community. Third, and finally, the sermon arises from and moves into the larger witness of the baptized people of God.

In the *Continuing Conversion of the Church*, Darrell Guder notes that *Mission and Evangelism: An Ecumenical Affirmation*, published in 1982–83, says, "A vital instrument for the fulfillment of the missionary vocation of the Church is the local congregation." He then remarks that if the document were written today, it would probably be revised to read, "*The* vital instrument . . ."[121] That conviction permeates the missional theological conversation and is a basic impulse behind this missional homiletic. It is imperative and essential for preaching to equip the congregation for its missional vocation. Yet what does it mean to say that the congregation is the basic unit of Christian witness?

First, it is the basic unit because we must consider the gathered Christian community as logically prior to individual Christians who are members of it. Barth makes this point as he transitions from "The Event of Reconciliation Is Sanctification" to "The Holy Spirit and the Upbuilding of the Christian Community." He argues that the individual Christian "exists on the basis of and in the meaning and purpose of the community."[122] That is to say, one cannot understand an individual Christian except to understand that person in the context where he or she is in fact an individual Christian—in the Christian community. Moreover, the Christian

---

[121]Darrell L. Guder, *The Continuing Conversion of the Church* (Grand Rapids: Eerdmans, 2000), 145.
[122]Barth, *CD* IV/3.2, 615.

community is logically prior to the individual Christian. Barth argues that it is only an appearance that the Holy Spirit creates Christian love, and this leads to individual Christians, and then the Christian community, and thus the church. In fact, an individual person becomes a Christian in a definite historical context, as a part of the Christian community. For instance, Barth notes, the justified person is found in the Apostles' Creed as part of the community, when one confesses, "I believe . . . in the holy catholic church." Moreover, one might think of the context in which a person would recite that baptismal creed: in and to the congregation on the occasion of one's entrance into the community.

This is not to dissolve the individual into the community such that one loses sight altogether of the individual Christians who are gathered, upbuilt and sent as a community. Rather, it is to say that the community is logically prior to the individual, and one must always keep both in view. Whenever one considers the individual Christian, one is considering this person in his or her interrelationship to the Christian community; whenever one considers the Christian community, it is in interrelationship with the individual members who are a part of it. To say that the congregation is the basic unit of Christian witness is to say that the congregation as a reciprocally related community of individual members is the basic unit of Christian witness. It is not simply the congregation as community, but as community and individuals, as the "gathered and scattered" church.

Second, the Christian community is the people of God in a particular time and place. It is important to note that when I refer to a Christian community, and when Barth does as well, it is in reference to a local congregation, a parish or a fellowship—a distinct and located group of people. In one sense the community is located in a rich sociocultural context, which can be described and analyzed through a variety of social-scientific theories and methods. However, in a more generally applicable sense, as Barth argues, the community is located in a dialectical "sphere." This sphere is, on the one hand, what Barth calls "the sphere of God's providence." That is to say, the Christian community always finds itself in a place and time where Jesus Christ is Lord, where God is sovereign. Even if it does not appear to be the case, even if the community meets resistance and there is much that opposes God's will, nevertheless the community exists in the sphere of God's providence. Human history with all of its events is preceded, accompanied, and its future determined by the will and action of God, and it exists under the parental providence of God.

Yet on the other hand, the community is located in a sphere of human confusion. This is not a state that humanity is in but rather the way Barth characterizes the activity of human persons. God's good creation is not obliterated, but human persons persistently intertwine God's good creation with the negation of God's good creation. For instance, human persons take the good gift of intelligence and use it to harm their neighbors; they take the ample supply of creation and exploit it for selfish gain. Referring to this entangling that humans do, Barth writes, "It is not the glorious or shameful acts, but their compromises, which give to their history its distinctive aspect from the human standpoint."[123] It is not that we are blind but that we squint and "with this squinting eye that [we] try to live."[124]

Thus, the Christian community finds itself located in a place and time where God is sovereign and where humanity is engaged in the entanglement and confusion of God's good creation and the negation of God's good creation. There is much that may be discovered and understood about the sociocultural location of a Christian community, especially for homiletics, in terms of language, traditions, symbols and rituals. Nevertheless, theologically speaking the location of the Christian community is in the sphere of God's providence and human confusion. The unique commission of the Christian community is not simply to bear witness to this twofold state of affairs but most importantly to live as the people of God to whom it is given to know the new reality in Jesus Christ.

As I argued earlier in discussing the content of the confession, in Jesus Christ God has assumed human form in order to be the human one whom God intended in the good creation, a human who, in Eberhard Busch's terms, is accepted by God and who accepts God. In Jesus Christ, the apparent finality of the tension between God and humanity has been reconciled, as Jesus Christ has removed human confusion, restored order and concluded peace between God and humanity. In Jesus Christ, God himself has become the one who does not look with "squinted eye," who

---

[123]Barth, *CD* IV/3.2, 696.
[124]Ibid.

does not see the world as an inevitable entanglement of God's goodness and the negation of God's goodness, but one who sees clearly and resists temptation, who is faithful to God even unto death. Moreover, in the resurrection God affirms that Jesus is in fact this truly human one, and in his resurrection he reaches out to proclaim to humanity that all of this has in fact been accomplished in him.

The local congregation as it exists in a particular time and place is the Christian community whom God's Spirit has empowered to respond in faith to the confession of Jesus Christ and to know by faith this new reality that is hidden in the apparent state of world affairs. Moreover, this is the community whom the Spirit is gathering, equipping and sending to live and exist in the world in light of and on the basis of this new reality. The community's knowledge of the new reality is by faith, yet that does not mean the life of the community is timid. Rather, it acts with complete confidence in Jesus Christ, making purposeful decisions and choices that indicate the new reality to the world.

Indeed, the Christian community is a people who are in the world and a part of the world, living on the same level as the world and not hovering above it or planted within it as aliens. The church exists as Christ exists, bound to him as his witnesses. This means the Christian community is in solidarity with the world and is for the world as Christ himself is for the world; the Christian community is in the flesh as Christ himself was in the flesh. In understanding the Christian community as the earthly-historical form of Jesus Christ, it is very important to qualify that the Christian community does not become Christ for the world, somehow substituting itself in his place. Rather the community takes its form and dimension from him, bearing witness to him in its speech and action, its thought and choices.

Moreover, the community is empowered to do this by the Holy Spirit working within it. The Holy Spirit is the power that joins the community to Jesus Christ, that enables it to confess Jesus Christ, to know the new reality by faith and to live on the basis of the new reality amid the confusion of world affairs. Barth understands the relationship between the Holy Spirit and the Christian community as dynamic and historical rather than static and immobile. In essence, this means that the identity of the community as the body of Christ is not a static state of being but an active state of existence. The union is continually effected by the Holy Spirit as the Spirit gathers, sanctifies and sends the church to bear witness to him.

Finally, and only in this sense, the Christian community is a parable of the kingdom of God. As the community bears witness to Jesus Christ, forming and patterning itself after him, it becomes a representation of the kingdom of God to the world. To put it another way, as the community lives under Christ's lordship it demonstrates a likeness of what it means to live under the reign of God, reconciled to God, faithful to God and obedient to God's will. At no time will the community be the kingdom of God—for the community is always being sanctified, continually being converted. Yet by the empowering of God's Spirit, the community can be a likeness or a parable of the kingdom.

Thus, we return to the question that began this excursion: what does it mean to say the local congregation is the basic unit of Christian witness? First, it means the focus shifts from the individual Christian—for instance, the individual preacher or teacher—to the local Christian community, and the individual is then seen in interrelationship to the Christian community. For homiletics, this means the focus on the preacher is misplaced unless the preacher is understood in his or her interrelationship to the Christian community. Or the focus on the listener is misplaced unless that listener is understood as an individual who is gathered into the Christian community and shares in the community's identity and calling. Second, it means the local congregation is the community that exists in the sphere of God's providence and human confusion, yet that by the empowering of God's Spirit confesses Jesus Christ and knows a new reality by faith. Moreover, the local congregation is the community God's Spirit empowers to bear witness to the new reality as the body of Christ in the midst of world affairs. The local congregation is the community that, in its gathered and scattered life, demonstrates a provisional representation of life in the kingdom of God.

Before turning to consider the relationship between preaching and the witness of the congregation, it is worth connecting this understanding of the local congregation to Lesslie Newbigin's oft-quoted description of the congregation as "hermeneutic of the gospel." Newbigin's idea connects not only with the description here of the local congregation but also with

points raised earlier in our discussion of confession as the most appropriate mode of preaching in our postmodern situation. In making his
argument for the congregation as hermeneutic of the gospel, Newbigin is
describing the difficulty of confessing the gospel in a Western society that
has been shaped by an Enlightenment rationality, is characterized by a
"reigning ideology of pluralism," and where confessions such as the cross
and resurrection of Jesus Christ are not considered "public truth" but
"private opinion." He makes this case in *The Gospel in a Pluralist Society*
and in a chapter near the end asks the question "How is it possible that
the gospel should be credible, that people should come to believe that the
power which has the last word in human affairs is represented by a man
hanging on a cross?" He responds, "I am suggesting that the only answer,
the only hermeneutic of the gospel, is a congregation of men and women
who believe it and live by it." Of course, he acknowledges, there are many
other activities by which we communicate the gospel to the world, yet, he
writes, "I am saying that all these are secondary, and that they have the
power to accomplish their purpose only as they are rooted in and lead
back to a believing community."[125] Without taking on Newbigin's full argument about the challenges posed to the church by a "pluralist society,"
nevertheless it is in precisely this sense that I believe the local congregation is the basic unit of witness to Jesus Christ.

The next step in understanding the equipping nature of missional
preaching is to explore the relationship between the distinct confession
of preaching and the varied witness of the congregation. Recall first that
I have defined preaching as the specific form of proclamation that occurs
in the liturgy of public worship in response to the reading of scripture.
Thus it is only one discrete form of proclamation. Furthermore, it is not
novel to say the congregation has a varied witness or that "proclamation"
encompasses more activities than preaching. Indeed, this is both implicit
and explicit in the homiletical proposals we have explored here. What is
noticeably missing, however, from these homiletical nods toward other
forms of the congregation's witness is any sense of the unique role of the
sermon in relationship to these other forms of witness. If preaching is a

---

[125]The quotations in this paragraph all come from Lesslie Newbigin, *The Gospel in a Pluralist Society*
(Grand Rapids: Eerdmans, 1989), 222-33.

specialized form of proclamation given to and located within the Christian community, and if it is understood as part of the whole "faithful action" of the community, then what is that relationship? What is the unique work of preaching within the multiform and varied witness of the church? I contend that the unique witness of preaching can be characterized by three distinct yet related activities that have been alluded to already in various ways: centering, contextualizing and kindling.

First, preaching centers the congregation in its confession of Jesus Christ, who is the new reality to whom all other forms of witness point. This is in indeed Barth's description of preaching as he delineates the twelve ways in which the community performs its task of service. Recall that he is reluctant to use the term *die Predigt* because it is an overburdened word, but he does use it in this specific sense. Preaching is the explicit proclamation of the gospel in the assembled community, "in the midst of the divine service." What is at issue in preaching? Barth asks. "Decisively that the community, and with it the world, should remind itself or be reminded explicitly of the witness with which it is charged, that it should find reassurance as to its content, that reflected in it Jesus Christ Himself should speak afresh to it, that it should be summoned afresh to His service in the world."[126] There is much in this description that reflects Barth's unique understanding of preaching, which is necessary to unpack here. Specifically, in the remark that "reflected in it Jesus Christ himself should speak afresh to it," Barth is referring to his sense that Jesus Christ, in the power of the Holy Spirit, is always the one who preaches—even as the human preacher preaches. Nevertheless, the important element here to notice is that in preaching the community is reminded of the witness with which it is charged, reassured of its content and called afresh to Christ's service in the world.

As the community carries out its witness, it does so in a wide variety of forms and ranging across all areas of public and private life. The crucial question is, what unites these various forms of witness; what is their common center? In one sense it is the new reality of Jesus Christ to which they all bear witness. The constant renewal of this center is vital

---

126Barth, *CD* IV/3.2, 867.

to the witness of the church because, as Barth argues, the new reality of Jesus Christ is the very possibility of the community's witness. The community exists only as it exists in Christ, bound to him as his witnesses. If the varied forms of witness of the community become severed from their basis in Jesus Christ, they lose their coherence as many forms of one witness. More deeply, they also lose their power and potential. The power hidden within the witness of the church is the working of God's Spirit to enable the church to hear the confession of Jesus Christ and bear witness to him. The Spirit of God is the power that enables the witness of the church to have any possibility of effect, and the Spirit of God bears witness to none other than Jesus Christ.

We also see this centering function of preaching in David Lose's understanding of the confession of preaching. Lose approaches this through his engagement with the postliberal homiletics of Charles Campbell. The goal of Campbell's proposal of preaching the narrative identity of Jesus Christ is to impart to the church its communal identity as "followers of that rendered character, Jesus Christ."[127] Indeed, Lose shares Campbell's goal, but he believes that narrative does not have the ability to do what Campbell argues it can do. As I discussed at length above, confession is the more appropriate way to center the church in a communal identity and offers the critical distance necessary for the community to respond in faith as followers of the one who is confessed. Moreover, the confession of preaching forms the congregation in a communal identity, and it is in just this sense that I am suggesting here that preaching is centering confession.

However, it is not enough to say that preaching is a centering confession, and this brings us to the second aspect of the distinctiveness of the witness of preaching. It is also a contextualizing confession. In one sense, this is true as we have seen it presented in the homiletical proposals in this project. In preaching the preacher comes from the community, is sent by the community as a representative of that community, and carries to the encounter with the text the richly contextual life of that community. The preacher goes to hear the confession of Jesus Christ coming through the text and speaking directly to the contextualized ex-

---

[127]Lose, *Confessing Jesus Christ*, 120.

perience of the community, which includes both the preacher and the congregation. The response of the preacher to the confession of the text, the sermon, is a contextual confession.

Yet missional theology particularly highlights another sense in which the sermon is a contextualizing confession, as preaching helps the congregation to discern its unique missional vocation. In a general sense, the missional vocation of the congregation is to bear witness to Jesus Christ, and preaching as centering confession equips the congregation to do just this. Indeed, the missional researchers of *Treasure in Clay Jars* found in the congregations they studied that a sense of communal identity was essential, "shared pervasively in a congregation that knows it is caught up into God's intent for the world." This shared sense of identity shapes the community and the members of it. However, as George Hunsberger writes, "When attentive to the voice of God, a congregation discerns not only that vocation that is shared across the whole church, but also its particular calling to express that vocation in its own place and time."[128]

Hunsberger continues that these congregations discerned their specific calling in relation to *where* they were contextually, *when* they were in the flow of history, *who* they were in relation to their tradition, and *why* they were in terms of their purpose of demonstrating God's coming reign. In a missional homiletic, when the preacher takes a congregation with her to the text in preparation for preaching, these are the types of missionally contextual questions she brings. She is not simply asking what the needs of the community are, what their strengths or challenges are, where they need to be encouraged in faith or summoned to deeper discipleship—though these are important questions. The missional preacher also asks questions about missional contextuality: What is our context geographically, culturally, socially? What is our location in the course of history and in the changing world in which we live? Who are we in relation to our tradition, and what does our context have to say back to our tradition? Why has God placed us here in this time and place? What particular aspect of God's reign might God be calling us to demonstrate? Certainly not all of these questions will be a part of every dialogue with a text. But they are

---

[128]Barrett et al., *Treasure in Clay Jars*, 38.

there with the preacher in the encounter with the text, and they give contextual shape and dimension to the confession of Jesus Christ that the
preacher hears and is called to proclaim.

In the churches studied in *Treasure*, the ministry of preaching was vital
in helping the congregation discern its contextual missional vocation and
continually center the community in it. Preachers did this through specific
and repeated messages, sometimes very simple statements of the community's vocation, and through intentional cultivation of a "missional
awareness." Indeed, the contention of missional theologians is that the
broad reductionism of the North American church is one in which
members believe that the church exists to dispense the benefits of Christ
in one form or another. Cultivating missional awareness is the long-term
project of helping a congregation see that the benefits of Christ are theirs
so that they may bear witness in the world. To use a well-worn phrase, the
church is blessed to be a blessing. In some instances, researchers have
found that this missional awareness of contextual vocation arose through
a catalytic moment, such as the arrival of a new pastor, or slowly developed
over a long period of time, or came through the conscious reflection of the
community. Nevertheless, however this distinctive sense of vocation develops, the role of preaching is crucial. The confession of preaching helps
to center and renew the community in its contextual vocation.

It is important to recognize several qualifications here. First, this distinctive missional vocation is not something a preacher simply imports
into a congregation. Though the preacher may indeed be a catalyst of
discernment, a sense of missional vocation is something that is pervasive
in the life of the community, an identity that is intricately woven into the
context of the community and is shared by the members of the community. As the researchers noted in the First Presbyterian Church in
Bellevue, Washington, "The pastor in his preaching worked to cultivate
a 'missional church' perspective."[129] *Cultivate* is the important word. A
distinctive understanding of missional vocation must take root and grow
within a local congregation; it cannot simply be announced from the
pulpit or printed on the back of a bulletin.

---

[129] Ibid., 48.

Moreover, this growth of a distinctive missional vocation is ultimately a work of God's Spirit. It is in this sense that Hunsberger speaks of the charism of a congregation, which is to say the spiritual gifting of a congregation. Hunsberger writes:

> The gift of the Spirit to fulfill the calling comes in the course of the faithful response. It becomes evident only over time what that gift, that charism, has been. Once evident, its presence in the pulse of a congregation's life is a gift to the whole church toward the fulfillment of its missional nature. And in fact it is a gift from God to the world that is coming to know Christ because this charism has come to expression in this congregation that takes its vocation seriously.[130]

This must serve as a word of both encouragement and warning. It is encouragement because as a congregation pursues its missional vocation and is faithful to its calling, it may be assured that God's Spirit will empower it with the gifts it needs to bear its witness. Yet it is a warning that the fulfillment of missional vocation is not a program or initiative that can simply be implemented by the congregation's leadership. Even more to the point, it is not a method that can be used to revitalize dying congregations who have seen their membership and attendance decline. A sense of distinctive and widely shared missional vocation in a community, and the gifts that must come to fulfill that vocation, are ultimately gifts of God's Spirit.

Thus, preaching is centering confession that grounds the congregation in its faith in Jesus Christ and contextualizing confession that helps shape a distinctive sense of missional vocation. Finally, the confession of preaching is distinctive among the varied forms of witness in the community because it is kindling confession. The word *kindling* is used here in the sense of arousing and inspiring, of "igniting" the confession of the community. Lose refers to this when he discusses the distinctiveness of preaching in relation to the larger conversation of the faithful. He writes that preaching is a catalyst, a "prompting, focusing, shaping, and nurturing" within the community's larger conversation. In one sense, and this is largely what Lose means, this happens by virtue of the nature of

---

[130]Ibid., 58.

confession itself. A confession, as assertive discourse, calls for a response. The preacher's sermon, as a confession that purports to refer to reality and speak the truth, calls for response—an affirmation, a challenge, a rejection, a clarification, a question spoken by the one who has heard. In this sense, the confession of preaching regularly sparks the confessional conversation of the community.

In addition, the confession of preaching kindles through its engagement with scripture. Scripture as a missionary document has a formative role in the sense that it equips the church for witness, or forms the church in its identity as God's people. In approaching scripture from a missional perspective, in some way the preacher asks how this text formed God's people for missional faithfulness then and how it does so today. In asking the question "How does it do so today?" preaching is nurturing and "kindling" the ongoing witness of the community.

John Dally picks up on this theme in *Choosing the Kingdom* when he argues that preaching should engage the biblical images and descriptions of the kingdom of God so that those metaphors come alive in the imagination of the congregation, sparking them to see how the kingdom of God may be present among them in their context. Or, as Guder writes, "People do not automatically know how the reign of God works. Citizenship in the reign of God is learned."[131] The biblical images and metaphors of the kingdom of God, the accounts of God's people in their struggles—sometimes successful and sometimes not—to be faithful to God, and especially the narrative accounts of the life of Jesus Christ, who embodies the reign of God, are all kindling for stoking the witness of the community. As the preacher engages these biblical texts from a missional perspective through the interpretive matrix of Jesus Christ and contextualizes them toward the missional formation of the community, then preaching becomes confession fueling the community's ongoing witness.

Preaching as a kindling confession that ignites the flame of the church anew each time it is performed connects us to a much broader theme present in Barth's understanding of preaching. In this discussion we have been describing preaching as the ongoing, centering, contextual-

---

[131]Ibid., 72.

izing confession that slowly helps form a congregation in its distinctive missional vocation and equips them to bear their witness to the world. Indeed, I would argue that this is how most preachers and congregations experience the ministry of preaching, week to week and year to year. Yet in a sense Barth argues that preaching is always creating the church anew. Barth writes:

> To this extent all preaching is on the human level a new constitution, and outwardly a new manifestation, of the community as a fellowship of ministry and witness. For in all true preaching there is made a new and specific reference to that which, according to the Gospel which it has to attest, has been accomplished by God and is manifested to be real and true. True preaching is, in fact, preaching of Jesus Christ, of the radical alteration of the situation between God and man, between heaven and earth, as it has been effected in Him.[132]

This is, perhaps, the most full sense in which preaching is kindling confession. Whenever Jesus Christ is confessed, Christ himself in the power of his Spirit is gathering the community to be his witnesses. In the power of his Spirit, he is creating the community anew at its deepest level, to be a provisional sign of his reign, of the coming kingdom of God and the reconciliation of God and humanity that he has accomplished.

In this sense, to recall Barth's multilayered understanding of the doctrine of reconciliation, the individual and the community do not experience the various movements of Christ's reconciliation as a linear progression. It is not that one appropriates justification and the community is gathered, and then one is sanctified and the community is upbuilt, and then one is called and the community is sent. These aspects of reconciliation to God in Christ are treated separately for analytical purposes. Rather, in the experience of the individual and community, this justification, sanctifying and calling, this gathering, upbuilding and sending is a continuing event of appropriating the new reality, a continuing event of hearing the proclamation of Jesus Christ and responding in faith and obedience. Moreover, by God's grace and Spirit, it happens whenever the gospel is preached.

---

[132]Barth, *CD* IV/3.2 , 868.

To summarize so far, the congregation is the basic unit of witness to Jesus Christ, and preaching is a confession that centers, contextualizes and kindles the witness of the congregation. Finally, missional preaching arises from and moves into the witness of the baptized community. In a sense, I am saying again that missional preaching is contextual, but here I mean that missional preaching is contextual as a confession that arises from the whole witness of the Christian community and then leads into its further witness. I have already argued that a missional interpretation of the text and missional preaching should arise from the lived experience of the community. Yet often this "lived experience" is taken to mean only the community's needs, struggles, burdens and challenges—the "problem" to which the "solution" of the gospel corresponds. Here I want to stress that the lived experience of the community also includes its witness to Jesus Christ as the Holy Spirit is at work within and among its members. This witness, which is ultimately the activity of God with God's people, gives rise to the specific proclamation of the gospel in the preaching moment. Moreover, this specific proclamation, these words that powerfully correspond to and interpret deeds, leads into further witness.

Again Newbigin is helpful in elucidating this point. He argues that the ministry of preaching, and indeed the whole witness of the church, is set in the context of the ongoing reign of God. Moreover, the witness of the church continues in the pattern of Jesus Christ's own ministry, wherein his verbal teaching and deeds of power corresponded, and who is himself the reign of God. In the same way, Newbigin argues, the church must understand its word, works and presence as one unified witness. He writes:

> Why should people believe our preaching that the kingdom of God has come near in Jesus if they see no sign that anything is happening as a result, if they can see no evidence that disease and ignorance and cruelty and injustice are being challenged and overcome? Why should they believe our words if there is nothing happening to authenticate them?[133]

Words and deeds must be held together in the witness of the church, for words interpret deeds, and deeds authenticate the words. Similar to New-

---

[133]Lesslie Newbigin, *Mission in Christ's Way: A Gift, a Command, an Assurance* (New York: Friendship Press, 1988), 11.

bigin's argument that the congregation is the "hermeneutic of the gospel," here the gospel, especially in its radical and countercultural claims, becomes credible to a watching world through the life of a community in which God is at work. Again drawing on Newbigin's words, preaching is credible when behind it lies "a costly engagement with the powers of evil, with all the powers that rob men and women of their humanity, and . . . [when it calls] men and women to share in the same costly engagement."[134]

In this way, missional preaching arises from and moves into the witness of the community. Missional preaching does not simply arise from a preacher's study of the text in a quiet room, though that is indispensable. It also arises from the experience of Christian men and women in the community as they have struggled to bear witness to the gospel in every aspect of their lives and as God has empowered their witness to be, in fact, witness to Jesus Christ. It arises from a pastoral ministry that is engaged with the community in its struggle to bear faithful witness and that watches closely for signs of the activity of God in its midst. This again refers us to what Cardoza-Orlandi means when he says missional preaching does not simply address the needs of the community or help its members discern God's activity, but joins the community's struggle to live out its faith in its place and time to the rich Christian tradition.

The preacher must keep this struggle in view because this struggle is the test of the formation to which missional preaching intends. Indeed, the confession of the congregation, made in words and deeds as members of the community lead their varied lives, is the both the fruit and the test of missional preaching. Darrell Guder elaborates on this:

> The test of missional formation in the gathered community is the lay apostolate. The concern is for how our members live and why they live that way when we are not gathered. The concern is how we gather for one-seventh of our time in order to be equipped for the apostolate of the sixth-sevenths of our time.[135]

Of course, Guder is being overly optimistic in his division of one-seventh and six-sevenths. The more common experience in North American churches is that the community gathers for one hour during the

---

[134]Ibid., 12.
[135]Guder, "Missional Hermeneutics: The Missional Vocation of the Congregation," 141.

week and rarely for more, and thus it spends only a minuscule fraction of its time together. Yet this only reinforces the point: preaching, which often makes up one-third or more of the one hour per week that the community is gathered, must be closely connected to the life of the community when it is apart. The vast proportion of the witness born by the Christian community is born in the daily lives of its members. Missional preaching must arise from this daily witness, center it in the confession of Jesus Christ, and kindle further witness as the community scatters again.

What might a preacher look for in the daily witness of the community as signs of God's activity and faithful witness? I think the patterns discerned in *Treasure in Clay Jars* are most promising in relation to this question as they are richly suggestive of what missional formation looks like in the North American context. Taken together they form a lens through which the preacher might consider the daily life of the congregation and look for signs of faithful witness and God's activity. For example, the third pattern of missional faithfulness is taking risks as a contrast community. In this sense, the missional community understands itself in light of the gospel, is raising questions about the implications of the gospel with regard to cultural captivity, and is taking risks "for the sake of the gospel."[136] As the preacher interprets a text, questions about the implications of the gospel and cultural captivity will arise. However, these questions must also be directed into the daily life of the congregation. Moreover, the preacher asks these questions not simply to look for examples of how the community is culturally captive, but also to see how lived discipleship interacts with the wider culture. The preacher is looking for instances of risks that are taken for the sake of the gospel, risks that place the community and its members in contrast to the surrounding culture.

For example, in light of biblical teaching on the Sabbath, it is common to lament the state of Sabbath-keeping and reverence for the Lord's Day in the United States. Often sermons are preached that both encourage Sabbath-keeping and simultaneously take aim at a sports and leisure culture that supposedly undermines discipleship and draws many people

---

[136]Barrett et al., *Treasure in Clay Jars*, 74.

away from weekly corporate worship. Of the sermons I have heard on the topic, most seem to yearn for a utopic 1950s America when, in blessed memory, the whole family went to church every Sunday. Sermons that come at the issue from this angle often encourage the hearer to go back to a simpler and better time, often citing a variety of benefits to be gained in emotional, spiritual, mental, physical and familial health.

Yet if one looks at this issue through the lens of taking risks as a contrast community, different insights and questions emerge. First, what is indisputably a sad state of Sabbath-keeping in the wider culture also looks like an opportunity for distinctive Christian witness. We are now at a point in North American cultural life in many places where reserving even a Sunday morning for corporate worship is a countercultural and contrast activity. Such a practice raises questions among people outside the Christian community about why one would set such time aside and thus becomes an opportunity for members of the community to share their faith and give "an accounting for the hope that is in [them]" (1 Pet 3:15). When one Little League coach says to another, "I can't make the games on Sunday morning," it is an act of witness that opens a natural and honest opportunity for further witness.

Second, when seen in this light, Sabbath-keeping also carries with it real risk. Individuals who keep the Sabbath may find themselves at odds with friends, declining invitations that others readily accept, and perhaps be considered "too religious" according to the standards of the wider culture. Parents who tell a child that he or she may not play a sport because the games conflict with corporate worship may find that their child is the only one among his or her friends not able to participate. Adults may find that they do not have the time their peers do for hobbies or vacations because they set time aside for weekly worship and rest. Business owners may find they need to say no to clients and customers who want services on the Sabbath. Employees whose employers ask them to work a schedule that conflicts with corporate worship have perhaps the hardest decision because their livelihood is at stake. Keeping the Sabbath in light of these potential consequences is risky because it puts relationships, reputation and livelihood at stake and regularly causes a person to consider why she is making the decisions she is making.

The preacher who approaches Sabbath-keeping through this lens might then ask, what can equip this community to take such a risk and freely share with others the reasons for their decision? What does the confession of Jesus Christ, heard through the interpretation of a text, have to say to this important area of discipleship? How does it address the hidden assumptions that lie behind a no-Sabbath culture, and how does it address the real challenges and risks a community will face as they live out their faith in this way? Moreover, who in the community is making a risky decision to keep the Sabbath, and what is that decision and experience like for them? How did they come to the personal decision to do it, what challenges have they faced, and how they have seen God at work through their faithful witness? If the preacher were to find one in the community who could share his or her experience, that testimony might even form the bulk of a sermon.

This is simply one pattern and one area of discipleship, but the example serves to demonstrate the point. The patterns of missional faithfulness found in the *Treasure* research lead us to view the daily witness of a Christian community through a missional lens. Moreover, these patterns are especially helpful for preachers in the United States because they arise from research into missional churches in this context. The patterns of missional faithfulness may well be different, for example, in sub-Saharan Africa or in Western Europe. Living out the implications of the gospel is thoroughly contextual, and the blind spots and areas of cultural captivity will vary from context to context. Nevertheless, patterns of missional faithfulness such as these evoke new insights and questions for the preacher, lead the preacher to ask in the preparation of the sermon about the ongoing faithful witness of the community to the world, and help him or her craft a sermon that equips the community for future faithful witness.

In his book *Missional Preaching*, Al Tizon examines at length how one's preaching ministry might be guided by missional patterns. Essentially, in *Missional Preaching* Tizon lays out the foundation of a missional perspective in part one and then turns to the goals of missional preaching in part two. When he turns to the goals, he addresses the issue that we are also discussing here: How does missional preaching equip the community for its confession to the world? Tizon names seven goals of missional preaching and they bear some resemblance to the patterns I examined in chapter three: preaching for inculturation, preaching for the alternative community, preaching for holistic transformation, preaching for justice and reconciliation, preaching for whole-life stewardship, preaching for *shalom* (life and peace) and preaching the scandal of Jesus. In these goals, Tizon means to guide the homiletical discussion to consider the shape of the community that is formed in a preaching ministry. This is far larger than goals for individual sermons; it is about the long-term implications of a preaching ministry in a community. Tizon's list is a description of the characteristics of a missional community and thus a vision toward which the preacher can work over a long period of time. While these goals are not developed in research as the *Treasure in Clay Jars* patterns have been, they arise from the experience and context of a North American and an evangelical Christian in North America.

Tizon's approach of aiming at goals raises an important question about how a preacher might appropriate goals or patterns in a preaching ministry. Are they patterns that can be discerned in the life of a congregation, as the *Treasure* authors suggest, or are they goals to which the preacher aims in shaping the missional identity of a congregation? The authors of *Treasure* are clear that they chose the word *patterns* to indicate that this is not a model of a missional congregation, nor is it a program that can be implemented. Indeed, throughout their literature, missional theologians strongly resist the urge to make missional faithfulness a formula for church leadership or, worse, church growth. Yet Tizon, who has not been a part of the Gospel and Our Culture Network, moves in the direction of a formula for the creation of a missional church through preaching. Is this a good move, or are we heading into the dangerous territory of making missional preaching another corporate-style leadership technique for building a better church? Should a preacher take these patterns and preach toward them with the goal of sewing them into the community fabric, or should they simply be markers of missional faithfulness that guide the preacher in discerning the activity of God in the community? I think the answer is both. These dimensions of missional faithfulness are both goals and patterns for the preacher. As the preacher looks back on the lived experiences of the community, they are patterns of missional faithfulness that reveal the activity of God. Yet as the preacher looks forward to the future life of the community, these patterns naturally become specific dimensions of corporate and individual life that one wants to intentionally cultivate through preaching and other means.

Whether patterns or goals, these marks offer the preacher lenses for carefully attending to the daily life of the community in order to discern God's activity in the midst of his people as he empowers the community to bear its distinctive witness and equips them to bear its witness in the future. As Newbigin argues, if the gospel is to be credible to the world it must be seen in a living community. If preaching is to be believable, it must have both behind it and in front of it a communal life of discipleship that confesses the new reality. Moreover, the preacher's task is to center the community in the confession of this new reality, connect this confession to the lived experience and witness of this particular people, and kindle their ongoing witness to the world.

This work is the most distinctive dimension of missional preaching. The Christian community is the primary Christian witness, made up of those God has commissioned to bear witness to Jesus Christ in their particular place and time in both their corporate and individual lives. The unique role of the witness of preaching relative to the other forms of witness the community performs is to center the community in its confession of Jesus Christ, contextualize that confession to their distinctive missional vocation and kindle the larger confession of the community. The whole life of the community, its words and deeds, both individually and together, is a parable of the reign of God, a hermeneutic of the gospel through which a watching world might come to believe the good news. Missional preaching takes its place as a clarion voice that is joined to the larger chorus of proclamation.

Conclusion

From the beginning, this book has been a conversation about missional preaching. It began, for me personally and in this book, as a response to Lesslie Newbigin's question put forth in *Foolishness to the Greeks*, reframed in homiletical terms: What would be involved homiletically in a genuinely missionary encounter between the gospel and Western culture? In gathering this conversation and responding to that question, I have articulated what I call a "missional homiletic." That is to say, I have proposed a homiletic that orients itself around the sent nature of the church as the community that is sent into the world by the triune God to bear witness to Jesus Christ. The conversation partners in this proposal have been homileticians who orient their understanding of preaching around the concept of witness; Karl Barth's ecclesiology, which understands the vocation and task of the church as witness to Jesus Christ; and the research and writing of missional theologians who have studied missional congregations in the United States. The contributions of these conversation partners have led to the following understanding of missional preaching: preaching confesses Jesus Christ through a missional interpretation of scripture in order to equip the community for its confession to the world.

As with any conversation, the time comes when it must end—or at least pause—and so we come now to the conclusion. When one has finished a lengthy and involved dialogue—or spent hours reading a book—one thinks back over the conversation. Questions arise, such as, "What did I learn in that discussion? What stands out as most significant? How does this conversation connect with other areas of interest and learning? What questions does this raise, and what do I need to do to pursue them further?"

These are the type of questions I have in mind as I conclude this conversation, and this concluding chapter is a brief attempt to address them. First, I want to point to what I believe are the distinctive contributions of missional preaching to the broader homiletical conversation. This discussion will also briefly summarize the major themes of the book.

First, I hope we will take seriously the proposal of a communal preaching ministry within a local congregation. Within every congregation there are people whom God has gifted and called to the ministry of preaching and who should be part of a preaching community within that congregation, though they may not be ordained to preach or may not have fulfilled the requirements for ordination in their tradition. The important distinction is that they are called and gifted by God and that their call and gift is confirmed by their community. It is on this basis that they are authorized to preach and thus form a fellowship of preachers within that community.

The question of who is authorized to preach is vital both to homiletical studies in recent decades and missional theology. In homiletics, the issue has been framed in terms of authority or authorization to preach and how one receives such authorization. Theorists have pointed on the one hand to the error inherent in patriarchal systems that have excluded women from the ministry of preaching and on the other hand to the postmodern dismantling of all traditional structures of authority such as ordination, education and even scripture and reason.[1] In missional theology, the issue has been framed in terms of clericalism and a clerical paradigm in which only a special caste of Christians are allowed to "minister." Missional theologians have argued that whether one sees the preacher as a priest, a pedagogue or a professional, in all cases there is a basic understanding that only those with special training and licensing are allowed to participate in a "ministerial task" such as preaching. The laity, on the other hand, are not ministers but those who receive the blessings dispensed by the clergy.

The proposal of a communal preaching ministry seeks to address both homiletical and missional concerns by situating the authority to preach in giftedness and lifting up the importance of a community of voices in a congregation rather than only a voice. A communal ministry such as this

---

[1]For an account of the displacement of preaching from traditional structures of authority, see John S. McClure, *Other-Wise Preaching: A Postmodern Ethic for Homiletics* (St. Louis: Chalice Press, 2001).

has partial antecedents in earlier homiletical proposals, for instance in what Ronald Allen calls "feed-forward" groups wherein a small group of listeners work with the preacher to interpret the text and move toward the sermon. It is important to note that these kinds of groups come nearer to my concept of a communal preaching ministry when they undertake the theological work of bringing their lived experience to the text in order to discern contextual meaning. Yet the notion of a feed-forward group still does not envision a community of preachers, only a community of interpreters. Regular preaching is still reserved for licensed clergy.

By contrast, I am proposing that we move from feed-forward communities of interpreters to communities of preachers who gather to interpret scripture and share preaching responsibilities. This shared responsibility brings multiple voices into the process of interpretation and preaching, which guards against any one perspective totalizing the gospel discourse in a community. Moreover, I am proposing that this community is based on giftedness and calling, which guards against clericalism rooted especially in education and gender. Embracing such a communal preaching ministry would mean real changes for preachers and congregations, as preachers learn to identify and collaborate with other preachers in the congregation and congregations learn to welcome and affirm other preachers in the pulpit. This would also mean changes for homileticians who teach preachers, as preachers would need to learn not only how to preach but also how to nurture other preachers.

I also think it is important in the homiletical conversation to take seriously the essential content and criterion of faithful preaching, which in my view is the person, work and name of Jesus Christ. This is certainly not novel to missional preaching, and as we saw it is a major piece of David Lose's *Confessing Jesus Christ*. However, I am proposing that not only is the confession of Jesus Christ important to connect preaching with the historic Christian proclamation, as others claim, but also to connect preaching to the various other forms of Christian witness and interpret them in light of the ultimate reality to which they point. In his ecclesiology, Barth suggests a variety of forms of witness the Christian community might undertake both in speech and act. Likewise, missional theologians suggest various ways in which the community bears its witness, many of them more in deed than word. What thread holds these forms of witness together as the common proclamation of the Christian community, preventing them from becoming simply random acts of kindness? The answer is they all point beyond themselves to the new reality revealed in Jesus Christ, finding both their impulse and their direction in him.

Yet especially in the case of deeds, this reference is not immediately clear. It requires interpretation and verbal proclamation. Preaching is the form of regular proclamation that ties the multiform witness of the Christian community together as witness to Jesus Christ; it is the form of witness that sounds the one note common to the whole symphony of Christian witness. Moreover, preaching centers the various words and deeds of the community in this new reality and by that continually nourishes and kindles the greater witness of the church. Unless Jesus Christ is the essential content of preaching, then preaching is disconnected from its historical tradition, disconnected from the larger witness of the church, and disconnected from the power working within it that gives it the possibility of real effect.

For decades homiletics as a discipline has been much more interested in the "who" and "how" of preaching than the "what." Particularly in light of postmodern challenges, homileticians have focused on questions such as "Who is the preacher? What is the best metaphor to understand that identity?" or "How does a preacher interpret a text? What is the proper hermeneutic?" and "How does a preacher communicate most effectively with an audience?"—which has tended often to become "How do people understand?" Relatively lost among these questions has been the subject of "what" is preached![2] Yet the content of preaching is vitally important, and I would argue more important than the "how" or "who" of preaching. Ultimately preaching is empowered not by the persona of the preacher or the preacher's rhetorical skill but by the Holy Spirit working within and alongside the preacher's words to bear witness to Jesus Christ. There is certainly an identity, hermeneutic and rhetoric appropriate to this core

---

[2]There have been attempts to address the "what" of preaching, and perhaps most notable is Charles Campbell's *Preaching Jesus*. In hindsight, however, it is interesting to note that his proposal frames the question of "What do we preach?" in terms of the hermeneutical question of "How do we interpret the text?"

confession and it is the task of homileticians to propose them for the church. Yet homileticians cannot take the essential content of preaching for granted or leave it blank, to be filled in by the preacher's own tradition. It is integral to the task of preaching, connecting preaching both to the historic Christian tradition and to larger, multiform witness of the contemporary church.

In addition, I hope for more conversation around what is a missional hermeneutic for preaching. A missional hermeneutic approaches the text from the perspective of the mission of God and the missionary nature of the church, seeking to discern how the text might form God's people for their witness today. Specifically, and first, the missional hermeneutic I propose understands Jesus Christ—who is the essential confession of all Christian proclamation—as the interpretive matrix of the biblical text. This means that Jesus Christ, his death and resurrection and the new reality revealed in him, is the lens through which one views a text, and he sets the parameters for its interpretation. Indeed, the task of biblical interpretation is to bring the text and lived experience into a dynamic interplay within the framework of this gospel. This missional hermeneutic assumes the missionary formative intent of the text. The scriptures were written to form God's people for their witness, participating in God's mission in the world. This is true of both Old and New Testaments, as Israel was commissioned as a light to the nations and the early Christians to be witnesses to Jesus Christ. The texts written to these communities are intended to equip and shape them to fulfill their commission. Moreover, by the illuminating power of the Holy Spirit, these scriptures may have the same effect today. Reading scripture on this assumption means the preacher asks how the text might have shaped God's people for mission then and how it might do so today.

Inquiring into the contemporary formative potential of the text brings the preacher to consider the context of the congregation, and this must also be from a missional perspective. This means understanding the community first and foremost as the people of God sent to bear witness to Christ in a particular place and time. This people has attendant characteristics such as ethnicity, socioeconomic status, education and culture, but these characteristics are understood in the context of their vocation as the people of God. As Michael Barram proposes, bringing the vocational locatedness of the congregation into the interpretation of the text means asking questions of the text related to the witness of the congregation. Moreover, it means asking questions that get at the blind spots in a community's witness and that seek to reveal areas of life where deeper conversion is needed. In order to ask these questions, for the preacher to see the blind spots, there must be dialogue with the "other," both the other who exists within the local Christian community and the other who comes to the community from a very different context.

Thus the missional hermeneutic I propose includes the interpretive matrix of Jesus Christ, the missional formative intent and effect of scripture, and questions that address the vocational locatedness of the Christian community in its time and place. Together, this hermeneutic offers an interpretation of a text that is centered in missional vocation, is in critical dialogue with context, and aims at equipping the congregation for witness. As I have said, this proposal is only a sketch, and the discussion around missional hermeneutics is very much in early stages. Still, this sketch is unique in the homiletical discussion, particularly as it brings the missional formative intent of scripture and questions about vocational locatedness to bear in interpretation. This is a distinctive contribution of this project, and I am hopeful that I and perhaps others will do more in developing a missional hermeneutic for preaching.

Fourth, and finally, I think it is very important, not only to missional preaching but also to homiletics, to situate the witness of preaching in relation to the broader and multiform witness of the congregation. This is perhaps the most distinctive contribution of missional preaching to the larger conversations in homiletics. Most typically, the homiletical lens is zoomed in on the preacher, focusing on this one form of witness. This one form of witness, however, can be properly understood only when one zooms out to take in the larger context of preaching, which is the whole witness of the church. We can fully understand preaching only when we see it in this context and in its relationship to the other forms of witness.

The larger context of preaching is the congregation, understood first and foremost according to its theological identity as the people of God and the primary Christian witness. While there are individual Christians and witness is undertaken by individuals, both Christians and Christian witness should be understood first in light of the community as a whole. Moreover, the larger world in which the community exists should also be seen first in its theological sense as the "sphere of God's providence" and the "sphere of human confusion." In other words, whatever else may be said about the world, it is both where the sovereign God is at work and where human beings entangle God's goodness and all that opposes God. In this context the new reality of Jesus Christ is revealed, and in this situation the community bears its witness. Indeed, the community is a parable of the kingdom of heaven, a glimpse of life under the reign of God.

In pointing to the distinctiveness of this understanding of the community within the larger conversations of homiletics, it is helpful to distinguish it from at least two other common conceptions. The first is the Christian community as an aggregation of listeners, relatively atomized and having no explicit common connection, whose dominant characteristics are their human needs, problems, concerns and perhaps hopes and dreams. Rather, I am saying the Christian community is first a people who have a common calling to bear witness to Christ, and then within that framework the community is made up of individuals with individual joys and concerns. The second common conception is the Christian community as an audience, viewed from a variety of perspectives such as anthropology, psychology, sociology and rhetoric. While these perspectives are useful in understanding the Christian community, they must not eclipse the theological identity of the people of God; their identity *kata pneuma* is far more important than their identity *kata sarka*.

Furthermore, preaching is centering, contextualizing and kindling confession within the Christian community. What is the distinctive contribution of preaching to the multiform witness of the community? It is distinct because it regularly centers the various forms of witness in the one to whom they all point, Jesus Christ. It is distinct because it contextualizes the witness of the community for a people in a particular time and place. The vocation common to all Christians is to bear witness to Christ, but that vocation is expressed in specific ways according to the giftedness of each community and the particular location in which it finds itself. Regular preaching in the Christian community helps the congregation to discern its particular, contextual vocation and thus to bear not only its common witness but also its distinctive witness. It is distinct because it is kindling confession, a confession that, as Barth argues, creates the church anew each time it is done. Regular preaching continually ignites the ongoing witness of the church, much as one feeds a fire by regularly adding fuel.

Moreover, preaching arises from and flows into the witness of the Christian community. When the preacher prepares the sermon, she has behind her all the words and deeds inspired by the Spirit in the community over the past weeks, months or years. She has in front of her a vision of what the Spirit may do through this community in the coming weeks, months and years. The sermon is not disconnected from this but lives in a dialectical relationship with these other words and deeds of witness. As Newbigin argues, without the works of the Holy Spirit in the life of the community, the words of the preacher are empty. Yet with these works the preacher's words are accompanied by visible signs that confirm their truth and illuminate their meaning. Here one may be tempted to think of an "illustration" that sheds light on a preacher's abstract idea, but there is more here. When I refer to the works of the Spirit in the life of the community, I mean more than a well of sermon illustrations. Rather, I mean the other and indispensable side of verbal proclamation, the deeds of power by which God confirms the truth of the gospel we have heard.

Again, one may see the distinctiveness of this proposal by setting it in contrast to other conceptions of the lived experience from which preaching springs and into which it leads. One might argue that preaching arises in response to the need of the world and to the specific needs and problems of the community that gathers to hear the sermon, as Lose argues specifically and Florence implicitly. Or one might argue that preaching arises in response to the desire to make sense of lived experience, both joys and sorrows, to see life whole and understand the meaning of it. Indeed, preaching does respond to the need of the world and preaching does help make sense of lived experience—but it does not spring from need or from the desire for meaning. Rather, Christian preaching arises, as is paradigmatic in the Acts 2 account of Pentecost, in response to the deeds of power performed by the Spirit of God, which bear witness to the new reality of Jesus Christ. Preaching is in response to the works of God, both in the past and present, and by grace leads into the works of God in the future.

Thus, I see the homiletical contributions of this proposal for missional preaching moving along four lines: (1) a community of preachers who equip a congregation, (2) the necessity of confessing Jesus Christ as the essential and common content of proclamation, (3) a missional hermeneutic for interpreting scripture and (4) understanding preaching in relationship to the multiform and primary witness of the community. I also hope that missional preaching finds a place in the larger conversation of missional theology. Practical theology is not simply the application of theology to the practices of ministry. Rather, it is a mutual critical engagement between theology and the practices of ministry. The practices of ministry are open to revision in light of theological norms, but theological norms are also open to revision in light of the practices of ministry. Moreover, in the interaction between practical theological disciplines (such as homiletics) and other theological disciplines (such as missional theology), there should be mutual critical engagement. I have not intended this conversation to be the application of missional theology to homiletics. Rather, my intent is that missional theology too may be challenged by its engagement with homiletics, and I see this potential along at least two lines.

First, it continues to be surprising that missional theologians have not engaged in deeper dialogue with practical theological disciplines. In many ways missional theology is oriented around an ecclesiology of sending, hence the title of the seminal book *Missional Church: A Vision for the Sending of the Church in North America*. As ecclesiology, missional theology is closely connected to and in conversation with the practices, structures and life of the church in North America. This is at least in part why missional literature has been so well received by church leaders in North America. It seems obvious, therefore, that a focus on ecclesiology would bring the discussion into close contact with the disciplines that are oriented around the practices of ministry, but that has not been the case.

Missional literature has addressed ministerial leadership in the congregation but with very little engagement with the historical disciplines of homiletics, Christian education or pastoral care. For instance, in chapter eight of *Missional Church*, "Missional Leadership: Equipping God's People for Mission," the authors describe characteristics of missional leadership and urge that preparation for church leadership move beyond "preaching and teaching" to take in the wider scope of "apostolic leadership" in the formation of communities. In the most recent follow-up to *Missional Church*, *The Missional Church in Perspective: Mapping Trends and Shaping the Conversation*, the chapter "Missional Practices of Church Life and Leadership" likewise addresses the broader character-istics of missional congregations and how those communities are shaped. Here the argument again is made that ministerial leadership needs to move beyond specific practices of ministry and move toward the more general category of leadership and the formation of communities

In my view, both as a homiletician and pastor, this perspective fails to acknowledge at least two things. First, both historically and in the contem-porary context, ministerial leadership is exercised primarily through the practices of preaching, teaching and the "cure of souls." Certainly mis-sional theologians are right to say that these activities should not be re-stricted to ordained clergy and the laity should be equipped to join in these ministries. Nevertheless, neither should these practices be glossed over in favor of a more general concept of leadership. This is especially risky if the concept of leadership is fleshed out by a commercial or corporate par-adigm more than by historic Christian practice. When pastors are called to serve churches or plant churches, it is precisely these ancient practices in which they are engaged and which constitute the bulk of their ministry.

Moreover, and second, the study of each of these areas of ministry is long and rich. As has been shown in this conversation and a few other works, engagement between practical theology and missional theology produces a rich and nuanced understanding of the specific tasks of lead-ership in the missional church, and more such work is needed. Missional theologians need to press beyond the general category of "missional lead-ership" into the specific practices of ministry that constitute pastoral lead-ership in a church. This means engaging with the practical theological disciplines that focus on those practices.[3] Missional theology has the po-

---

[3]In particular, I would highlight Benjamin T. Conner, *Practicing Witness: A Missional Vision of Christian Practices* (Grand Rapids: Eerdmans, 2011) and Clayton J. Schmit, *Sent and Gathered: A Worship Manual for the Missional Church*, Engaging Worship (Grand Rapids: Baker Academic, 2009) as examples of excellent engagement between practical and missional theology.

tential to reform the way we understand preaching, teaching and pastoral care, especially in terms of equipping the baptized for their common ministry. Nevertheless, the practical theological disciplines also have much to teach missional theology about the practice of pastoral leadership.

The second line of dialogue I see relates to the conception of the local congregation in the study of missional theology. What we have learned in practical theology is that congregations are enormously complex sociocultural organizations. For instance, when seen through the lens of anthropology in a work such as Lenora Tisdale's *Local Theology and Folk Art*, a congregation is a complex cultural web of symbols and stories. These stories and symbols are sometimes complementary and sometimes at odds, and they combine to form a complex semiotic web through which people understand themselves and the community. In addition, and this is where most work in homiletics has been done, those who fill the pews have complex individual identities that both share in and are separate from the identity of the congregation. Even individuals cannot be defined by one cultural identity but have a complex sociocultural identity representing a variety of familial, religious, political, professional and social influences.

For instance, the study "Listening to the Listeners," referenced in the last chapter, demonstrates through research that each listener hears a sermon through his or her own hermeneutical framework and often the message heard is very different from what the preacher intends. Stories and symbols referenced in the sermon take their place in the hearer's own hermeneutical web, and the meaning is reshaped there. In a sense the listeners make what they will of the sermon according to their own interpretive frames of reference. Any preacher who has stood at the door and listened to congregants share what they heard in the sermon can bear witness to this truth! Moreover, preachers can appeal to scripture, tradition, reason or experience, but all of these are under challenge in the postmodern environment and any of them may be questioned and rejected by the individual hearer. As postmodern homileticians have taught us, preachers speak "as one without authority," standing only on the conviction of belief and the working of the Spirit.

It appears in missional literature that missional theologians do not take sufficient account of the sociocultural and religious complexity of congregations and the individuals in them. In *The Missional Church in Perspective*, the authors acknowledge the cultural complexity of a "globalized world," but that complexity does not appear to find a place in the understanding of the congregation. Throughout missional literature, the basic image of the average congregation is as a group of Christians who gather weekly to receive the blessings of Christ administered in some form by the clergy. The intent of missional theologians is to change this basic image so that congregations see themselves as called to witness in the world and shaped for that witness through their life together. There is much in that description with which I resonate, but it also strikes me as vastly oversimplified.

Specifically, the unspoken assumption seems to be that there is a relatively homogenous, coherent group called a "church" or "congregation," which can be set in distinction to a world that is "out there." Yet when you press more deeply, there is as much world "in here" as "out there." There is not a clear line between church and world, and there is a complex mixture in every individual Christian and congregation. When the preacher stands to deliver the sermon, she is not simply speaking to the Christian faithful who have gathered from their lives in the world and will soon return back into it. She is also speaking to a group of people who very much bring the world with them—who are the world—who come to worship for a host of reasons both sacred and secular and many of whom have mixed feelings at best about their own Christian identity. This makes equipping the church for witness a vastly more complicated task.

Homileticians point toward this when they stress the identity of the preacher as witness, or as confessor, or as one who testifies. In a complex congregation filled with even more complex individuals, the most a preacher can do is bear witness to Jesus Christ as he is encountered through the living voice of the biblical witness. This is what Thomas Long means when he argues that the preacher is not best understood as a herald announcing the truth from on high or even a pastor who has the solution to the problems of the people. Likewise, I would add that a preacher is not best understood as a missional leader who is able to equip a congregation with all they need to fulfill their vocation. There is a necessary tentativeness in the metaphor of witness and a circumscription of the authority, expertise and power of the preacher. Homileticians have come to this through an understanding of the deep complexity of postmodern congregations and Christians. As missional theologians describe the church, both as it is and as they hope it to be, their description needs to be at least as complex as their description of the post-Christendom and postmodern world in which the church finds itself.

I continue to believe that Lesslie Newbigin was right when he argued that the only hermeneutic that can make the gospel credible to the watching world is a community of people who live it. It is for that reason I am committed to the conversation around missional preaching. It is why I believe that preachers need to develop communities of preachers within their congregations, because no one preacher is capable of equipping a community for its vocation. Preachers need to center the congregation in the good news of Jesus Christ; they need to employ a missional hermeneutic in the interpretation of scripture; they need to attend specifically to the ways their sermons connect to the larger witness of their communities and the work of God among them. Preaching that does this has the potential of forming congregations who see themselves as a living parable of God's kingdom, a demonstration to the world of God's gracious reign.

Moreover, it is for this reason that I am convinced that homiletics needs to attend to the ways in which preaching can form the witnessing community and equip the people of God to confess Jesus Christ to the world in words and deeds. For too long homiletics has focused exclusively on the individual in the pulpit who speaks to listeners in the pew. In a Christendom setting and a clerical paradigm, perhaps this focus made sense. Yet Christendom is largely gone, and it is the task of the whole people of God to take up their vocation to witness. Homileticians, whose focus continues rightly to be paradigmatic preaching, must widen the focus to include the ways in which preachers and preaching can shape and equip the witnessing community. Likewise, missional theologians need to engage more deeply with the practices of ministry that have historically constituted pastoral leadership and the disciplines that have long studied and taught them.

As Newbigin saw, the church today is engaged in a missionary encounter with Western culture. It is the task now—in many ways, as it always has been—for congregations, preachers and teachers to bring out from the storehouse treasures old and new that may help the church to meet the challenge of the present age.

Bibliography

Allen, O. Wesley. *The Homiletic of All Believers: A Conversational Approach to Proclamation and Preaching.* Louisville: Westminster John Knox, 2005.

Allen, Ronald. "The Turn to the Listener: A Selective Review of a Recent Trend in Preaching." *Encounter* 64 (2003): 167-96.

Auerbach, Erich. *Mimesis: The Representation of Reality in Western Literature.* Princeton, NJ: Princeton University Press, 1953.

Barrett, Lois Y., et al. *Treasure in Clay Jars: Patterns in Missional Faithfulness.* Grand Rapids: Eerdmans, 2004.

Barth, Karl. *Die Kirchliche Dogmatik.* Zurich: Theologischer Verlag, 1986.

———. *The Doctrine of Reconciliation.* Vol. IV/3.2 of *Church Dogmatics.* Edited by G. W. Bromiley and T. F. Torrance. Edinburgh: T & T Clark, 1958.

Bauckham, Richard. *Bible and Mission: Christian Witness in a Postmodern World.* Grand Rapids: Baker Academic, 2004.

Bond, L. Susan. Review of *Confessing Jesus Christ: Preaching in a Postmodern World,* by David J. Lose. *Homiletic* 28 (2003): 27-29.

Bosch, David J. *Transforming Mission: Paradigm Shifts in Theology of Mission.* American Society of Missiology. Maryknoll, NY: Orbis Books, 2011.

———. *Witness to the World: The Christian Mission in Theological Perspective.* Eugene, OR: Wipf & Stock Publishers, 2006.

Brothers, Michael. "The Role of Distance in Preaching: A Critical Dialogue With Fred Craddock and Post-Liberal Homiletics." PhD diss., Princeton Theological Seminary, 2003.

Brownson, James V. "A Response at SBL to Hunsberger's 'Proposals . . .' Essay." Paper presented at the Gospel and Our Culture Network, 2009.

———. *Speaking the Truth in Love: New Testament Resources for a Missional Hermeneutic.* Christian Mission and Modern Culture. Edinburgh: T & T Clark, 1998.

Burke, Kenneth. "Four Master Tropes." *Kenyon Review* 3 (1941): 421-38.

Busch, Eberhard. *The Great Passion: An Introduction to Karl Barth's Theology.* Grand Rapids: Eerdmans, 2010.

Calvin, John. *Institutes of the Christian Religion.* Edited by John T. McNeill. Translated by Ford Lewis Battles. Philadelphia: Westminster Press, 1960.

Campbell, Charles L. *Preaching Jesus: New Directions for Homiletics in Hans Frei's Postliberal Theology*. Grand Rapids: Eerdmans, 1997.

Cardoza-Orlandi, Carlos. "What Makes Preaching Missional?" *Journal for Preachers* 22 (1999): 3-9.

Conner, Benjamin T. "Practicing Witness: A Contribution to the Theology of Christian Practices Issuing from a Conversation Between Missional Theology and Craig Dykstra's Theology of Christian Practices." PhD diss., Princeton Theological Seminary, 2009.

———. *Practicing Witness: A Missional Vision of Christian Practices*. Grand Rapids: Eerdmans, 2011.

Dally, John Addison. *Choosing the Kingdom: Missional Preaching for the Household of God*. Herndon, VA: The Alban Institute, 2007.

Farrer, Austin. *Austin Farrer: The Essential Sermons*. London: SPCK, 1991.

Flett, John G. "God Is a Missionary God: Missio Dei, Karl Barth, and the Doctrine of the Trinity." PhD diss., Princeton Theological Seminary, 2007.

———. *The Witness of God: The Trinity, Missio Dei, Karl Barth, and the Nature of Christian Community*. Grand Rapids: Eerdmans, 2010.

Florence, Anna Carter. "Preaching as Testimony: Towards a Women's Preaching Tradition and New Homiletical Models." PhD diss., Princeton Theological Seminary, 2000.

———. *Preaching as Testimony*. Louisville: Westminster John Knox, 2007.

Gerrish, B. A. *Saving and Secular Faith: An Invitation to Systematic Theology*. Philadelphia: Fortress, 1999.

Goheen, Michael W. "Continuing Steps Towards a Missional Hermeneutic." *Fidelis: A Journal of Redeemer Pacific College* 3 (2008): 49-99.

González, Catherine Gunsalus. "The Baptismal Lens for Missional Preaching." *Journal for Preachers* Easter (1995): 27-30.

Guder, Darrell L. *The Continuing Conversion of the Church*. Grand Rapids: Eerdmans, 2000

———. "From Mission and Theology to Missional Theology." *Princeton Seminary Bulletin* 24 (2003): 36-54.

———. "Missional Hermeneutics: The Missional Authority of Scripture." *Mission Focus: Annual Review* 15 (2007): 106-21.

———. "Missional Hermeneutics: The Missional Vocation of the Congregation—and How Scripture Shapes that Calling." *Mission Focus: Annual Review* 15 (2007): 125-42.

———. *Unlikely Ambassadors: Clay Jar Christians in God's Service*. Louisville:

Office of the General Assembly, Presbyterian Church (U.S.A.), 2002.

———. "Walking Worthy: Missional Leadership After Christendom." *Princeton Seminary Bulletin* 28 (2007): 251-91.

Guder, Darrell L., et al. *Missional Church: A Vision for the Sending of the Church in North America.* Grand Rapids: Eerdmans, 1998.

Gwyn, Douglas. "A School of the Prophets: Teaching Congregational Members to Preach." In *Preaching in the Context of Worship,* edited by David M. Greenhaw and Ronald J. Allen. St. Louis: Chalice Press, 2000.

Hall, Douglas John. *Confessing the Faith: Christian Theology in a North American Context.* Philadelphia: Fortress, 1998.

Harrisville, Roy A. Review of *Confessing Jesus Christ: Preaching in a Postmodern World,* by David J. Lose. *Word and World* 25 (2005): 350-54.

Hauerwas, Stanley. *With the Grain of the Universe: The Church's Witness and Natural Theology.* Grand Rapids: Brazos Press, 2001.

Healy, Nicholas M. "Karl Barth's Ecclesiology Reconsidered." *Scottish Journal of Theology* 57 (2004): 287-99.

Hunsberger, George R. "Proposals for a Missionary Hermeneutic: Mapping a Conversation." *Missiology: An International Review* 39 (2011): 309-21.

Jiménez, Pablo. "Missional Preaching." In *The New Interpreter's Handbook of Preaching,* edited by Paul Scott Wilson. Nashville: Abingdon Press, 2008.

Johns, Cheryl Bridges. "Acts and the Task of Missional Preaching." *Journal for Preachers* 22 (2006): 16-21.

Kaiser, Walter C., Jr. *Mission in the Old Testament: Israel as a Light to the Nations.* 2nd ed. Grand Rapids: Baker Academic, 2012.

Kay, James F. "Preacher as Messenger of Hope." In *Slow of Speech and Unclean Lips: Contemporary Images of Preaching Identity,* edited by Robert Stephen Reid, 13-34. Eugene, OR: Cascade Books, 2010.

———. *Preaching and Theology.* Preaching and Its Partners. St. Louis: Chalice Press, 2007.

———. "The Word of the Cross at the Turn of the Ages." *Interpretation* 53 (1999): 44-56.

Kittel, Gerhard, and Gerhard Friedrich, eds. *Theological Dictionary of the New Testament.* Vol. III, Grand Rapids: Eerdmans, 1965.

Lischer, Richard. Review of *Confessing Jesus Christ: Preaching in a Postmodern World,* by David J. Lose. *Theology Today* 60 (2004): 582-84.

Long, Thomas G. "And How Shall They Hear? The Listener in Contemporary Preaching." In *Listening to the Word: Studies in Honor of Fred B. Craddock,* edited by Gail R. O'Day, 167-88. Nashville, TN: Abingdon Press, 1993.

———. Review of *Confessing Jesus Christ: Preaching in a Postmodern World*, by David J. Lose. *Interpretation* 58 (2004): 216-18.

———. *The Witness of Preaching*. 1st ed. Louisville: Westminster John Knox, 1989.

———. *The Witness of Preaching*. 2nd ed. Louisville: Westminster John Knox, 2005.

Lose, David J. *Confessing Jesus Christ: Preaching in a Postmodern World*. Grand Rapids: Eerdmans, 2003.

McClure, John S. *Other-Wise Preaching: A Postmodern Ethic for Homiletics*. St. Louis: Chalice Press, 2001.

Murphy, Francesca Aran. *God Is Not a Story: Realism Revisited*. New York: Oxford University Press, 2007.

Murray, Jeffrey W. "A Dialogue of Motives." *Philosophy and Rhetoric* 35 (2002): 22-49.

Newbigin, Lesslie. *Foolishness to the Greeks: The Gospel and Western Culture*. SPCK Publishing, 1986.

———. *The Good Shepherd: Meditations on Christian Ministry in Today's World*. Leighton Buzzard, UK: Faith Press, 1977.

———. *The Gospel in a Pluralist Society*. Grand Rapids: Eerdmans, 1989.

———. *Mission in Christ's Way: A Gift, a Command, an Assurance*. New York: Friendship Press, 1988.

Osmer, Richard R. *Practical Theology: An Introduction*. Grand Rapids: Eerdmans, 2008.

Schmit, Clayton J. *Sent and Gathered: A Worship Manual for the Missional Church*. Engaging Worship. Grand Rapids: Baker Academic, 2009.

Scudieri, Robert. Review of *Missional Church: A Vision for the Sending of the Church in North America*, by Darrell L. Guder. *International Bulletin of Missionary Research* 22 (1998): 178.

Smith, Dennis A. Review of *Missional Church: A Vision for the Sending of the Church in North America*, by Darrell L. Guder. *International Review of Mission* 87 (1998): 574.

Stuempfle, Herman G. *Preaching in the Witnessing Community*. Philadelphia: Fortress, 1973.

Stutzman, Ervin R. "Preaching in the Missional Church." *preaching.org*. March 4, 2011. www.preaching.org/preaching-in-the-missional-church.

Tell, David. "Burke's Encounter with Ransom: Rhetoric and Epistemology in 'Four Master Tropes.'" *Rhetoric Society Quarterly* 34 (2004): 33-54.

Tizon, Al. *Missional Preaching: Engage Embrace Transform*. King of Prussia, PA: Judson Press, 2012.

Van Gelder, Craig. *The Ministry of the Missional Church: A Community Led by the Spirit*. Grand Rapids: Baker Books, 2007.

Volf, Miroslav. *After Our Likeness: The Church as the Image of the Trinity*. Sacra Doctrina. Grand Rapids: Eerdmans, 1997.

Wainwright, Geoffrey. *Lesslie Newbigin: A Theological Life*. New York: Oxford University Press, 2000.

Wright, Christopher J. H. *The Mission of God: Unlocking the Bible's Grand Narrative*. Downers Grove, IL: InterVarsity Press, 2006.

Name and Subject Index

Finding the Textbook You Need

The IVP Academic Textbook Selector
is an online tool for instantly finding the IVP books
suitable for over 250 courses across 24 disciplines.

---

ivpacademic.com
